JOURNEY TO FREEDOM

AND BEYOND

Robert M. Slane

Colonel
U.S. Air Force (Ret.)

Copyright © 2004 by Robert M. Slane. All rights reserved.

No part of this book, text or photos, may be reproduced, stored in a retrieval system, or transmitted, in any form, or by any means, electronic, mechanical, photocopying, recording, or otherwise, without the written prior permission of the author.

Printed in Canada

Editor, Ellen Beck
Design and typesetting, Roy Diment, VRG.
www.members.shaw.ca/vrg
Cover, Roy Diment

A cataloguing record for this book that includes the U.S. Library of Congress Classification number, the Library of Congress Call number and the Dewey Decimal cataloguing code is available from the National Library of Canada. The complete cataloguing record can be obtained from the National Library's online database at: www.nlc-bnc.ca/amicus/index-e.html
ISBN 1-4120-1672-X

TRAFFORD

This book was published *on-demand* in cooperation with Trafford Publishing.
On-demand publishing is a unique process and service of making a book available for retail sale to the public taking advantage of on-demand manufacturing and Internet marketing. **On-demand publishing** includes promotions, retail sales, manufacturing, order fulfilment, accounting and collecting royalties on behalf of the author.

Suite 6E, 2333 Government St., Victoria, B.C. V8T 4P4, CANADA
Phone   250-383-6864   Toll-free   1-888-232-4444 (Canada & US)
Fax   250-383-6804   E-mail   sales@trafford.com
Web site   www.trafford.com   TRAFFORD PUBLISHING IS A DIVISION OF TRAFFORD HOLDINGS LTD.
Trafford Catalogue #03-2049   www.trafford.com/robots/03-2049.html

10   9   8   7   6   5

Contents

Acknowledgements vii
Introduction ix

PART I GOING TO WAR
Grand Island, Nebraska 1
Prestwick, Scotland 13
Emergency Landing 17
Misplaced Watches 21
England 23
September 27 1943, Mission to Emden 25
October 3 1943, Night Instrument Training Flight 29
October 4 1943, Mission to Frankfort, Germany 33
A Reprieve 37
October 10 1943, Mission to Munster, Germany 39
October 14 1943, Mission to Schweinfurt, Germany 45

PART II PRISONER OF WAR
Captured! 55
Solitary Confinement 65
Stalag Luft III 71
The "X" Committee 89
Settling In 95
Adjusting to Prison Life 103
Escape Plan 107
Letters from Home 111
A New Plan 115
The Escape 119

PART III THE WAR MARCHES ON
Interrogation 131
A Solitary Life 135
The March Begins... 141
Hiding Out in Muskau 149

The March Continues…	153
Boxcar Blues	155
Prisoner At Nuremberg	157
Don't Let the Bedbugs Bite	161
Hunger Pains	165
Air Raids	167
Bomb Attacks	169
Journey Out of Nuremberg	173
A Taste of Freedom	177
Escape with a Friend	181
Search for Freedom	193
Eichstatt	199
Oflag VIIB	203
Stalag VIIA	207
Freedom at Last!	213
A New World Begins	227

PART IV AFTER LIBERATION

Camp Lucky Strike	235
Home At Last	239
Life Begins Anew	241
Survivor	247
Military Synopsis	265
The Later Years	267
Epilogue	277

Dedicated

TO THE MEMORY OF MY B-17 CREW MEMBERS

Who flew with me and fought the battle of their lives on the 14th of October 1943, as we returned alone from a mission to Schweinfurt, Germany. A special tribute is offered to Sergeant Claud J. Smith who gave his life for his country on that date.

Co-pilot	2nd Lt. Joseph A. Johnson 0804344
Navigator	2nd Lt Arthur G. Foster 0683233
Bombardier	2nd Lt. William C, Runner, Jr. 0735345
Engineer-Gunner	S/Sgt. Sherman W. Sly 38189731
Ball Turret Gunner	S/Sgt. Louis L. Brown 13110500
Radio Operator-Gunner	S/Sgt. Victor H. Kuhlman 37275843
Left Waist Gunner	S/Sgt. Robert S. Soloman 34425673
Right Waist Gunner	S/Sgt. Charles J. Groth 32504726
Tail Gunner	Sgt. Claud J. Smith 18166608

AND

TO THE MEMORY OF MY JET-BOMBER B-47 CREW MEMBERS

Who perished in the crash of a B-47 in Canada on the 30th of November 1956.

Co-pilot	2nd Lt Richard J. Martin AO-3057185
Navigator	2nd Lt. Donald S. Petty AO-3038433
Navigator	1st Lt. Max H. Workman AO-2229782

Flight Officer Robert Slane, January 1943.

Acknowledgements

First and foremost I must acknowledge and express my love and grateful appreciation to my Mother, Myrtle Roper Slane. She saved all of my letters written to my family from the years 1940 through 1945. The correspondence she saved included the letters and cards received from me and those written about me while I was held as a Prisoner of War in Germany from October 1943 to May 1945.

Special thanks and gratitude must be afforded to the work accomplished by Ewell Ross McCright. McCright saw seven members of his crew killed before he bailed out of a burning B-17 Fortress on January the 23,rd 1943. Taken prisoner by the Germans, he was imprisoned in Stalag Luft III. It was during his imprisonment in Stalag Luft III, that he was assigned by Lt Col. Clark, the head of Escape Activities, to interview and maintain a brief historical record of every prisoner of war assigned quarters in the <u>South Compound</u> of Stalag Luft III. This ledger record included the date "shot down," the date and place captured, crew position and type of aircraft flying when shot down, the target of the mission, whether wounded or not and any previous locations where the flyer might have been imprisoned before arrival at Stalag Luft III.

Despite many searches, forced marches and many other hard ships, Ewell McCrieght managed to save these records. Ewell Ross Mc Crieght died on the 24th of April, 1990.

Fortunately for us and for historians Ewell McCright had a great friend who accepted the responsibility for gathering the ledger material accumulated by McCright and after additional research published a book that includes all available information from those ledgers. That friend was Arthur A. Wright and the book is "BEHIND the WIRE," Stalag Luft III, South Compound. Arnold Wright is a resident of **Benton, Arkansas.**

Arnold A. Wright undertook the task of publishing the ledgers in their entirety and in his book he included additional information relative to prison life that was extracted from letters, interviews and personal contact with former prisoners of war. I am personally indebted to Arnold Wright as I received a copy of his book in 1994 and he has granted me permission to use the statistical data from the McCright ledgers.

The letters of love and support from a little student nurse while I was a Prisoner of War in Germany helped me to survive and of course it was important that she was still waiting when I returned. Her love and support has continued through the years and her encouragement has been part of the stimuli to keep plugging away at a book that seems would never be completed. That student nurse is Mary Lee Valentine and I changed her name to mine, but she will always be my "Valentine."

Introduction

Although many years have passed since World War II and much of what occurred during those years has faded into the past; there are certain events that are forever etched in my memory. I still see the faces of my B-17 crew members just as I first saw them in 1943. Those faces are still young and filled with the buoyancy of youth. I can still hear the cough and feel the vibration of an aircraft engine as it awakens with the rough, jerky motions of a propeller that without warning suddenly settles into a smooth, beautiful, see-through circle of air. I remember the feeling of exhilaration when skimming over the tops of stratus clouds that are layered like a ruffled sheet covering the earth as far as the eye can see.

I remember the helpless feeling when flying through a barrage of dirty looking puffs of flak and watching as a train of these black demons gets closer and closer until you can see the red glow of destruction and hear the muffled sound of the exploding shell. I can still see the red tracers of enemy 20mm arcing over head and fading into distant space. I can hear the shattering sound of guns within our aircraft as the gunners fought for our lives to deter an enemy that was determined to down our aircraft.

I have vivid recollections of the cast of characters who occupied Room 4 in Block 136, in the South Compound of the German Prison Camp at Stalag Luft III - my home for fourteen of the eighteen and a half months that I was a prisoner of war in Germany. I will always remember standing at the feet of a dead Corporal who had been murdered by a guard at Stalag Luft III. That date was Easter Sunday, 1944.

There is no forgetting the snow and piercing, icy cold wind as we prisoners struggled to stay on our feet and to keep moving during a forced march in the dead of winter. I remember well, the stench, filth, and hunger as I traveled for three days and nights locked up in a 40 and 8 French box car with over sixty fellow prisoners.

Most of all I remember the feeling of despair as the days passed and freedom seemed so remote that I sought God's help to give me the courage to attempt escape and I resolved that I would accept what ever His plans for my future might be.

Never to be forgotten is the feeling of exhilaration during those short periods of freedom when I finally did escape.

I note that, after the 2nd Schweinfurt mission on 14 October 1943, a command decision was made that for the remainder of the year there would be no bomber missions scheduled against targets deep in enemy territory during clear weather unless fighter escort was available all the way to and from the target. However, this story is not about decisions related to the air war or to the significance of a particular target.

My experiences are typical of thousands of men who fought in the air war over Europe. Others have stories of action and events that they encountered during successful completion of a combat tour. Many did not live to see the end of combat over Europe - others flew and completed their missions during a period when fighter protection was available all the way to and from the target, but there was always the danger from flak or loss of oxygen or loss of engines. Any aircraft that fell out of formation for one reason or another was always exposed to increased danger. With respect to the crew members who were shot down - some were killed by enemy gunfire; others parachuted to safety only to be captured and sometimes killed by irate citizens. Many died in the crash of their aircraft. Some were badly injured and were hospitalized prior to imprisonment. There were those fortunate enough to survive and receive aid in escaping to a neutral country. Many, like myself, had no opportunity to escape and became prisoners of war.

This is my story,
Robert Slane

XII

This photograph was taken at Grand Island Nebraska, in August 1943, just prior to our overseas deployment to England. All 39 Officers are 1st Pilot, B-17 crew commanders. I am the fifth person counting from the right, in the group that is kneeling. We were the "Bowman Provisional Group." Major Bowman is seated, center-forward.

PART I

GOING TO WAR

PART I GOING TO WAR

Grand Island, Nebraska

It is August 23, 1943. My B-17 bomber flight crew is busy scrambling to gather their flight gear and personal belongings for storage in our "factory fresh" B-17G aircraft located at the Army Air Base, Grand Island, Nebraska. We have all just returned from a ten-day furlough, which had been granted after completion of the third and final phase of our combat crew training. I returned a day early, worried that some unforeseen circumstance might cause a delay in our deployment to a combat theater of operations. The other crew members had scattered to locations all over the nation to make their final visit with loved ones before departing for combat.

Lt. Joe Johnson, the co-pilot, is from Tacoma, Washington. He has recently married. I met his wife Bette just before we departed Spokane Washington, after completing our third phase of combat training at Geiger Field, an airbase located near Spokane.

Lt. Arthur Glenn Foster, the navigator, was also recently married. His wife, Gloria, was able to visit Glenn prior to our leaving Geiger Field. Glenn was the last crew member to join our crew. He reported for crew assignment in July 1943 shortly after graduating from navigation training. Glenn Foster and Gloria are devout Mormons. Gloria will remain in her home in Salt Lake City as she awaits Glenn's return.

Lt. Bill Runner, our fun-loving and musically inclined trumpet player/bombardier, has family in Bridgeton, New Jersey. With the exception of S/Sgt Charles Groth, our right waist gunner, Bill had the greatest distance to travel. Charles Groth, the oldest member of our crew, is a seasoned thirty years of age and a "tough talkin'" New Yorker from Brooklyn. His bark is much greater than his bite. The enlisted crew members have generally accepted him as their unofficial spokesman.

The only married enlisted crew member is Sgt Claud Smith, who lists his hometown as Newport, Arkansas. Of special significance to me and to the other crew members is the fact that Claud has received final approval of his application for pilot training, but has made the choice to delay acceptance until after he completes his combat tour as the tail gunner on our crew.

S/Sgt Robert Soloman, a tall, handsome Mississippian, is the left waist gunner. Robert, with his athlete's build and disposition, played minor league baseball. His good looks have him branded as a "ladies' man," but he scores well with me as a highly qualified gunner.

Late to join the crew was our radio operator/gunner, S/Sgt Victor H. Kuhlman. Being from Nebraska, Victor had the shortest distance to travel on leave. Slightly built and not very tall, he is noted for his wry sense of humor.

Hailing from Fairfield, Oklahoma is S/Sgt Sherman Sly. This serious, quiet-spoken man is my right arm with respect to keeping the aircraft engines operating within their proper limits and operating the fuel transfer system. His duties during combat include manning the top turret guns.

The man who commands special respect from every crew member is S/Sgt Louis L. Brown from Franklin, Pennsylvania. In addition to assisting the engineer in his duties, Louis mans the ball turret gun position that is located in the belly of the aircraft. This turret is considered the most hazardous of all the gun positions. Brown has a larger build then most men who volunteer for that position, and I marvel that he has the courage and self-control to fold his body into a pretzel to fit into the ball-turret.

I am 2nd Lt. Robert Slane, the first-pilot and crew commander of the above-mentioned crew. With respect to my own leave, I first went to Santa Monica, California and then accompanied my brother and sister to Trinidad, Colorado to visit my parents. This had been my first furlough since enlisting as a private in the Army Air Corps in 1941. Despite my many trials and tribulations during the past two years, I had finally accomplished my lifelong goal of becoming a military pilot…

PART I GOING TO WAR

I left home on August 5, 1941, my eighteenth birthday, to enlist in the Army Air Corps. On that date, the local recruiting office in Trinidad, Colorado gave me a train ticket to Denver and then provided transportation to the adjacent Army camp at Ft. Logan, Colorado. I arrived at Ft. Logan that same day and had a physical examination scheduled for the next morning. I was so excited that it was three days before I could slow my heart rate down to an acceptable level. Consequently, I wasn't sworn in until August 8, 1941.

I weighed 119 pounds. The quartermaster had no khaki trousers small enough to fit my waist. The solution was to provide me with a set of blue fatigue clothing with the promise that when I was assigned to an Army "Boot Camp," I would receive the standard issue of clothing.

Having finally passed the physical I was, for some unknown reason, placed on a train headed for Ft. Sill, Oklahoma. When I arrived, I was informed that there had been a mistake. The Army was not conducting "Boot Camp" at Ft. Sill and I should have been sent to Jefferson Barracks, Missouri or Ellington Field, Texas. I still wore only the fatigue uniform, but it seemed to make no difference to anyone at Ft Sill. I was told to report to Base Headquarters every morning, which I did for three days. I reported to an army sergeant at 6 A.M. and was handed a large basket and a knife. For three days, it was my job to cut out dandelions on the lawn in front of the Headquarters building.

On the fourth day, I was put on a train to Ellington Field near Galveston, Texas. I was still wearing fatigue clothing. I finally received new and proper-fitting khaki uniforms during personnel processing at Ellington Air Field.

While undergoing recruit training at the Ellington Field "Boot Camp," I learned that the Army Air Corps was accepting applications for enlisted pilot training. The minimum age to become an "Aviation Student" was eighteen. The minimum age to apply for Aviation Cadet Flight training was, at that time, twenty years.

I immediately applied for pilot training as an Aviation Student. I would graduate as a Staff Sergeant Pilot upon completion of the course. The application was returned to me with instructions to re-submit when I arrived at my first base of assignment after completing the "Recruit Training" at Ellington Air Base.

My new base of assignment was Lerdo Air Base at Bakersfield, California. Upon arrival at Lerdo Air Base, I re-submitted my application. There was a delay, as I had to be scheduled for a physical. Finally, in mid-October, I was sent to March Field for the flight physical. Again, my heart rate was so fast that I had three re-checks before finally passing that portion of the physical. I was notified that I had passed the physical, with one exception: I had a "deviated septum" in my nose, but was told that with corrective surgery my application would be approved.

I returned to my base at Lerdo with instructions to get scheduled for the corrective surgery. It was another two months before I was finally permitted to go to Hoff General Hospital at Santa Barbara, California for the operation. Upon return to my assigned base at Lerdo, I discovered that my application had been returned to me with a note stating that the time for completing the corrective surgery had expired, and that if I was still interested in the program I should "re-apply."

Disheartened but not about to give up, I started the application process anew. In the meantime, I continued my duties as an aircraft mechanic. During this period, I was promoted to corporal and assigned duty as a crew chief. My primary responsibility was the daily maintenance of a BT-13, an aircraft basic flight trainer. My flight line "boss" was a Staff Sergeant named Whitfield. It was with his help that I was finally able to get rescheduled for another flight physical.

Instead of graduating in an early pilot class in 1942 (Class-42D), I graduated in Class 43A on January 4th, 1943. In the interim period, between application acceptance and graduation as a military pilot, a new change had come into effect. Instead of graduating as Staff/Sergeants, all Aviation Students were graduated as Flight Officers (F/O). We received Warrants instead of Sergeant stripes or Commissions.

My station assignment after graduation from flight training

was Gowen Field in Boise, Idaho. Arriving as a fledgling B-17 co-pilot, I was immediately assigned to a newly formed crew to begin Combat Crew phase training. I was placed on a crew with a first-pilot who had received formal B-17 pilot transition training at Sebring, Florida, as had the majority of first-pilots.

It was at about the mid-point of our first phase of training that our crew first-pilot began having problems with his night vision. He was given a series of depth perception tests and had difficulty in passing the standard night vision checks. At this juncture of our training, I had an advantage over most co-pilots in that my pilot had permitted me to do much of the flying, including take-offs, landings and formation flight. When our crew's assigned pilot was temporarily grounded pending further evaluation, I was given a series of flight checks, and in late March, 1943, at the age of nineteen, I took over the crew as first-pilot. I remained first-pilot throughout the remainder of our phased combat crew training at Gowen Field in Boise, Idaho; Geiger Field in Spokane, Washington; and Pendleton Air Base at Pendleton, Oregon. For a short time, my flying school classmate, F/O Joe Ferguson, was co-pilot. Joe Johnson joined the crew as co-pilot during our phase training at Geiger Field.

Since I had taken on first-pilot responsibilities, I was recommended for promotion from Flight Officer (F/O) direct to 1st Lt. This promotion request was denied. The denial stated that in order to be promoted, I must first receive a commission as a 2nd Lt. The title made little difference to me as my only desire was to continue on as a pilot with my own crew.

The promotion to 2nd Lt. came on August 13th, 1943. I received assurance from the Provisional Group Commander, Major Bowman, that now that I had received a Commission as a 2nd Lt., he was initiating action for my immediate promotion to 1st Lt. The other three officers assigned to my crew had been Aviation Cadets and had received their Commissions as 2nd Lt's. upon graduation from their respective flight classes. Despite the fact that my officer crew members "outranked" me, there was never any question as to who was in charge of our Combat Crew.

All crew members were present when we reported to inspect our new aircraft. We were quite certain that our destination would be somewhere in the South Pacific as a jungle kit had been placed at each crew position in the aircraft. Additional jungle kits had also been stored in the mid-section of the aircraft. An assignment to combat in the South Pacific was just fine with us, as we felt we had a special and personal score to settle with the Japanese.

Our final "graduation" exercise had been a low-level navigation flight from the Army Air Base at Pendleton, Oregon to a geographic point located some five hundred miles out in the middle of the Pacific Ocean. After reaching this geographic point, we were to return and make landfall near the city of Oceanside, Oregon.

Upon our return, Glenn Foster made a perfect landfall. We cerebrated by flying along the beach at Oceanside. It was our misfortune, or perhaps *my* misfortune, that one of the beach vacationers was an army Colonel. This man made note of our aircraft number and called the air base to report that a B-17 crew had "buzzed" the beach area while flying at a "dangerously" low altitude.

After landing, I was instructed to report to the Squadron operations officer. The first question posed by the 'Ops' officer was, "Who on your crew is from Seaside, Oregon?" Of course, no one on the crew was from Seaside and I had to acknowledge that I had in fact "checked out" the beach area. The operations officer didn't appear too upset, but he needed to respond to someone higher in authority. He finally agreed to report that "the crew was unsure of their location and had been forced to fly along the shore line to find a landmark, thus the reason for the relatively low flight." It was difficult to accept a statement that seemed to reflect the inability of the crew to navigate, but in view of the possibility of more drastic action, it was a reasonable explanation. I was hopeful that this response would be accepted as I wanted my crew to "get out of Dodge" without any further discussion of the "overseas orientation" flight.

It wasn't until the day before departure that we were finally briefed on our overseas destination. The "Bowman Provisional

Group" (36 B-17 crews and aircraft) was scheduled to deploy to England! The decision to send us to fight in the European conflict was a surprise to the crew and to me, but we weren't displeased at the thought of combat against the Nazis. We were young and excited at the prospect of putting our months of training to use in actual combat, be it Europe or the South Pacific.

August 25th was a day of preparation and briefings. The aircraft were scheduled to depart the next day with a ten-minute spacing interval between each takeoff. I learned that a Captain from higher headquarters was going to accompany my crew on the first leg of the journey. I wondered if my crew had been selected for monitoring because of the 'Seaside' incident.

We were up early on the morning of August 26th. This was the day when we would begin our flight to a land we knew only through geography, history, and stories. Ireland, England, and Scotland — most of us had only dreamed of visiting those magical places. Yes, we were excited, and a little fearful, too. But we had the vibrancy of youth to carry us through whatever the future held for us.

Most of the crew reported to the aircraft to help prepare it for the long overseas flight. I wanted Joe Johnson and the navigator, Glenn Foster, with me at the weather briefing. It was at this briefing that I met Capt. Nye, who would be accompanying my crew on this deployment.

The weather at Grand Island was typical for late August and we had clear skies; however, at the weather briefing, we were apprised of a deep line of thunderstorms and a fast-moving cold front that extended from the Great Lakes area south to the Carolinas. I discussed the weather conditions with Captain Nye, and he indicated to me that it was my responsibility to make all decisions with respect to the flight. Because other aircraft had already taken off to fly our same route and had not yet reported any trouble, I decided we would go ahead as scheduled.

Precisely at 8:15 AM, I applied full power to the engines and began the takeoff roll. Our aircraft was at a gross weight that required more runway than our normal training aircraft. This combat configured airplane was a late "G" model and had additional fuel tanks and more protective armor than the earlier models we had used in training. The fuel tanks had been loaded to their fullest capacity. As we broke ground and began a slow climb, the engineer noted that fuel was flowing from one of the left wing tanks. When I checked the wing surface, I could see that a fuel cap had probably not been correctly fastened.

I notified the tower that we had a fuel leak and that I would be bringing the aircraft back for an emergency landing. I had no trouble getting the aircraft back on the ground, but I found that I needed almost full power to maintain correct landing speed. This was the first time I had ever landed a fully loaded B-17. I was surprised that in order to maintain correct airspeed I had to use almost full power at touchdown for the landing.

As we suspected, the fuel leak was due to an improperly fastened fuel tank cover. With the problem now corrected, I made a second take off and we were on our way to our first destination—Bangor, Maine.

As we approached the line of thunderstorms, it became obvious that the tops of the thunderheads were towering above our altitude. We all put on oxygen masks, knowing that we would be above 10,000 feet during any attempt to over-fly thunder storm areas. As we approached the clouds, it became even more evident that with the heavy fuel load we had no chance of topping the swirling, rapidly building clouds. We discussed attempting to fly south around the squall line, but that route would offer no solution if the squall line was as far south as had been predicted in the weather briefing. I made the decision, with Captain Nye's concurrence, that we would select areas where there appeared to be breaks between the thunderclouds and attempt to fly around the dark areas where we could expect the most rain and turbulence. We managed to pick our way through the first line of thunderstorms, deviating from course at times to avoid areas that looked particularly ominous.

About thirty minutes after clearing the first line of thunderstorms, a second line of towering clouds were sighted dead ahead in our flight path. This was obviously the fast-moving squall line predicted by the weather forecaster. We diverted to a southerly direction and found an opening that appeared to offer a passage between two cloud buildups. We entered this new arena of clouds, only to find that there was no clear route of passage. We were effectively blocked in all directions. I reversed flight but the turbulence increased, and suddenly St Elmo's fire was dancing along the windshield as we flew into an area of heavy hail. It became apparent that the return route to Grand Island would be just as dangerous as the one ahead, so I turned back to our original heading.

It was at this point that Capt. Nye replaced Joe Johnson in the co-pilot's position. He agreed that at this juncture it would be best to continue the flight on course and hope to fly through and get ahead of the line of thunderstorms. The hail continued. The sound of the hailstones striking the aircraft was deafening. There were periods when we were flying in total darkness, and we could see from the cockpit that the wing forward surfaces were receiving large dents. We were in "updrafts" and "downdrafts," losing or gaining two or three thousand feet, depending on the severity of the air motion. The airspeed varied as much as one hundred miles per hour and would often drop to zero. About all we could do at that point was maintain normal power settings and try to keep the wings and fuselage level.

Capt Nye and I alternated controlling the aircraft and kept up a conversation, hoping to allay the fears of the crew members who were depending on us to keep the aircraft under control. Captain Nye's presence in the cockpit provided additional assurance to the crew and to me. He was an experienced B-17 pilot, and any resentment I may have harbored as a result of his assignment to fly with my crew for this overseas flight was drowned in the fury of the storm.

We continued flight in the described severe weather conditions for about twenty minutes, which seemed like an eternity. We flew in non-turbulent clouds for about twenty or thirty more minutes before we finally broke into the clear. The remainder of the flight was uneventful, as was my landing at Bangor. The flight had been extended due to the weather. I landed the aircraft after eight hours and fifteen minutes of flight.

Captain Nye acknowledged that we had just flown through the worst weather conditions he had ever encountered in his flying career. His comments with respect to the crew were complimentary, and I acknowledged to him that his presence in the cockpit had provided additional assurance to the crew that we would make it through the bad weather.

Upon arrival at Bangor, we found that only two other crews had made it through the weather to Bangor. Several crews had diverted to alternate bases and some had returned to the air base at Grand Island.

Inspection of our aircraft revealed "golf ball" sized dents in the leading edges of the wings and the wing deicer boots were ripped to shreds. The cover protecting the loop antenna for the radio compass was cracked open and the canvas sections of the forward gun turret were shredded. Since we were on a priority mission, there was a maintenance crew assigned to work all night to do what repairs were necessary for our continued flight.

I was up early the next morning with Joe Johnson and Sherman Sly to check on the work accomplished. We flew a test flight in the local area to insure there was no damage to any of the engines and to check out our radio compass. The engines operated fine, with no sign of problems.

The next leg of our journey was the flight from Bangor, Maine to Gander Bay in Newfoundland, which was the departure base for our destination in Scotland. After a five-hour flight we arrived at Gander Bay and made our final preparation for the flight overseas.

We flew to Gander Bay without Captain Nye, as he was continuing his journey to England with another crew from the Bowman Provisional Group. He told me that his job was to get a sampling of the quality and training of the replacement crews. He explained his simple criteria for selecting the crews he would fly with: He wanted to fly with the youngest crew commander as well as the oldest, most senior crew commander. My crew was selected because I was the youngest. 1st Lt. James A. Mullinax was the oldest, most senior crew commander. Captain Nye's flight to the British Isles would be with Mullinax. I was relieved to know that his flight with me had not been related to the flight along the beach at Seaside, Oregon!

Capt Nye's words to me before departure were, "Slane, shave that thing off. It makes you look kind of silly." He was referring to the 'fuzz' I had grown since returning from leave. The entire crew had decided that since we were going to the South Pacific we would all grow beards. Although the majority of the crew had shaved after learning that our destination would be Europe, I had not yet shaved. Captain Nye's remark was sufficient to cause an immediate change in my appearance.

Front row (l to r) Navigator - Glenn Foster, 1st Pilot - Robert Slane, Co-pilot - Joe Johnson, Bombardier - Bill Runner.
Back row (l to r) 1. Radio Operator/Gunner - Victor Kuhlman
2. Right Waist Gunner - Charles Groth 3. Tail Gunner - Claud Smith
4. Engineer/Top Turret Gunner, Sherman Sly
5. Ball Turret Gunner/Asst Engineer - Louis Brown
6. Left Waist Gunner - Robert Soloman

Prestwick, Scotland

It was August 31, 1943. We tried to get as much crew rest as possible because we were scheduled to depart Gander that evening. We would fly all night and arrive in Prestwick, Scotland during daylight hours in the British Isles.

We had another heavy weight takeoff, this time over the water. The weather people had made me a chart showing the levels where I could expect icing conditions. The deicing boots hadn't been repaired and I wanted some assurance that we wouldn't be flying in weather where icing conditions were anticipated.

Glenn spent hours going over his navigation charts, plotting our travel route. On the way to Bangor, Sherman Sly had charted our fuel consumption. According to our calculations, we should have a good reserve in case there was unexpected weather in Britain.

Finally, we were airborne and on our way! Was it really happening? I had a deep feeling of pride for the work and accomplishments of my crew, and I took time to silently give thanks to the Lord for His help in getting us through the storm and making this day possible.

I leveled the aircraft at our planned altitude and turned the controls over to Joe. I wanted to walk through the bomb bay, where our personal gear is stored, and check with the enlisted crew. There was a card game just starting. Everyone appeared to have fully recovered from the shock and fear that was evident during our encounter with the stormy weather enroute to Bangor, Maine. There was a time during that flight when everyone was hanging on to whatever they could reach. A parachute ripcord had been inadvertently pulled and the parachute had spilled out into the fuselage. A replacement parachute had been obtained at Bangor.

I wasn't sleepy and remained fully awake as the hours slipped by. We were flying below an overcast sky, frequently through lower layers of stratus clouds. There was no turbulence, but there could be potential problems with icing. Sherman Sly checked fuel consumption against his plotted curve. The consumption rate was somewhat higher than his predicted fuel curve. I noted that Glenn Foster had made several trips back into the bomb bay. Glenn was off the intercom system, so I queried Bill Runner as to what Glenn was doing with his frequent trips to the bomb bay. Bill indicated that Glenn was looking for something, but he didn't know exactly what.

We had been airborne about five hours when I glanced back into the bomb bay corridor and noticed that Glenn was once again back in that area and had enlisted someone to help him search through the equipment bags. I asked Bill Runner to tell Glenn that I wanted to talk to him on interphone as soon as he was back at his navigation station.

While talking to Bill, I felt someone touch my arm. It was Glenn — in tears. His words to me were, "You've got to turn back. I left all my star charts back in Grand Island." I was firm when I responded that we were "not turning back under any circumstances." I pointed out to him that if we turned back now we would face headwinds all the way and that it would probably take us longer to return to America than if we continued toward our destination in Scotland. Seeing that he was becoming even more distraught, I pointed out to him that with the solid overcast above us we probably would never get a star shot anyway so he should navigate with what he had available. I wanted him to try and put any thought of the star charts out of his mind.

Glenn had been so obsessed with finding the star charts and fearing the consequences if they couldn't be found that he had overlooked the fact that the charts would be useless in the type of weather we were encountering. I told him to have confidence in his preplanned flight route since I knew he had spent hours preparing for the flight. I also reminded him that the aircraft radio compass had a directional capability and that we had been briefed to try and home-in on the powerful radio beam located at Shornhorst, Scotland. Once this burden had been lifted from him, Glenn went back to work using the skills that had enabled him to rise to the top of his military navigation training class.

We had been airborne almost nine hours when fuel consumption began to be of major concern. Sherman Sly showed me the consumption curve plotted against the one programmed. The difference was alarming. Fuel consumption had been plotted during the flight from Grand Island to Bangor. With normal power settings, fuel consumption was exactly as had been planned during that earlier flight. I questioned Sherman regarding possible engine work that might have been performed on the ground at Bangor, but he knew of no engine work that had been required or performed.

Bill Runner, overhearing the conversation, said that he had gone back to the aircraft the night we landed and noticed that the cowling had been removed from all four engines and that two ground mechanics were on a stand, appearing to be working on one engine. He said he gave no further thought to what he had seen since the cowling was probably being removed to check the amount of hail damage to the engine cowlings. The engine cowlings, like the leading edges of the wings, had dents from the hailstorm. My immediate thought was that there might be people at Bangor who were engaged in sabotage activity. My questions to Sherman and Louis Brown were an attempt to find out if there was any chance that the fuel flow mechanism could have been altered in such as way that it could not easily be detected.

Since I received no positive answer to that question, I decided that this problem should be put aside and addressed at another time. Instead, I would address the immediate concern and review the charts to try to come up with changes in altitude or power settings that would further reduce fuel consumption. I lowered the altitude, adjusted the power settings and we pressed on.

Emergency Landing

We had been airborne for eleven hours. It was daylight and the sun was shining. We picked up the radio beacon located at Shornhorst, Scotland and altered our course ten degrees to the left. Prior to our departure from Gander Bay, we had been warned that the Germans often sent out false radio signals to draw approaching aircraft off course. This signal was in line with the plotted course Glenn had on his navigation map, so I was confident we were still on course.

One by one, the low fuel warning lights began to flash. Soon all four lights shone a steady red. Victor Kuhlman had been instructed to send out an emergency SOS, as there was a possibility that we would run out of fuel before landfall. Glenn and Bill were still in the nose of the aircraft, ready to evacuate to the radio room to assume ditching positions on a moment's notice. The rest of the crew, with the exception of Sherman Sly, were in the radio compartment in their ditching positions.

I had designated Claud Smith to be in charge of the evacuation and release of the life rafts if we were forced to ditch. Sherman was still forward, standing where he could immediately decide whether it was feasible to transfer fuel to any engine that had begun to die from fuel starvation. Joe and I had unbuckled our parachutes so we would be free to get out of our seats after the aircraft had landed in the water. I had instructed Glenn to look for a landing field near the Irish coastline. If we made it to land, I would land at the first field sighted. If we had multiple engine failure, I would make a crash landing in the most suitable location I could find.

The engines droned on. I held altitude at two thousand feet as we monitored the direction of the ocean swells below us. The ocean looked like a huge glass plate. The greenish-blue water had a shimmering, shiny look that hid the quiet turbulence lurking below the surface. The wind was from our left. I told Joe that if we had to ditch, we should turn about forty-five degrees to the left of course and land parallel to the small white crests that marked the surging waves. Joe agreed. He asked where I intended to evacuate the aircraft. I pointed to the pilot's window. Joe, who weighed one hundred and eight-five pounds, indicated that he would not be able to get through the co-pilot window. I agreed and told him that if the engines began to fail, he and Sherman were to go back to the radio room for the water landing.

Twenty more minutes passed and the engines were still turning. I don't know how many silent prayers were being said, but I felt something besides fuel was keeping them alive.

Bill Runner was the first to see the tiny speck of land just ahead of us. We were elated but cautious. There was still no certainty that we would make landfall before the engines failed.

In a few minutes, the full picture of a magical fairyland was visible. All shades of green and gold were reflected in the quilted patches of land. We continued flight over land, my stomach knotted with apprehension. I could feel beads of water trickling down my face as we swept over the beautiful countryside.

I had no sooner said, "Prepare for crash landing," than I saw an airfield and a runway dead ahead. We were over the runway so fast that I only had time to rock my wings to indicate we were in emergency. I ask Glenn to fire a red flare, but before he could respond, I saw a green light flash from what appeared to be a small tower. The aircraft was in a turn at the time, so I continued to bank, drop the gear and make a short field landing approach. Within three minutes of sighting the runway, we were on that runway. A loud cheer emanated from the radio room. The sense of relief I felt when the wheels touched that runway can never be adequately described.

I taxied the aircraft off the runway and waited for a few minutes for instructions to a parking location. A man in a jeep flagged us with a 'Follow Me' sign, and we taxied onto a tarmac and cut the engines. An American major, the commander of the detachment at this emergency air base, stood by the aircraft as we parked.

As it turned out, the location, which was named "Nuts Corner," had been one of the bases listed in our flight "flimsy" for use in an emergency. At the time of the emergency landing, I had no knowledge of the base's ownership.

The Major welcomed us to Ireland, pointing out that if I had landed on an airfield not too far to the south, my crew would probably have been interned in the Irish Free State or "Eire" as it was called. I briefly explained to the Major the reason for the emergency landing, emphasizing my belief that our aircraft had been sabotaged. The major indicated that erroneous fuel tank indicators might have caused the problem.

As we were unloading our gear for a night's stay, I noticed that the Major and one of his assistants were on the aircraft wings checking each tank with a fuel dipstick. After checking the tanks, he approached me, shaking his head. He hadn't been able to detect fuel in any of the tanks. If there was any fuel left in the tanks, the level was so low that the residual would not be detected because of the slope of the wings. The faulty gage theory had been disproved. We had had no major deviations from course, no increases in power settings, and the weather had not been a factor.

I repeated to the major my belief that our aircraft had been sabotaged. He appeared skeptical but acknowledged that there had been aircraft on this same deployment route that had disappeared without a trace. He agreed to make a record of my suspicions and forward the information to a higher level of command.

We were taken to the visitors' quarters with a promise from our host that he would have transportation available for a trip into Belfast for dinner at one of the Irish pubs.

It was a happy, excited, and talkative crew as we were transported by motor truck to the city. The people at the pub had been forewarned of our arrival and the food was ready. I ate lamb for the first time in my life and enjoyed every bite, and there was plenty of stout brew. The servers were women with brogues so thick we had difficulty understanding their speech. But what warm and friendly people they were! We had truly been blessed this day.

I finally had to remind everyone that we were planning an early flight in the morning to our final destination—the airfield at Prestwick, Scotland.

Misplaced Watches

The next morning, we made a short one-hour flight to Prestwick. Upon arrival, we were parked and informed that the aircraft would remain at Prestwick. We were somewhat surprised as we'd been under the assumption that the crew would be assigned directly to one of the operational bomb wings and that "our" B-17 aircraft would accompany us.

Joe and I left the airplane to accomplish the turnover paperwork. A Scottish ground crew was already at our location, checking some of the equipment on board that was destined for the depot at Prestwick. Our flight crew was busy gathering up their personal belongings for transfer to a waiting "lorry." When we returned to remove our personal flight gear and maps, Joe remarked that his wristwatch was missing. We had both placed our wristwatches on a ledge above the instrument panel. My watch was also missing. A check with our flight crew was made. None of them had been in our area, but two people from the local depot had been seen entering the cockpit. We had all noticed that there had been no friendly greetings from this ground crew when they met the aircraft to download the equipment scheduled for delivery to the depot. I used our aircraft radio to report the theft to personnel in the control tower.

We stayed overnight at Prestwick and departed for a crew replacement center late the next afternoon. Our watches were never recovered and thus, we left Scotland without the feelings of good will that had been so generously bestowed upon us by the Irish in Belfast.

I was given a train order. It read "LT. Slane and sixty-nine others." We were to depart by rail for London at about 10 PM from the rail station at Kilmarnock, a town near Prestwick. In London we were to change trains and continue by rail to Hemel Hempstead.

We arrived at Hemel Hempstead at about 8 AM on September 4th. We traveled by bus to Bovington, the combat crew replacement and training center, where we received theater indoctrination training for about two weeks. The individual crews were then assigned as replacement crews to various B-17 combat units stationed in England.

England

On September 17th, 1943, we finally arrived at our assigned combat unit. My crew and 2nd Lt. Marco Demara's crew were assigned to the 91st Bomb Group located at Bassingbourne, near Cambridge. Our crew was further assigned to the 401st Bomb Squadron. I was introduced to the Squadron Commander, Major Gillespie and the Operations Officer, Captain McPartlin.

I was assigned quarters in a large brick building. My roommate was Captain Harry Lay, a seasoned combat pilot. Captain Lay had completed the required twenty-five combat missions and had volunteered to fly five additional sorties. If he completed the thirty missions, he would be the first pilot in the 91st Bomb Group to volunteer and accomplish this extraordinary task. For all I knew, Captain Lay might have been the first pilot in this theater to volunteer for an additional five sorties.

The quarters were a welcome surprise. I had expected Quonset huts, but these were permanent quarters. I had hoped to be with the other officers on the crew, but was told that the building to which I was assigned provided quarters for only the first-pilots and that co-pilots had their own building. Bill Runner and Glenn Foster were together at another location. The enlisted members of the crew were housed in a building at a different location.

On my first orientation flight in the local area, I rode the co-pilot's seat. The entire crew and I flew again on the 24th and 25th of September. One flight was a simulated combat mission with a formation join-up. Several other units had joined up with the 91st Bomb Group aircraft and I flew in a three-ship formation as part of this "Battle Wing." What appeared to be hundreds of B-17s joined this "simulated" combat force.

Monitoring my flight procedures was an experienced, mission qualified, co-pilot who explained some of the tactics that would be used. I felt confident that I would be able to fly in tight formation during combat.

After completing twelve flight hours of additional training, I was ready for combat. On September 26th, I flew two more hours.

My crew and I were ready. We were scheduled to fly our first combat mission on September 27th, but wouldn't know the target until mission briefing that morning.

September 27, 1943
Mission to Emden

My full crew was at the initial briefing; however, we found out that on this first mission, Victor Kuhlman would be replaced by a substitute radio operator, Sgt. J. H. Clifton. An 'instructor' gunner, T/Sgt. G.W. Boyle, was replacing our Charles Groth. I had been told by other pilots that for the first five missions, it was common policy to have a combat-experienced pilot fly as first-pilot while the crew-assigned first-pilot would gain experience by flying as co-pilot. I was thankful that this policy was evidently not going to apply to me on this, our first combat sortie.

We were briefed that P-47 fighters would escort the bomber force all the way to the target and all the way back to England. This was advertised as a 'first.' My crew was excited. Other than to tell them to be professional, to try and stay calm, and to watch out for each other, I had no special words of advice.

Take-off was uneventful and there were no problems in the join-up. I flew formation off the right wing of the lead aircraft in the middle element and stayed locked in close to the element leader. The target was the port city of Emden. Most of our flight would be over water. Another squadron in the group had joined us. One of their three ship elements was flying just ahead, above and to the right of our aircraft. We were flying at an altitude of 23,000 ft.

The flight to the target was relatively uneventful. My gunners could see fighter aircraft in the distance; most of their discussion centered on the identification of the aircraft type. As predicted, the P-47s' were in evidence. T/Sgt Boyle, the instructor gunner, called out to say that he thought some of the gunners flying in the bomber aircraft on the extreme right of the formation were shooting at our own aircraft. I was so busy flying formation that I could only listen and visualize what was occurring around me.

"As we approach the target, we see flames flowing from a B-17 that is positioned above and to the right of our aircraft. The flames are emanating from an area adjacent to the inboard side of the No.3 engine. The aircraft remains in formation as we turn at the initial point and start the bomb run. Its bomb doors are opened in preparation for bomb release. Flames are now sucked up into the bomb bay and a raging fire is visible. After bomb release, the bomb bay doors remain open. The aircraft begins to drift to the left and falling debris from the right wing is striking our airplane. I am forced to drop back and to the left and as I do so, the hatch on the ball turret comes whistling by our aircraft. A body slowly emerges from the turret, then suddenly releases, and quickly drops out of sight. The aircraft then noses down and forward, making a slow turn to the left. I ease back into formation and have Joe take control of our aircraft. Looking down and to the left, I watch as the aircraft slowly rolls upside down. Then suddenly there is nothing! This B-17 fortress has evidently exploded and all that can be seen are small pieces of scattered debris. In the next few seconds, four parachutes bloom out below the area where the aircraft disintegrated."

Our waist gunner, Robert Soloman, also witnessed the entire episode. Terrifying and unreal, that scene will not easily be forgotten.

After departing the target area and flying back over water on the return leg of the mission, I received a call from Louis Brown. He reported that he did not see our bombs release when the lead aircraft released their bomb load. Bill Runner, the bombardier, immediately made a check and verified that we still had a full bomb load. This news was disappointing, as we should have made a visual check of the bomb bay immediately after bomb release. I told Bill that we would worry about mistakes made when we returned to our home base, but in the meantime we would have to jettison the bombs since the policy at that time was to not return to England with live bombs.

The bombs were subsequently jettisoned in the North Sea while we were still near the German coastline. One other aircraft in our squadron had the same problem; they also jettisoned their bombs. This time a visual check was made to confirm that all bombs had been jettisoned from our aircraft.

My crew fired at enemy aircraft at intervals throughout the mission, but with so many aircraft firing at the same enemy, it was difficult to claim any positive kills. Several enemy fighter-aircraft were claimed as being shot down, but none by my crew. Since I saw no enemy planes making head-on passes at our particular formation, I assumed the P-47's had helped save the day for us. The only bursts of flak that I saw were not near any B-17 formations.

There were no weather problems on return and we remained in formation flight until break up for landing. I felt that we had done a credible job of flying close formation in our flight element. There were no crew problems reported and the crew had good radio discipline. We would get credit for a combat mission, but failure to release our bombs on the target mitigated any thoughts of celebration. We hoped to do better on the next mission.

We had flown our new "G" model B-17 on her first mission. "Everyone had suggestions for her name but we decided that Bill Runner's "Vagabond Lady" was most fitting. We also had the names of wives or girlfriends painted on the outside surfaces adjacent to our crew positions. "Mary Lee" for Mary Lee Valentine, was painted on the left side of the cockpit just beneath my pilot window.

On that mission, the only minor damage to "Vagabond Lady" was to the engine cowlings and the right wing surface caused by debris from the burning aircraft previously mentioned.

BOMBS AWAY "BEWARE the FLAK"

October 3, 1943
Night Instrument Training Flight

A night instrument training flight was on the schedule. With a three-man crew, we flew for three hours making "blackout" landings using a light system developed by the British. The system was devised to prevent enemy aircraft from encroaching onto an airfield. It was a fascinating system of using green, red and yellow lights to control descent altitude. The runway suddenly became visible to the flight crew just before landing. Joe Johnson and Sherman Sly, the flight engineer, were aboard the aircraft with me. I made three landings using this system; Joe made a couple of low approaches.

Because we flew last night on the training mission, I was a little surprised to be on the schedule the next day.

I hadn't yet met many pilots from the other crews in the 401 Squadron. My roommate, Captain Lay, had flown another mission to Emden on the 2nd of October and was now on a seven-day leave at a place called Standbridge Earl's Rest Home. He had only one more mission to complete his thirty. Because our schedules seemed to conflict, I had had little opportunity to talk to him. He was quiet and seldom initiated any conversation. He also talked in his sleep at night and appeared very restless.

The combat crew losses in the B-17 Groups were high. My enlisted crew members were quartered with other enlisted flyers — some newly assigned and some seasoned combat veterans. Stories of death, injury and loss of crews and aircraft were discussed openly. The statistics quoted for completing twenty-five missions depended on the "teller of the tales." The generally accepted figure for mission completion was that only one in five crew members would be fortunate enough to make twenty-five missions. Injury, death, missing in action, prisoner of war, or grounding for fear of combat supposedly accounted for the other four who did not complete the twenty-five-mission requirement.

I didn't attempt to argue with what could be the truth with respect to the attrition rate; nor did I expect my crew members to block their ears to this type of discussion – but on the way to the next mission's briefing, I felt I should try and generate some positive views with respect to what we were trying to accomplish. I pointed out that many of the stories of crew losses were related to loose formation flying. Our role at that time was to stay in formation with our assigned element leader and to take special precautions so that in the heat of attacks by the enemy, we wouldn't forget to take care of each other or check oxygen levels or make certain that we released our bombs as soon as the lead aircraft made release. Most important, I wanted them to double check that after release, all bomb racks were empty. I still had received no information as to why the bombs hadn't released on our first mission to Emden.

Flight over England (photo: Joe Harlick)

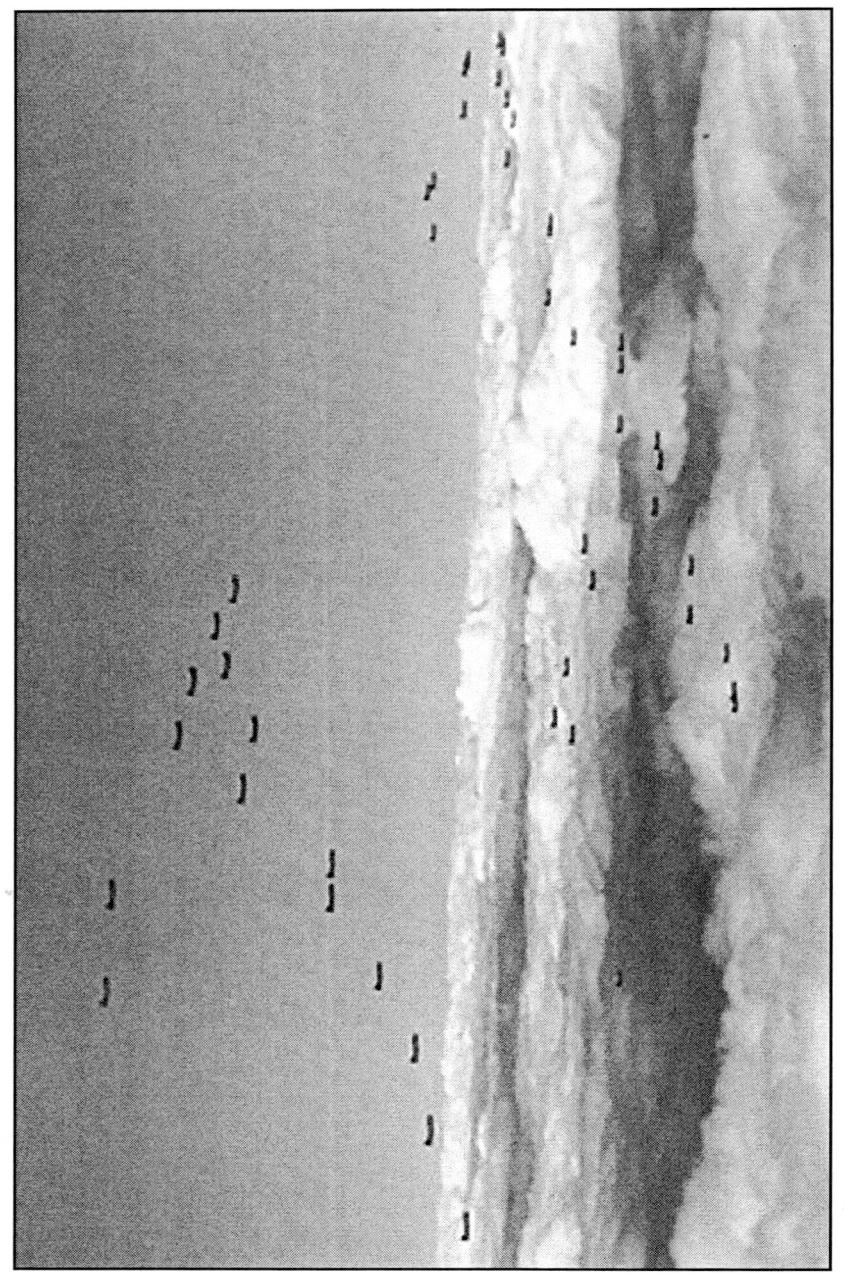

48 B17's in stacked formation (photo: Joe Harlick)

October 4, 1943
Mission to Frankfort, Germany

Five 401st Squadron aircraft flew this mission. I noted that three of the five scheduled crews from the 401st Squadron had also been scheduled along with my crew to fly the mission to Emden on September 27th (Crew first pilots - Pitts, Slane, Evers, Verrill and Phillips.)

Our aircraft joined the formation after take-off without any particular problems. We were flying the crew assigned aircraft, No. 742, Vagabond Lady. Although the B-17 formation was under enemy attack shortly after crossing the English Channel, the formation stayed intact and proceeded on course without loss of any aircraft in our Squadron. The first indication of a problem within our aircraft was a report by the radio operator that the oxygen level in the system was being rapidly depleted and that the gunners were having difficulty refilling the portable walk-around oxygen bottles. We were in formation at the time, flying at 26,000 feet, and had not yet arrived at the point where we would make our final turn toward the target. All crew members were notified to check their oxygen systems to insure that the regulators were at the proper settings. An incorrect setting on a regulator could cause 100% oxygen flow. If left in that position, that particular oxygen system could be depleted. I was on the same system as the navigator and we could not detect a problem with our system. There was apparently a leak in the main system utilized by all stations aft of the bomb bay so the emergency walk-around bottles would have to be filled from the forward systems.

I sent Sherman Sly back to check on the problem. He reported that the oxygen was depleted from the main system servicing the rear positions in the aircraft and that everyone on that system was using emergency oxygen bottles that required frequent refilling.

The bomber formation was approaching the initial point for final turn to the target when for the first time we encountered accurate flak bursts at our altitude. I hadn't had time to address the oxygen problem, but there was at least some assurance that for the time being the flight crew had sufficient oxygen support.

With the bombs released, it was time to re-evaluate our situation. Louis Brown, the ball turret gunner, had to leave his position as his auxiliary oxygen supply had been depleted and other crew members had been unable to refill the turret auxiliary tank. The gunners couldn't effectively add their support to the defense of the formation as they were often away from their stations refilling the cumbersome portable "walk-around" units. Oxygen was being depleted from the two forward oxygen systems at an alarming rate.

There was little choice but to depart the security of the formation and descend alone to an altitude where we could continue flight without the necessity of oxygen. There was a chance that the cloud layer below us could provide suitable cover for protection from enemy fighters.

It was with considerable reluctance that I dropped out of the formation. We observed radio silence so the rest of the formation was unaware of the reason for our sudden departure with no apparent combat damage and four operating engines. Only six hours earlier, I had sought to reassure the crew that staying in formation would be our key ingredient for survival. I now had to take action to void that key ingredient. It was a difficult decision.

I began a steep descent at maximum airspeed, hoping to reach the blanket of clouds before enemy fighters could react. It was too late, as one of the waist gunners reported sighting two Me 109 German fighters above our aircraft in a spiraling dive trying to get within firing range. At about the seven thousand foot level, a stream of 20mm shells streaked over the cockpit and faded into air space ahead of us. Louis Brown was trying to position himself back into the ball turret as we were at a level where oxygen was not required. Charles Groth was assisting him. Two gun positions unmanned at a critical time!

Looking out the left window, I could see holes where enemy gunfire had raked the wing. Suddenly I sighted another Me 109 flying just off our left wing, but in a direction opposite to our flight path. Robert Soloman was firing at this aircraft. I placed the B-17 in a turn to the left in an effort to keep his guns trained on the enemy.

The enemy aircraft sighted off the left wing disappeared from view. I continued the turn back to our original heading and leveled off just as we entered the cloud layer at three thousand feet. Still in a steep descent, we knifed through this layer of clouds and broke out below the clouds. I stopped the descent and immediately climbed back to the protective cover of the clouds. We had been in the clouds for two or three minutes when we suddenly broke out into a clearing. Just ahead—not more than 30 yards—was an Me-109 German fighter!

This aircraft was flying on our magnetic heading; the pilot had obviously been searching for us. The left gear was down and the pilot had the canopy open. The German pilot was leaning left and looking down and to the left, completely unaware of our position behind him.

I shouted to Foster and Runner to open fire since the German aircraft was dead ahead, almost in a position where with a little forward thrust I could chop off his tail with our left outboard propeller. I made a second call to fire, but we had descended at such a high rate of speed and changed altitude so rapidly that the guns in the nose were temporarily frozen.

After a short period, during which time I debated whether or not to continue formation with the German fighter until the guns cleared, we re-entered the cloud cover. I decided it would be prudent to stay in the clouds, as other enemy aircraft were in the area. We flew several off-course headings in the clouds before finally setting course for England. Over the channel, the cloud cover broke and fortunately we were picked up by a Spitfire and escorted to the coast of England.

We finally returned to home base at Bassingbourne. We were the last aircraft to return from this mission to Frankfort. I was extremely proud of my crew and their cool performance while under attack.

Our aircraft, Vagabond Lady, was badly damaged; both wing main spars had received enemy fire and the wings were scheduled for replacement. As it turned out, we had made our last flight in our assigned, crew-named aircraft.

USAAF NOSE ART RESEARCH PROJECT

Named by William Runmer, bombardier on Robert Slane's crew, Vagabond Lady went down on 3rd November. Slane and his crew were shot down on the Schweinfurt mission of 14th October, both men survived as prisoners of war (J. Starcer)

A Reprieve

During periods between combat missions, various crew members were scheduled for classes related to their crew responsibilities. Identification of enemy aircraft was practiced by all crew members. Both the navigator and bombardier received continued training in handling the fifty-caliber, twin guns in the nose turret. Glenn Foster studied a new secret devise to aid in navigation that I believe was referred to as a "G" box or the "black-box." The gunners reported to a range where skeet shooting and other devices were utilized to increase target accuracy. The pilots continued to practice instrument flying by simulating various types of conditions in a ground flight trainer.

Our training was suddenly interrupted when the crew was notified that they were receiving forty-eight hour passes and were free to travel to London for a short stay. Glenn decided he would visit his uncle, a Captain in an Army unit located relatively close to Bassingbourne. Joe Johnson, Bill Runner and I took the same train to London and stayed at a hotel operated by the American Red Cross. We went to a play and saw a couple of movies.

For me, the most important part of this short vacation was the discovery that two of my pilot classmates were also on pass and staying at the same hotel. Both men had been in England for several months. They had joined B-17 crews as co-pilots and after accumulating missions had been checked out as first-pilots. Verl Fisher, who had twenty-one missions, was flying as a deputy lead and was still a Flight Officer but flying in a position that was normally filled by a captain. B.H. Holmes had completed twenty-four missions and had only one more to go. He said that he had needed a rest before going on his final sortie.

The forty-eight hours just flew by and we returned to the squadron. We were scheduled to fly on the next day's mission. All flight crew members had returned except for Glenn Foster; hopefully he would return in time for the briefing for the combat mission the next day.

October 10, 1943
Mission to Munster, Germany

Glenn Foster had not yet returned from pass so my crew was assigned a substitute navigator. At the mission briefing I noted that the 401st Squadron was supplying four crews in support of the mission to Munster, Germany. (The first pilots were Lt. R. A. Pitts, Lt R.M. Slane, Lt. K.B. Rutledge and Lt. E.R. Verrill.) Our crew-assigned aircraft, "Vagabond Lady" was still in the hanger for repairs so we were assigned to fly a B-17 named "Sir Baboon McGoon," a name familiar to those who follow the "Li'l Abner" comic strip. This aircraft was an "F" model, although it had been retrofitted with some of the improvements found in the newer "G" models. The additions included a twin gun nose-turret, thick glass windows and heavy armor plating to protect the pilots' seats. This aircraft didn't have the increased fuel capacity available in the newer "G" models.

Take-off was made in near zero visibility and each aircraft followed instrument climb-out procedures. As we joined the formation after breaking out above the clouds, the navigator reported to me by interphone that he was feeling nauseous. I contacted Bill Runner, the bombardier, and requested that he assist the navigator by insuring that he was receiving sufficient oxygen. After completing a large arc, the formation continued climbing to our assigned altitude and set course on the pre-planned route.

As we departed the English coast, I received another call from the navigator, who had previously stated that this was his fifth mission. This time the navigator insisted that I abort the mission due to his illness. When he received no immediate response from me, he informed me that he had been sick and had vomited on all his previous missions and, in fact, had never completed a single mission because the pilots had to abort the aircraft prior to reaching enemy territory. In each case, the abort was due to his illness.

His story was unbelievable and the course of action he suggested was totally unacceptable to me. I refused to abort the mission and advised the navigator that he would just have to do the best he could under the circumstances. I also requested Bill Runner to come to the cockpit area, whereupon I advised him to keep a close watch on the navigator and to keep me informed of his condition and report any unusual actions that might be exhibited by this man.

Our formation of B-17's encountered considerable gunfire from enemy aircraft and on several occasions, German FW-190- fighters flew directly into and through our formation. All the gunners were busy and the sounds and smell of gunfire occupied every compartment in the aircraft. We released the bombs on our assigned target and Vic Kuhlman, our radioman-gunner, provided verification that the bomb racks had been emptied.

I had been receiving periodic reports from Bill Runner on the condition of the navigator. Bill reported that the navigator showed no evidence of being sick, but that he had remained seated the entire flight with his back against a bulkhead. He had offered no assistance in firing the turret guns and showed no interest in following the flight path of the formation. He had on his flak helmet and flak vest and was seated on Bill Runner's flak vest. His only conversation with me had been to repeat his request to abort the mission. His only conversation with Bill was to ask him whether we were aborting the mission. After observing the navigator's actions for several hours, Bill climbed up to the pilot's station and expressed his opinion to me that the man was not sick but feigning sickness.

On the return flight enemy resistance was light and we could find no evidence that our aircraft, Sir Baboon McGoon, had received battle damage. My greatest concern was the indication that our fuel consumption was excessive. This aircraft with its modifications was considerably heavier than most "F" series B-17's, and the increase in power settings necessary to stay in formation was very noticeable.

Prior to reaching the English coastline, our flight had to break formation as we descended into heavy weather. The thick clouds had reduced visibility to the point where formation flying was impossible. When the first low-fuel warning light illuminated, we were still flying over water. I notified the crew that we would be landing at the first air base we could locate.

Despite the efforts of the bombardier and radio operator, we were unable to obtain an accurate fix. Our problems were amplified by the apparent inability of the substitute navigator to provide any assistance. I finally found a small break in the clouds that offered confirmation that we were over land and reduced power for further descent. When we over-flew an airfield, I got a glimpse of B-24 Bombers on a parking ramp. For a brief period, there was an opening in the clouds and I had some hope that we would be able to land at the air base.

As I began a turn in an attempt to line up parallel to the sighted runway, the fog closed in and the airfield disappeared. I had just completed the turn when the two engines on the right wing began to lose power. All the low-fuel warning lights were now illuminated. Sherman Sly, who was monitoring the engines, quickly transferred enough fuel to prevent complete fuel starvation. It was evident that I had precious little time to get the aircraft on the ground.

There was insufficient fuel to increase the power settings to climb back to an altitude where the crew members could parachute to safety. I headed the aircraft back in a northeasterly direction, as the maps had indicated the area was flat farmland and less populated than the area around Cambridge and Bassingbourne. The crew was directed to take their crash landing positions but I wanted the engineer, Sherman Sly, to remain in his position between the pilots to be ready to transfer fuel to any engine that might falter. Joe Johnson was to remain in his co-pilot position. I was flying the aircraft about two hundred feet above ground level. The fog was intermittently very dense with some breaks that permitted Joe and I to see the ground.

It was "white knuckle" time for both of us as we searched for a break in the dense fog. The area off to the right of our course suddenly provided us with a glimpse of an opening into what appeared to be a plowed field. I banked to the right, cut the power and began a rapid descent. We flew over a short fence as I leveled out for the gear-up landing. The flaps had just started down as I raised the nose of the aircraft just prior to touchdown. The aircraft skipped over the ground and after traveling a relatively short distance, we re-entered the fog layer and skidded blindly forward until the aircraft came to a sudden stop.

Fortunately, there were no obstacles in our path. For just a moment after the aircraft stopped moving, there was dead silence as though we were all trying to comprehend what had just occurred. I looked over at Joe's ashen face. My adrenalin level had peaked and I was suddenly very relieved, very tired and very grateful that we were all safely on the ground.

There was a buzzing noise in the cockpit. I reached over and cut the ignition switches. The decision to land and the crash landing itself had come within seconds of each other and there had been no time for checklists or discussion. All I had said over the interphone was, "Hang on, we're going in."

I opened the side window in the cockpit and was greeted by several of the crew members who had already evacuated the aircraft. The fog was so thick that we could see nothing of our surroundings. Sherman Sly had been standing by in case the pilots needed help keeping the engines running and he was holding on to the back of my seat for support during the crash-landing. His bravery in time of crisis will never be questioned.

The first two people to suddenly appear out of the fog were two young English boys who had been pushing their bicycles along the roadway. They had heard the approaching aircraft and feared for their lives as the plane flew overhead and the sounds of the crash landing echoed through the fog. One lad named Tom Perkins left to seek help for our crew. It wasn't too long before we had a member of the Home Guard volunteer to guard our aircraft until additional support help could arrive.

We had landed in a beet field owned by an English couple, Sheila and Tony Harvey. Their home was located just beside the beet field, probably not more than one hundred yards from our downed aircraft; however the fog was now so thick that visibility was limited to twenty or thirty feet. We had not seen the house prior to the crash landing.

The Harvey's opened up their home to four members of the crew and me, and arranged with a neighbor to provide food and a bed for the remaining crew members. The Harvey's had two young sons. The unexpected arrival of our crew and a bomber aircraft on their land was a strange, fascinating and exciting event for them.

I contacted the 401st Squadron by phone and reported the status of the crew and the temporary demise of our aircraft, "Sir Baboon McGoon." A truck was scheduled to arrive the following morning to return us to our Squadron at Bassingbourne.

A NEW NOSE replaces the one punched out by the chin turret. Here the new Plexiglas "goldfish bowl" is being put in place over the bombardier's compartment. During the earlier stages of the work, a dummy nose covered the opening to keep out rain and prevent damage to the instruments and controls inside. Up on the side of the fuselage you can see the plane's emblem, the comic-strip character from whom Sir Baboon took his name, represented running with his war club on the road to Berlin. The McGoon presented a relatively simple repair job, being less damaged than most

October 14, 1943
Mission to Schweinfurt, Germany

Lt. Robert Slane - Age 20 - Pilot/ Crew Commander of a ten man B-17 Bomber Crew - stationed at Bassingbourne England. 401st Bomb Sq., 91st Bombardment Group, 8th Air Force. Crew assigned to fly B-17 aircraft #42-5714, a 323rd Bomb Sq. aircraft.

There was an early wake-up call on October 14th, 1943. My navigator, Lt. Foster, had returned from pass and my crew was scheduled to fly this mission without substitute.

Just prior to the mission briefing, we had been informed that our flight position would be "tail-end Charlie" and that the group leader would be my roommate, Captain Harry Lay. This was to be Harry's thirtieth and last mission with the 91st Bomb Group. Lt/Col Milton would accompany him as co-pilot and mission commander.

It was still dark and very foggy as we were trucked to our aircraft after the briefing. We were the last crew out of the truck, arriving at an aircraft from another squadron. (Aircraft 42-5714, 323rd Squadron.)

While unloading our gear, I was met by the distraught aircraft crew chief. He informed me that there must have been a mistake as his aircraft was not "combat ready" and had never been scheduled for combat. In response to my question concerning its use, he informed me that it was an older aircraft that was used only locally, primarily for instrument flying. While this discussion was taking place, the bomb-loading crew arrived and began loading the bombs. I had no time to discuss this situation further with the crew chief as it was obvious the aircraft was on the schedule if bombs were being loaded.

We discovered the aircraft had the old-style "bladder type" oxygen system. This meant that we would need extra oxygen masks since these systems would invariably get clogged up with ice at high altitudes. My crew had flown with this type of equipment when flying older model B-17's during training missions prior to our overseas assignment. The "demand" type oxygen system on the later model aircraft had corrected this problem.

Once the crew chief realized that his aircraft was indeed going into combat, he did everything possible to assist my crew in obtaining additional oxygen masks and ammunition. He was concerned about the "high-timer" engines. The extra weight from the additional ammunition was one of my concerns so both the flight crew and ground crew monitored the distribution of the additional ammo.

The weather remained so wet and foggy that we wouldn't have been surprised if the mission had been scrubbed. But after a long wait, the green "go" flare appeared and we were on our way. Once on the runway, the only visible directional mark was the white center stripe. It was a full instrument take-off and climb-out using air speed, climb rate and timing procedures.

We were the third aircraft to locate Capt. Lay's lead aircraft. After waiting for some time for other aircraft to join up, I pulled into formation on the right wing of the high element leader. As we started on course, it became increasingly obvious that several aircraft assigned to our formation had either aborted or were having difficulty locating the formation. The left wing position in Capt. Lay's lead element remained vacant for a considerable length of time. I debated whether to fill that slot, but eventually another B-17 finally pulled up into that position.

Enemy aircraft of all types began attacking at coast-in. ME-109's and FW-190's were the principal attack aircraft coming in from all directions while JU-88's, ME-110's and Hinkle 111's were observed flying parallel to our formation just out of range of our gunner's fifty-caliber guns. These aircraft were reporting our position and firing rockets into the formation. Any aircraft that was crippled or unable to stay in tight formation could expect to be singled out for mass attack by the enemy. On the way to the target FW 190's were lining up ahead of the formation and then making head-on attacks; doing a split-S maneuver after passing under the B-17 formation. It was during these attacks that the navigator, bombardier and lower turret gunner were most effective in providing defensive fire from our aircraft.

At the initial point (IP), the fighter attacks lessened and intense enemy flak was encountered. Just after bomb release over the target, our aircraft received what appeared to be a direct hit by a burst of flak. The No. 4 engine caught fire. Fortunately, we were able to feather the propeller, extinguish the fire and remain in formation with three operating engines.

After "bombs away" and leaving the target area, the fighter attacks resumed and all gunners fired at the enemy. I heard S/Sgt Brown, the ball turret gunner, and several other crew members call out "kills", but there was no time for discussion as everyone was too busy fighting off the enemy.

Approximately forty-five minutes after departing the target area, we were still in formation. For the first time during this mission, I turned over control of the aircraft to Lt. Joe Johnson, the co-pilot. We were holding our own and the three operating engines were holding steady, despite higher than normal power settings.

It was at this time that FW-190's were observed flying above our formation and releasing what appeared to be bombs down, into and through our formation. I was helping Sherman Sly, the top turret gunner, to locate the enemy fighters flying overhead. Suddenly our aircraft was struck by heavy enemy gunfire. The right inboard engine (No. 3) was hit, severing fuel and oil lines. The main oxygen tank located in the passageway below the pilot exploded with a loud "bang."

At the same time as the explosion, Joe Johnson let go of the control wheel and hunched down and forward, covering his head and face with his arms. His shoulders shoved the control wheel forward, causing the aircraft to immediately start a severe descending dive out of formation. From my seated position, I was unable to force Johnson to release the control wheel. I unbuckled my seat belt and while standing in the aisle, used all my strength to finally force him back to an upright, seated position. These actions were immediate and necessary before I could regain control of the aircraft.

I had recovered control of the B-17 but we were out of formation and had descended about fifteen hundred feet below our formation. I feared that Joe had been hit by enemy fire but he wasn't injured. The only explanation offered by Johnson was that when he heard the oxygen tank explode, he thought a 20mm cannon shell was about to explode in the cockpit.

Regardless of the cause, our aircraft was now out of formation and severely crippled with two inoperative engines. I was unable to feather the propeller on No. 3 engine. Fortunately, there was no fire, despite an obvious fuel leak in the inboard section of the right wing. We continued to drift further behind our formation and, in fact, found ourselves briefly in the middle of another group of B-17's that were at a lower altitude following the route of the 91st Bomb Group leader. That formation soon also left us behind.

It was a battle trying to keep the aircraft airborne without exceeding the engine operating limits on the two remaining engines. Main system oxygen had been destroyed and the emergency oxygen was near depletion. The bladder-type masks were a major problem. I descended to eighteen thousand feet where we could operate for a time without oxygen. There was no cloud cover below us to help in evading the enemy.

During the thirty or forty minutes after departing the formation, our crew was under constant enemy attack and it was a life or death struggle to survive. Enemy fighter-bombers were now attacking us from side angles. The last words I received from the tail gunner, Claud Smith, were "Skipper, there are seven ME-109's trailing us with their gear down. They're making single passes – gear up – and attack." I told Sgt. Smith to "get one for me."

The crew still had a limited supply of ammunition and we retained the hope that we could fend off the attackers and return to England utilizing the two remaining operating engines. I wanted to maintain altitude until we were closer to the enemy coastline before starting a descent with two engines inoperative on the right wing. A descent too early could result in having to ditch in the North Sea.

During this period of struggle for survival, I heard several crew members announce hits and possible destruction of enemy aircraft. I remain convinced that S/Sgt Louis Brown, the ball turret gunner, and other members of my crew destroyed as many as four enemy aircraft during the unrelenting attacks by the Germans.

Suddenly and without warning, No. 1 engine lost power. From my position, it appeared that the two top cylinders had blown. Smoke was coming from that area and flames were coming from the lower part of the engine. My attempts to feather the propeller were futile. I hit the bailout warning bell and gave the verbal order to bail out. All crew members acknowledged — with the exception of Sgt. Claud Smith, the tail gunner. Lt. Johnson and S/Sgt Sly assisted each other with their chutes. The bomb bay doors were opened and both men jumped out.

As the crew members were departing the aircraft, I received word from Vic Kuhlman, the radio operator, that Sgt. Smith was unconscious with no apparent wounds. Kuhlman had gone to the rear of the aircraft to obtain additional emergency oxygen bottles. After this report, I received no response from any crew members in the rear of the aircraft. All forward members of the crew, with the exception of the navigator, Glenn Foster, had departed the aircraft. Foster had not yet bailed out but had assisted Lt Runner, the bombardier, in evacuating the aircraft. Runner was suffering from mild anoxia and appeared to be confused; however, thanks to the valiant efforts of Lt. Foster, his bailout was successful.

Foster came to the cockpit area wanting to know if I was going to "crash-land" or "bail out." He would do whatever I was going to do. I told him I was going to parachute out, but that I had received word that Sgt Smith was unconscious in the rear of the aircraft. I wanted him to check on Smith. If he was in the aircraft but unconscious, I instructed him to try to get Smith to an exit and, if possible, throw him from the plane concurrent with pulling the parachute ripcord. After that was done, he was to notify me and immediately bail out. If Smith was not in the aircraft, Foster was to notify me and then bail out without further delay. Foster acknowledged and headed for the bomb bay.

Shortly after Glenn Foster entered the bomb bay on his way to the rear of the aircraft, a JU-88 coming in from the right rear, strafed the B–17, putting gunfire in the fuselage and in the cockpit area just to the right of the pilot's control column. The co-pilot's windshield and the right cockpit window were shattered, as was the co-pilot's instrument panel. I was not injured but my left leg felt numb from the shock of the explosion in the cockpit.

All crew members, with the exception of Foster and possibly Claud Smith, should have been out of the aircraft before the initial hits from the JU-88 were received. The landing gear on the B-17 had been placed down after the bailout order was given in the mistaken belief that the aircraft would not be fired on when it gave the 'wheels down' signal; and it became obvious that the crew was abandoning the aircraft. My first action was to retract the gear. I glanced to the left and saw the JU-88 pulling up into position just above and behind the left wing of our aircraft, possibly positioning for gunfire into the left cockpit. I immediately made a sharp left turn directly toward the JU-88 and kept the B-17 in a tight spiral turn to the left. I maintained maximum air speed while in this circling dive.

Since I hadn't received a report from Lt. Foster, I had to assume that the gunner, Sgt Smith, and possibly the navigator, were still aboard and could not bail out. I was flying at eighteen thousand feet when the JU-88 struck and the spiral dive was started. I could see a small clearing of land in the middle of what appeared to be a dense forest. I decided on a forced "crash" landing. No. 1 engine was still on fire, but I could see only white smoke and no flames. I kept the air speed above three hundred m.p.h. until level off about two hundred feet above the ground. The descent had been so rapid that the windshield and pilot's side window were frosted over.

As I flew over the small clearing, I opened the side window.

The airspeed was still high — two hundred and forty m.p.h. I saw Lt. Bill Runner on the ground at the edge of the clearing, wildly waving his arms as the aircraft went by. I made a tight circle to the right as I had full visibility from the shattered windshield and co-pilot side window. I couldn't maintain airspeed on one engine for an extended period so I completed the low-level circling maneuver and leveled off for the final approach.

The airspeed had slowed to one hundred and fifty. I slapped the flap lever down and flew flat for a high-speed gear-up landing. The aircraft crashed through a small wire fence and stopped just short of a larger wooden-wire fence and a ditch. I had unbuckled to take control of the aircraft from Lt Johnson, and from that period on had been so occupied with the recovery and control of the aircraft that I had no opportunity to get strapped back in. I made the crash-landing without benefit of the seat belt and shoulder harness!

With the bomb bay doors open, all the sounds of an aircraft making a belly landing were amplified. After the aircraft came to a full stop, the first sound I became aware of was the pounding of my own heart. I glanced at the left wing. The fire in No. 1 engine had been in the lower part of the nacelle. There was some smoke but no visible fire. The landing had evidently smothered the flames. I had cut the ignition switches just before touchdown. I glanced around the cockpit and remembered to push in the IFF destroyer buttons.

As I scrambled through the aircraft to the rear entrance, I called out Foster and Smith's names. There was no response. There was no one in the area of the main fuselage. Once outside the aircraft, I checked the tail-gunner's position. It was also vacant. I then assumed that all crew members had bailed out.

I initially departed the immediate vicinity of the B-17, fearing the JU-88 might strafe the downed aircraft. Seeking cover, I ran across the field to a hedge growth at the edge of the clearing. A few minutes after taking cover, the JU-88 flew directly overhead at a low altitude and then started a climbing turn away from my locaion.

With departure of the JU-88 from the area and no one in sight, I returned to the aircraft intending to destroy the B-17 by firing a flare into the No. 3 engine nacelle where fuel was still flowing down the wing-root. I found the flares but couldn't find the flare-pistol. I found the canister designed to destroy an aircraft but couldn't get the firing mechanism to work.

While thus engaged, I was startled to hear voices outside the aircraft. I immediately leaped out of the rear exit and began to run. I heard a sharp order to "Halt!" I glanced over my shoulder and saw a man holding a rifle pointed right at me. I stopped running, raised my arms and walked back to the aircraft. Two ME-109's flew over, dipping their wings. In front and to the right of the grounded B-17 was a 1936 Ford. Incredibly, two Germans in civilian clothes had driven directly onto the field apparently from a small village located at the south edge of the clearing, providing me with only ten or fifteen minutes of freedom after the crash landing.

I was held at the aircraft for a short period and during this time one of the Germans had discovered Sgt Smith's body behind the bulkhead located aft of the main entrance door. This area wasn't visible from the main fuselage interior and was an area that in my haste I had not searched. Sgt. Smith had evidently left his gun position and crawled forward toward the main fuselage interior. The Germans would not let me view his body. I was told that massive wounds to the chest had killed him. He could have been wounded during the fighter attacks, but in my opinion he was more than likely killed by gunfire from the JU-88. The radio operator, S/Sgt. Kuhlman, reported that Sgt Smith was unconscious during the time-frame that crew members were complying with my bailout order and stated he saw no wounds or any other indication that Smith had been hit by gunfire. I will always believe he was initially suffering from anoxia and would have survived had it not been for our last encounter with the JU-88.

I was taken from the vicinity of the aircraft before Sgt Claud Smith's body was removed.

PART II

PRISONER OF WAR

Captured!

After crash-landing my B-17 aircraft adjacent to a small village in France, I was captured by two men dressed in civilian clothing. I was searched and then placed in the front seat of a Ford car that the men had driven onto the field and parked near my downed aircraft. In the backseat of this vehicle, another prisoner was handcuffed and had both feet loosely tied. He had a broad face with wild blond hair and appeared to be of Slavic or Polish nationality. He cringed when one of our German captors threatened him with what appeared to be a hard rubber hose.

It was only a short drive off the field where I crash-landed to the outskirts of the village. We were removed from the car and taken down a dirt floor corridor between a house and a row of walled prison cells. The first cell door was opened and the other prisoner was shoved in. I was taken further up the corridor and placed in a similar cell.

When the door was closed, the cell was pitch black. The only source of light was a peephole in the door. The cell had a type of bench-bed about two feet off the ground. The walls were stone and concrete but the floor appeared to be hardened dirt or adobe.

I had been in the cell for about half an hour when the cell door was opened and I was led outside into the corridor. Two Germans in military uniform were waiting to question me. The questioning started with an inquiry as to whether I was hungry. Although I had no thought of food, I said "yes" because I felt I should eat to keep up my strength. The next questions were related to members of my crew: "How many were aboard the aircraft" "Was I concerned about their safety since some might be injured and need medical assistance?" I was unresponsive to any of these questions. I repeatedly showed them my dog tags and stated "name, rank and serial number." The interrogators did finally get my attention, though, when they pointed out that one member of my crew had been killed. I requested that they let me see and identify the crew member. This request was denied and I was returned to my cell. There was no further mention of food.

For the next several hours, I sat on the bench leaning against the wall. My mind was racing as I relived the events of the past few hours. I wondered what had happened to Glenn Foster. It couldn't have been his body the Germans discovered behind the bulkhead. Was it possible he had made it back to where the tail gunner, Sgt Smith, was reported to be unconscious? What happened to the flare gun? Why hadn't I carried matches so I could have destroyed the aircraft? Why did I go back once I was out of the aircraft and hidden in a thicket? I knew the answer to that question. I had to go back because it was my duty, my responsibility as the crew commander. If I had been able to destroy the aircraft, would the Germans have been able to identify the body found behind the bulkhead? Maybe it was best that I had been unable to destroy the aircraft for just that reason. What happened to Bill Runner, the bombardier who was waving from the ground as I came in over the field just before crash-landing? Did the rest of the crew make it safely to the ground? These were the types of thoughts that plagued me during those first hours of captivity.

My eyes gradually adjusted to the darkness of the cell. I found a wooden bucket in a corner near the door. I removed the lid. The stench was suffocating. It was obvious this bucket hadn't been emptied for a long time. I returned to the bench, using the fur collar of my flight jacket as a breathing mask until the smell receded.

I had been in the cell for four or five hours when I heard voices. My cell door opened and a German guard, lantern in hand, entered with a young man dressed like a motorcyclist. He had on a black leather jacket, leather pants and boots. He was about my size — 5 feet, 7 or 8 inches tall. He was dark-complexioned and spoke with what sounded to me like a French accent. He spoke some English. When he suddenly drew his pistol without warning or apparent cause, I thought he might be an agent in the

French Underground and was perhaps going to liberate me. That thought was short-lived as he grabbed my flying helmet and jerked it off my head. He then requested that I give him my watch. I did so, but refused when he demanded my pilot wings. After two attempts to take them from me while I resisted by covering the wings with my arms, he suddenly turned to the German guard, muttered something and left. The guard then departed and I was left to return to my own thoughts until morning.

The next morning, as more light was visible through the hole in the door, I had a better view of my surroundings. Just above my head, where I had been sitting all night, was a great circular web containing a spider with a body the size of a quarter. I shuddered at the thought that it might have been crawling on me. I managed to relocate my position on the bench away from the immediate vicinity of the spider and spent the next hour or so trying to figure out the best way to get rid of this new menace. Since I didn't have access to any weapon to kill it, I decided to leave well enough alone, with the hope that I could eventually get a guard to assist me in cleaning out the toilet and taking care of the spider.

About three hours after daybreak, the cell door opened and I was again taken out of the cell. I was escorted to a large room in the house. This room was full of men of all ages seated in different locations around the room. Some of the men were armed with rifles; others had sticks that could be used as weapons. They appeared to be ordinary workers and, for the most part, were dark haired and dark-complexioned. None spoke as the Germans put me on display; they just appeared to be curious. I assumed they were part of the local search force that the Germans were using to track downed allied airmen.

From that room I was taken to what appeared to be a kitchen. I was allowed to sit at one of the tables and was served a bowl of what looked like potato soup and a chunk of very hard, stale bread. The old woman who served me would not look directly at me and she was unresponsive to any conversation attempted by the German guards.

I didn't like the smell of the soup so I was able to gag down only one spoonful. The potatoes used in the soup tasted rotten. While I was trying to chew on the bread, the old woman poured herself a bowl of the same soup. Standing in front of the stove, she took a spoonful of the soup. She tried to swallow, but instead gagged and vomited the soup back into the bowl. She looked around the room. Seeing that the guard had his back to her and she was not being observed, she dumped the contents of her bowl back into the pot on the stove. She then turned toward me and looked me straight in the eye. A look of defiance had replaced the look of total indifference previously on her face. We were two people who shared a secret. Her hate for the Germans was obviously deeply rooted.

After leaving the kitchen, I again requested that I be allowed to see the body of my crew member. There was no response to this request, but I was told that the airman was named "Schmidt," that he had been shot in the chest and that the wounds were massive. I was returned to my cell with little accomplished except for the information about Sgt Claud Smith.

It was sometime in the afternoon that my cell door was again opened and I was taken out into the corridor. This time I was facing a Luftwaffe Officer who was wearing eagle wings surrounded by a wreath. I assumed he was a pilot, perhaps one of the pilots who had helped to down our aircraft. He had an English-speaking soldier with him. His only question concerned my age. He seemed amused when I pointed to the information on my dog tags and refused to answer his question. He made me take off my sheepskin-lined jacket. He then felt the material of my shirt, which was a thin, summer khaki long-sleeve. He may have intended to take the jacket, but didn't when he realized the shirt wouldn't provide much protection against the cold. The jacket was returned to me. After a brief conversation with the interpreter, the German officer spoke directly to me in German. I didn't understand him and his interpreter provided no assistance. Receiving no response from me, the Luftwaffe officer turned, talked briefly with the guard and departed. It was back to the prison cell for me.

I dozed for a brief time. When I awakened, I was relieved to see that the spider had climbed to a new and higher position in the web. I wondered if it could sense my desire to rid the cell of its presence. I didn't relish the thought that I might have to spend another night with the spider present in the cell.

Late in the afternoon, I heard increased activity in the corridor and the sound of marching footsteps. My cell door opened and a guard led me down the corridor. Outside the building was a line of about ten or twelve armed soldiers. My immediate thought was that the soldiers were a firing squad.

The guard guided me over to the corner of a building. I was shocked to see Joe Johnson, the co-pilot, and the engineer and top-turret gunner, Sherman Sly, coming around the building. I felt a surge of relief when it appeared they were uninjured. The three of us were directed to climb aboard a truck. The truck bed was covered with a canvas top and had seats along the sides and benches facing the rear of the truck. Four guards boarded the truck. One guard sat on each of the side benches and two sat on a bench in front of the tailgate, facing forward. Johnson sat next to me. We both faced the rear of the truck.

We had no way of knowing where we were going or what was in store for us, and admittedly, there remained some fear that we were going to face a firing squad. It was nightfall before we made our next stop. When three more members of my crew were placed aboard the truck, I had mixed feelings of joy and despair. Vic Kuhlman, the radio operator, was badly injured. He had made a successful bailout, but during descent had become tangled in the shroud lines. He struck the ground shoulder first and was in severe pain. He had received no medical treatment since capture. We managed to place him on one of the side benches in the truck. Lou Brown, the ball-turret gunner and Robert Solomon, waist-gunner, were picked up with Vic Kuhlman. Still unaccounted for was Charles Groth, the waist gunner, Glenn Foster the navigator, and Bill Runner, the bombardier. I had to assume that the body found in the aircraft was the tail-gunner, Claud Smith.

As we traveled, I attempted to read the road signs, but only the cities of Metz and Nancy were familiar to me. As we passed through many small villages, the thought that continuously crossed my mind was that we should try to escape. All of our escape training programs emphasized that, if possible, we should try to escape from our captors prior to being placed in a permanent POW prison, and that the opportunity for a successful escape would best be accomplished while being transported from one area to another. It seemed to me that positioning the two guards on a bench attached to the tail gate facing us was an invitation for us to leap up and push them over the back of the tail-gate.

I still had on heavy flying boots over my shoes. I would need to remove them before attempting to leap out the rear of the truck. I slowly unzipped one boot, but when I attempted to take the boot off, the guard sitting nearest me on the side bench spoke to me and pointed his gun at my chest. Needless to say, I didn't attempt to unzip the other boot. Even if I had been able to remove the boots, I knew there would be considerable risk in attempting to rush the guards. Never the less, every time the truck slowed, I thought about knocking the guard facing us overboard, leaping over the tailgate and disappearing in the darkness.

Realistically, I knew that any escape attempt would be foolhardy unless every crew member had advance knowledge of a plan and could react in a coordinated escape effort. Also, we had one member badly injured and his safety had to be considered. Still, the thought of being a prisoner and facing an unknown future caused an inward battle with my emotions as I contemplated a situation that offered little opportunity for a successful escape.

We finally arrived at a railroad station. The guards formed a circle around us and we were herded into a waiting room. The civilians were ordered to vacate the area, and then we were alone with the guards. Vic Kuhlman was in pain and shaking from shock and the chilly weather. We found a place for him to sit but the chills persisted. I finally went over to the table in the center of the room that contained a stack of blankets, took a blanket and we wrapped it around Kuhlman. One of the guards rushed forward shouting as he pushed me backward. His tirade continued as I tried to explain that our friend needed help. Another guard finally came forward, talked to his comrade and calmed him down.

When they were out of hearing range, Kuhlman said in a very low voice, "He says you didn't ask permission." For the first time I realized that Kuhlman could speak and understand German. He had heard and understood all their conversations, but was too frightened to let them know that he had been raised in a German-speaking household. Kuhlman told me that he could understand every word said in his presence by the Germans. This revelation was quite a surprise for all of us. I assured Victor that we would be careful not to reveal his secret. I requested that he listen carefully and let me know any information about our present location, proposed destination or anything else of significance relating to our status.

We were under constant surveillance by the guards, but were allowed to talk in low tones among ourselves. I asked Joe Johnson if he had been questioned about Sgt.Claud Smith. He indicated that he had not. He mentioned that he and Sherman Sly had been fed earlier in the day and that the soup was "delicious." He had eaten two bowls of the potato soup. I made no mention of my own experience; hopefully they had been served soup from another source.

After about a two-hour wait, we boarded a passenger train. The guards moved people out of their seats to make room for us. There was considerable grumbling by those who had to relinquish their seats. The other travelers appeared to be ordinary French citizens. It was difficult to fathom their thoughts regarding our presence, but it was obvious that we were not the first prisoners they had encountered.

The lights were dim in the train, and outside was total darkness. Kuhlman was in pain and every jolt of the train aggravated his shoulder injury. His low moans brought looks of sympathy from some of the surrounding passengers. One of the guards finally offered us a blanket. We placed the folded blanket under

Kuhlman's shoulder, and this action seemed to lessen his pain.

We spent the rest of the night on the train and arrived at a prison outside Frankfort, Germany early in the morning. We were lined up in columns, counted, and then marched into a prison compound. This was a "Dulag Luft," an interrogation center, where we were told we would remain until we were sent to a "permanent" prisoner of war camp. The 'officer' crew members were separated from the 'enlisted' crew members, and it was rumored that we would be sent to different permanent prison camps. We should have been aware of this, but I had forgotten that part of the lecture. I got a sick feeling as I watched my fellow crew members marching off to God knows where. Would I ever see them again?

My name was called and I was placed with a group of officer prisoners. Joe Johnson was called to join another group. My group, consisting of ten or so officers, was taken to a large room. The room was not a cell but an ordinary room with a locked door. I knew none of the other airmen, but in conversation discovered that most had been shot down on the Schweinfurt mission (14 Oct.43). There were no chairs, so most of us just slumped against the wall. Someone mentioned that we should keep our voices low and that the reason we were in a room without a guard was probably because our discussions would provide information of use to the enemy. There seemed to be some logic to that advice so our conversations became guarded.

For the first hour or so, the big topic was cigarettes. Who had a cigarette or tobacco? The heavy smokers were getting desperate. All the smokers began to search through their clothing. Matches were at a premium as most of the cigarette lighters had been confiscated. One man had "roll your own" cigarette paper and others were using toilet paper to make cigarettes. Pockets were turned inside out to collect any tobacco that could be extracted from the lint. Anyone who lit a cigarette would share with others. For most of us, this marked the beginning of a shared hardship that, in some cases, could mean the difference between life and death. I was thankful I didn't smoke.

One by one the names of prisoners were called out. Those who departed did not return to this "holding" room. I was one of the last to be called and was taken down a corridor, out into the open and into another block of prison cells. This area was where prisoners were held in solitary confinement. The cell was small, maybe six by nine feet. A single low-watt bulb was located in the center of the ceiling. High on the rear wall was a glassless, barred window. By standing on the cot, I could look out and view a sort of square courtyard. The buildings surrounding this square open area all appeared to be prison cells with the same type of window as the cell I occupied. During my imprisonment in this cell, I often saw faces peering out of these windows.

I had been in confinement for about three hours when I became aware of a guard looking at me through the small barred glass window in the door. It was standard procedure for the guards to periodically look in each cell, day and night. Once a day, each prisoner was escorted to a latrine in the building and permitted to use the facilities and wash up before returning to confinement. Since capture, I had eaten nothing except the stale piece of bread and I didn't take time to examine the contents of the small bowl of pea or bean soup served to me that first day of solitary confinement. I was very hungry and the soup was delicious. The black bread served with the soup had some kind of spread that had little taste, but it was palatable. The standard daily breakfast was a slice of bread with some type of hot drink that was a substitute for coffee. The mid-day meal consisted of a cup of barley or pea soup and a slice of bread. Supper was another slice of bread with a spread of some type of margarine or red jelly spread. It wasn't exactly a diet of "bread and water" but it was close to it.

I found that by pushing the cot up to the rear wall I could look out the barred window and listen in on the conversations of prisoners in adjacent cells. This method of communication must have been known to our captors but was evidently permitted. Perhaps it was a way of gaining information.

WESTERN UNION (29)

VH78 43 GOVT= WXX WMU WASHINGTON DC 25 547P

RALPH M SLANE=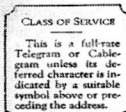

600 EAST MAIN ST DB=

1943 OCT 25 PM 4 29

THE SECRETARY OF WAR DESIRES ME TO EXPRESS HIS REGRET THAT YOUR SON SECOND LIEUTENANT ROBERT M SLANE HAS BEEN REPORTED MISSING IN ACTION SINCE FOURTEEN OCTOBER OVER SCHWEINFURT GERMANY IF FURTHER DETAILS OR OTHER INFORMATION ARE RECEIVED YOU WILL BE PROMPTLY NOTIFIED=

ULIO THE ADJUTANT GENERAL.

WESTERN UNION (49)

VA92 33 GOVT=PZ PXX WASHINGTON DC 18 1111P

RALPH M SLANE=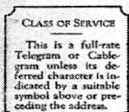

600 EAST MAIN ST DB=

1943 NOV 18 PM 9 50

REPORT RECEIVED THROUGH THE INTERNATIONAL RED CROSS STATES THAT YOUR SON SECOND LIEUTENANT ROBERT M SLANE IS A PRISONER OF WAR OF THE GERMAN GOVERNMENT LETTER OF INFORMATION FOLLOWS FROM PROVOST MARSHAL GENERAL=

ULIO THE ADJUTANT GENERAL.

Solitary Confinement

On the second day of imprisonment in the Dulag, I was at my window and listened to someone named Rose tell a story of his bailout. He had been in the nose of his aircraft attempting to put his chute on when the aircraft blew up and he was blown out of the exploding aircraft. Floating in the air right next to him was his parachute. Rose said he grabbed the chute, snapped it on and pulled the ripcord.

I was still trying to visualize Rose's story when the prisoner he had been conversing with began to tell his experiences. He began by saying he had delayed opening his parachute in order to lessen the chance for capture. He said that after he was on the ground, he had waved to his pilot as the B-17 was flown at low altitude over his landing area. He then described how shortly after waving to his pilot, a low flying German twin-engine plane had fired at him. He was unhurt except for a shell fragment that had gone through his shoe and become embedded under his big toe. I was stunned when I heard this conversation. I called out, "Runner, is that you?" Of course, it was Bill Runner, our crew bombardier! His response was immediate. He reported that he had been free for two days after bailout before seeking help from a man who appeared to be a French worker. He was taken to a house, given some food and was then turned over to the Germans. He had not escaped as I had hoped, but at least he was alive, unhurt and accounted for.

After two days of solitary, I found that I was getting an increasing number of itchy lumps on various parts of my body. I didn't know whether it was bed bugs from the straw mattress on the cot or fleas of some type. I spent part of each day exercising with periodic push-ups and squats to keep my legs in shape. I removed my outer clothing from time to time to search for and kill fleas. I had difficulty sleeping, as my mind kept reviewing the events that had suddenly changed my life. I tried to visualize the impact it would have on our families and loved ones back home. I wondered what my future would be like. I just couldn't seem to accept the fact that I was a prisoner and had no control over my own destiny. I made a firm resolve to provide only name, rank and serial number to anyone who might interrogate me. I prayed to God to give me strength and the perseverance to face any hardship that might befall me. I made a vow to myself that I would escape if the least opportunity presented itself.

On the forth day of solitary, I was taken to the office of my interrogator. A tall, distinguished-looking German officer was standing at his desk as I entered the room. Seated at another desk in the room was a young woman, who I assumed was the interrogator's secretary. I was invited to sit in a comfortable chair facing the interrogator's desk. At first the Luftwaffe officer spoke in clear English, reviewing some of the facts he already had. He noted that I was flying an aircraft assigned to another Squadron and wondered aloud if perhaps the 401st Sq. had suffered such a high loss rate on the previous mission to Anklam that the squadron could not fully support the Schweinfurt mission. I didn't know at the time what the loss rate was on the Anklam mission, but I did know it was high. That was probably the reason my crew had been assigned to fly an aircraft that had not only been assigned to another squadron but was at that time not even considered a "combat ready" aircraft by the aircraft's crew chief.

Receiving no response from me regarding his reasonably accurate assessment of the aircraft loss problem, he continued by telling me that I was a "little late" in arriving in England and that the majority of my provisional group had arrived ahead of me. Again he was right. We had delayed two days at Bangor, Maine for repairs from a hailstorm encountered in route to Bangor from Grand Island, Nebraska.

Standing behind his desk, he opened what appeared to be a large ledger or book. He then informed me that I was in pilot class 43A and had graduated on the 4th of January. After appearing to run his finger down a column, he advised me that many of my classmates were already "guests of the Reich." He asked me if I remembered a classmate named Chester Lott. He informed me that I would be able to join Lott at a main prison camp as soon as I was released from the Dulag.

It was now time for some questions, but first he asked about my health and general treatment. For the first time, I spoke and told him that my cell contained fleas or some type of bug and that I was concerned about infection from the bites. He stepped forward and had me raise my shirt above my abdomen. He viewed the swellings on my chest and then glanced at bites on my leg. He assured me that he would provide some relief but that he needed my assistance with just one problem. He then went on to explain that there had been some recent changes of personnel in the 401st Sq. and that he didn't have the name of the new commander of the squadron. He went on to say that he knew that a Captain McPartlin had recently taken over as operations officer and all he needed was for me to verify the name of the newly assigned Squadron Commander. Once again, I provided no response. The German officer then directed his secretary to call for a guard escort to return me back to my cell.

I was surprised to find that I was not taken to my previous cell but to a cell that appeared to be located in the same building where the interrogation took place. Adjacent to the large barred cell where I was placed was a shower room. After a few minutes in this new cell, a guard appeared with soap and a large towel. Apparently, my appeal for some relief from the fleas had been given some consideration. The guard indicated to me that I was to strip and he would collect my clothing for cleaning or delousing. I removed my wings and insignia and entered the shower room carrying only my underwear and shoes. The shower was the first chance I had to clean up since being captured, and the soap helped to relieve the itching and burning from the bites.

After the shower, I was returned to the adjacent cell but discovered that my clothing had not been returned. Fortunately for me, it wasn't cold in the cell as I was now without my flying jacket, flight boots, trousers, shirt and socks. As I sat on the cot in the cell wearing only underwear and shoes, I contemplated the turn of events and reviewed the one-sided discussion with the interrogator. It was very apparent that the German officer had recently gained a great deal of knowledge about our mission. I suspected he already knew the name of the squadron commander of the 401st Squadron. Major Gillespie was the commander, but I had no idea how long he had been the commander. In fact, my crew was so new in the organization that we were acquainted with only a few members of the B-17 crew force.

It was several hours before I saw anyone or heard another voice. By this time, it was apparent to me that it had been a big mistake to complain about the vermin bites. I was now in a location that was completely isolated from the other prisoners and there were no windows where I could peer outside. I remembered hearing other prisoners say that the average stay at the Dulag was seven days. Supposedly, by that time, the Germans had determined that the prisoner had no information of value or the information obtained was sufficient to satisfy the interrogator. There were rumors that several prisoners were still in solitary confinement after several weeks. These prisoners were probably ones who had been captured days or weeks after their aircraft had been shot down. Prior to being captured by the Germans, some of these prisoners had been hidden by "underground" operatives.

When the guard brought a cup of soup and bread late in the evening, I asked for the return of my clothing. The guard shrugged and left without further acknowledgment. I remained in my underwear for the next two days, seeing no one except a guard who escorted me to the latrine once a day and provided me with water and bread three times a day. I was no longer being served the daily cup of soup, and was becoming increasingly aware of being very hungry. The only advantage to the new cell location was that there appeared to be no new flea or bed-bug bites.

I still had no clothing on the third day of confinement after my interrogation. Some time in the morning, I was lying half-asleep on the cot when the cell door suddenly opened and a guard handed me a huge heavy overcoat. He grinned and exclaimed

"Rooski, Rooski" several times as he motioned for me to put the coat on. This coat had belonged to a large man. When I put it on, my hands were buried in the sleeves and the coat hung only inches above the floor.

The guard continued to grin as he led me out of the cell and back to the interrogation room. The same German officer-interrogator met me at the door of his office and pointed to the chair in front of his desk. His glance at me was also one of amusement. I tried not to show my embarrassment as I sat there with nothing on but shorts, shoes and the overcoat. The guard had addressed the officer as Hauptmann, so I realized that the officer was a Captain. Although he had introduced himself at the beginning of the first interrogation, his name continued to elude me.

The interrogation began with a question as to whether or not I had been assisted regarding the fleabites. He had me open the overcoat and gave a cursory glance at the condition of the swellings. After this brief examination, I told him that I wanted my clothing, flying boots and jacket returned. He responded that I had been provided an opportunity to tell him the name of the "new" 401st Bomb Squadron Commander and that my degree of cooperation would determine whether I would obtain my clothing. He further stated that my cooperation would also insure that I was sent to an established prisoner of war camp where I would receive clothing, have comfortable living conditions, letters from home and freedom from solitary confinement. I once again stated that I would provide only my name, rank and serial number.

The meeting was short. The German Officer informed me that, in view of my lack of cooperation, he could not predict when, if ever, I would be sent to the main prison camp. I was escorted back to my cell.

Late that same afternoon, the guard re-appeared and informed me that I was to be transferred to another prison camp. I told him I would not go willingly unless I had adequate clothing. A second guard showed up and after some discussion, left the area, only to reappear with something rolled up into a ball. Both guards entered the cell. It was obvious from their actions that they would not hesitate to use force if necessary to remove me from the cell.

I was handed an old blue heated flying suit that was like winter long johns – with a flap opening in the rear and a plug-in cord dangling at the waist. Designed to be worn under flying clothing and plugged into an electric heat outlet in the aircraft, these suits were utilized primarily by waist gunners and some lower ball turret gunners as protection from the freezing air at high altitudes. I had no choice but to put on the oversized monstrosity.

Outside the building a formation of prisoners was being assembled. The two escort guards left as soon as I got in line with other airmen scheduled for departure to a new prison location. For the most part, prisoners were wearing the clothes they had been wearing when they were captured. I was the only one with an open-flapped electric flying suit topped by an overcoat that once belonged to some Russian giant. Bill Runner was also in the formation. His reaction when he saw me was total disbelief, followed by laughter. I joined him in laughter, and in so doing, lessened the inward humiliation I was fighting to control. I decided I would just have to stop worrying about my appearance and concentrate on staying healthy and, most important, alive.

Stalag Luft III

After arriving at the rail station in Frankfort, we were marched through crowds of civilians to gain entrance to the main terminal. The guards were distributed along the slow-moving line of prisoners. Except for silent stares, there was little reaction from the onlookers. I felt particularly vulnerable with my strange attire and tried to keep my eyes focused on the line of prisoners ahead of me. I noted that the huge terminal had a glass ceiling and was surprised to see that despite our bombing raid on the 4th of October, there was not a single broken pane of glass in the massive ceiling. This was a mystery to me, as I was certain a rail terminal in Frankfort had been the primary target on that date.

We boarded small railroad cars. There were no windows in the section utilized by the prisoners, but there was one small, iron-barred opening for ventilation on the outside wall. A middle aisle separated two-man wooden high-back bench seats facing forward. At the rear was a small compartment utilized by the German guards. It had a glass front view that permitted the guards to monitor prisoner activities. Across the aisle and opposite the guard compartment was a small toilet-room. There was seating space for about forty prisoners in the railcar.

Bill Runner was seated just ahead of the guard compartment. I had hoped to get a seat with him, as I wanted to hear the details of his capture, discuss our present situation and perhaps come up with some sort of escape plan. By the time I had boarded, however, the seat beside him was taken so I moved to a seat in the middle of the boxcar.

The first hour or so of travel was relatively quiet in the rail car. Each prisoner faced an uncertain future. Some were still recovering from injuries. Others had not yet recovered from the shock of recent events. Death or severe injury to fellow crew members, survival of a parachute bailout or crash landing of an aircraft, capture and in some instances harsh treatment by the enemy and the recent period of solitary confinement had resulted in a sobering and deeply emotional response in all of us.

For the first time since being captured, we were offered food from Red Cross parcels. One of the guards distributing the food was friendly and very talkative. He announced that for many years he had lived in Chicago and was interested in knowing if any prisoners were from Chicago. His friendly attitude and discussion with various prisoners produced a change in the mood of the majority of the prisoners and soon the prisoners were talking with the German guards and sharing their experiences with each other.

Bill Runner, who possessed an engaging and outgoing personality, entered the compartment where the guards were seated and learned that we were being transported to a Prisoner of War camp at Sagan, Germany. The camp, an Allied Officer Prison primarily for aircrew members, was located southeast of Berlin.

My own thoughts were centered on only one objective — to escape before arrival at the new prison camp. I was able to get Bill Runner's attention and he came forward to my location. I told him I was considering leaping out of the rear entrance of the railcar during one of its frequent stops and that I would need his help. It was obvious that I couldn't wear the Russian overcoat during any escape attempt. The weather was quite mild outside but I would need a jacket of some type to wear over the heated suit. Bill volunteered his A-2 flying jacket.

Two of the guards were relaxing in their compartment, eating and chatting with various prisoners who were permitted to stand in the opening of the compartment. Their pistols were holstered and their rifles stacked in a corner. There were glass windows in the compartment. Anyone seated near the compartment could see outside and determine if the train was stopping at a station or pulling into a siding to permit another train to pass. Since Bill was seated near the compartment, he had the advantage of being able to see the outside surroundings and could signal me to go to the rear of the railcar. The plan was for him to engage the guards in conversation. I would leave my seat, walk down the aisle and then shove Bill into the compartment. In the subsequent confusion, I would exit the train through the rear opening. I pointed out to Bill that he would probably be at greater risk than me, but he felt he could explain to the guards that he was an innocent victim. Bill Runner indicated that he would risk his life to help me.

I put on Bill's A-2 jacket and sat with my feet in the aisle. The overcoat would be left behind. I could feel the adrenalin surging through my body as I sat there waiting for a signal from Runner. During this wait, two prisoners approached me. One was a navigator with his arm in a cast, who had been seated with me. He was the spokesman for both men. He had overheard part of the discussion I had with Bill Runner and he was very agitated. He expressed the fear that if I escaped I would be jeopardizing the lives of all the rest of the prisoners. It was his opinion that in all likelihood the guards would shoot the remainder of the prisoners. My initial reaction to his remarks was one of anger. I told him that if he was satisfied to be a prisoner, then so be it, but that all of us had a responsibility to escape if and when the opportunity presented itself.

I had to acknowledge to myself that, other than putting Runner in a precarious position, I had given no thought to the impact an escape attempt would have on the other prisoners. In fact, I had just assumed they all felt as I did, but perhaps without the same conviction. Some were like the navigator, recovering from wounds and unable to escape. Others were so traumatized by their experiences that for the time being they were just satisfied to be alive and out of solitary confinement. Regardless of a person's condition, I still felt it was important for everyone to have an escape plan.

The complaining navigator exchanged his seat next to me with another prisoner. It was apparent by his demeanor and actions that he was continuing to voice his fears to anyone who would listen. Bill Runner was aware that there was a problem of some sort and, once again, came up the aisle where we could talk. I told him of the dissention by my former seatmate, and after further discussion with him, I decided to delay any attempt to escape. I didn't know if my decision was based on the fearful attitude of a fellow prisoner or my own self doubts about my escape plan once it had been challenged. I really hadn't focused on the danger to Bill Runner, who would probably have faced retaliatory action by the guards if he had allowed me to push him into the compartment. Although I had little doubt that I could successfully exit the train, I had no plan other than to disappear in the darkness and attempt to distance myself from the immediate area by traveling at night and hiding during daylight hours. I knew that I would eventually need to find water, food and clothing, and that the "blue long johns" would need to be replaced.

Bill Runner returned to his seat wearing his A-2 jacket. That was the signal to those watching that there had been a change in plans. The dissenting navigator approached me wanting to talk, but I was in no mood for discussion and I waved him away. I was frustrated and angry with myself. I had likely given up my only chance to escape and I wasn't sure how much my own fear had contributed to the decision to forego the escape attempt.

Several hours passed before I was able to shift my mind to other thoughts. Finally, with my head resting on the bench backrest, I dozed off to a fitful sleep as the train yawed back and forth making frequent stops in sidings to allow other train traffic to pass. The Russian overcoat served a useful purpose after all — pillow, blanket and shock absorber.

It was late afternoon the following day when the train arrived at our final destination. Bill Runner and I had finally arrived at Stalag Luft III. It was the 28th of October, 1943.

We formed up in columns, joining other prisoners who were exiting their railcars. It was a short walking distance to the prison camp that was to be our new home. We entered an area called the "Outer Lager" for processing. Each prisoner was photographed and then handed a form to complete. The form had a Red Cross heading and, according to our captors, was required to be filled out in order for the Red Cross to verify our status.

While others seemed to have no difficulty completing the forms, I found that many of the questions were seeking information exceeding the "name, rank and serial number" response that had been our briefed guideline. I attempted to return the form with only basic information filled in. The form was returned to me with the warning that I would not be permitted to complete the processing until all the requested information was supplied.

The processing room soon emptied and I was the only prisoner remaining. Finally, an English-speaking man, who claimed to be a Red Cross representative, approached me and told me that I should provide the required additional basic information as that information was necessary to insure I was who I said I was. He pointed out that a home address was necessary to insure proper notification by the Red Cross of my prisoner status. I remained skeptical, but finally provided some additional information that was not military related, and the form was accepted.

The next step in processing was the issue of clothing — G.I. winter trousers and shirt, winter long johns, socks and a heavy G.I overcoat. For bedding, each prisoner was provided with two blankets, a covered straw pillow, a mattress cover and a bed sheet. We were told that we would be assigned "permanent" living quarters in one of the long low buildings located within the South Compound, but that for the first night we would have temporary quarters wherever there was available space.

Being new prisoners, we were taken to the entrance gate of the South Compound, Stalag Luft III. We were met by prisoner members of the Camp Staff who had been appointed to assist us in finding a place to eat and bed down for the night. We would be processed and assigned to permanent quarters the following day after our first "Appell" or roll call.

That first night I was assigned to a room occupied by six strangers. I slept on a mat on the floor and shared their food. The conversations that first night were guarded, since I wasn't certain what should be discussed and the occupants had to ensure that I wasn't a spy. I discovered that each new prisoner had to be interrogated and "cleared" by designated members of the prisoner staff before information considered "confidential or secret" could be discussed. Matters concerning prisoner activities had to be protected and some activities were handled by a strictly "need to know" rule.

The next morning, all the new prisoners were directed to stay in one group for the nine o'clock body count, our first "Appell." The remainder of the prisoner force lined up by individual barracks or "blocks." As the prisoners were dispersing after the count, I was suddenly grabbed from behind in a "bear-hug." The culprit was my good friend and pilot training classmate, Chester Lott. Chester's crew had been shot down during the mission to Kiel, Germany on June 13th, 1943. It had been the crew's first mission. Chester was the co-pilot. Prior to reaching the target, three engines had failed for no apparent reason. As the aircraft became a straggler, enemy FW-190's and ME-110's had begun a relentless attack, forcing the crew to bail out. Chester and his pilot, Lt. Robert Jackson, were captured as soon as their parachutes hit the ground. My German interrogator at the Dulag had been correct when he had informed me that Lott was a prisoner at a "permanent" camp.

My second surprise of the morning came when Joe Johnson, my co-pilot, emerged from the crowd of prisoners waiting to greet the newcomers. He had spent only two days at the Dulag in Frankfort before being released for transport to Stalag Luft III. Now, the only crew members unaccounted for were Glenn Foster, the navigator and Charles Groth, the right waist gunner.

To accommodate the large influx of new prisoners, it was necessary for each housing barracks or "block" to create additional bed space. This was accomplished by making tiers of bunk beds. Joe Johnson and I were assigned to Room-4 in Block 136. This was also Chester Lott's room, which he shared with seven other prisoners. Our arrival increased the room occupancy to ten. Joe had the lower bunk and I drew the upper one. Neither one of us complained; we were just grateful to finally be settled in a location where the occupants were considered friendly.

The first few days at Stalag Luft III were spent getting acquainted with other prisoners assigned to Room 4 and receiving an indoctrination in the "do's and don'ts" of prison life. The initial action by the American prison staff was to have an interrogator review each new prisoner's verbal description of the events that had led to his becoming a prisoner. This action was part of the verification process. By the time I arrived at Stalag Luft III, there were prisoners from most of the American flying units in the European theater, and it wasn't difficult to determine whether a new prisoner was the person he claimed to be. Chester Lott provided additional verification of my status.

Oberfeldweble Herman Glemnitz
Security Chief
Stalag Luft III

Daily "Appel" or roll call at Stalag Luft III, Sagan, Germany

PART II PRISONER OF WAR

"Glemnitz", Better Known as "Glimwitz"

Galatovics & Friends??

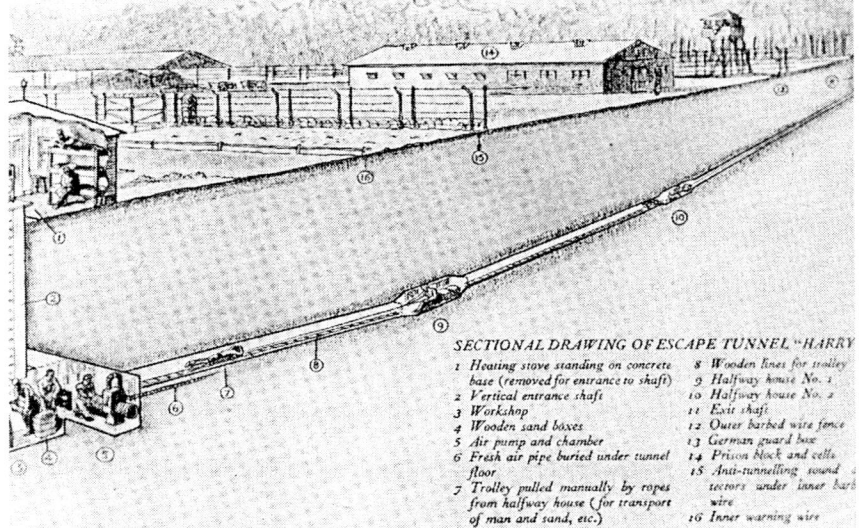

The Great Escape

Stalag Luft III Top: German Guard personnel
Bottom: Tunnel "Harry" North Compound

80　JOURNEY TO FREEDOM AND BEYOND

Original "Escape Photo," taken in September 1943

| Beschriftung der Erkennungsmarke Nr. | Lager: | Name: |

Bemerkungen:

Personalbeschreibung

Figur:	schlank
Größe:	1,67 m
Alter:	20 Jahre
Gesichtsform:	oval
Gesichtsfarbe:	gesund
Schädelform:	länglich
Augen:	d.braun
Nase:	gerade
Gebiß:	gesund
Haare:	d.braun
Bart:	
Gewicht:	63 kg
Besondere Merkmale:	
Deutsche Sprachkenntnisse:	

Typical Barracks - bunk beds, Stalag Luft III

Above and right, first letters mailed home after becoming P.O.W.

Stalag Luft No. 3
Nov. 7, 1943

Dear Folks, I would have written from ▬▬ Lug Luft, but I can't be sure that you received it and that you know I am a prisoner. We were shot down Oct. 1st ▬▬▬. Our oxygen was out and three engines hit with No. 1 on fire. I gave the order to bail out and everyone left ▬▬▬▬▬▬▬▬▬▬. I crash landed in a potato field ▬▬▬▬▬▬▬▬▬▬. I was captured immediately as was the crew. We are all quite well. Old Chester Lott and I live together here. We eat our own food. The Red Cross is wonderful. We would receive very little food if it were not for the Red Cross parcels. Don't worry about me and send a ▬▬▬ parcel whenever possible. You can get the necessary information from the Red Cross. I need heavy underwear, tooth brush and powder, handkerchiefs, chocolate, razor and blades, socks, and any dehydrated food it is possible to send, a pencil, a pocket knife and a few combs. Taber is here and lives across the hall from me ▬▬▬▬▬▬▬▬▬▬▬▬▬▬▬▬▬▬▬▬▬▬▬▬▬▬▬▬▬▬▬▬▬▬▬ want to know the circumstances. I beg of you not to worry. I can get along anywhere and will see you soon. Loads of Love, Bob

Stalag Luft No. 3
Nov. 7, 1943

Dearest Lee,

I hardly know what to write, but I just want you to know that I'm o.k. We were shot down Oct. 14th ▓▓▓▓▓▓▓▓▓▓▓▓▓▓▓▓▓▓▓▓▓▓ I crash landed in a potato field. ▓▓▓▓▓▓▓▓▓▓▓▓▓▓▓▓▓▓▓▓▓▓

I hope you received my other letters, and please write me as often as possible. I can only write you once or twice a month, but you may write as often as you please.

Tell Vickie that Bill was shot down in August, and I believe he is o.k. I had a letter on my dresser already sealed. I hope they sent it to you. Well, guess it was better not to have been married after all, but don't worry I'll be seeing you soon. If you can, write my folks. I'm not even sure that they know I'm a prisoner of war.

Gosh, winter will be here soon. This is a hell of a place to spend Christmas. You know in about three more months we can celebrate our anniversary. Take care of Horace. Tell him Pappy will be home soon. I must close. I love you, Bob

PART II PRISONER OF WAR

Kriegsgefangenenpost
Postkarte

An Miss Mary Lee Valentine

Empfangsort: 110 Idaho St.

Straße: Boise, Idaho

Land: United States of America

Vor- und Zuname: 1st Lt. Robert M. Slane

Gefangenennummer: 3201

Lager Bezeichnung: M.-Stammlager Luft 3

Deutschland (Germany)

11338 U.S. CENSOR

Kriegsgefangenenlager   Datum: Nov. 16, 1943

Dearest Lee — I wrote you last week but can't be sure you will receive the letter. I haven't much to write but want you to write me as often as possible. My prisoner number is on the other side of this card. Send your letters "via clipper". Be good and please write. I Love You, Bob

Kriegsgefangenenpost

Mit Luftpost / Par Avion / Postkarte

An: Mrs. Mary P. J. Reifel
Raph St.

Empfangsort: Santa Ana
Straße: California
Land: United States of America

Absender:
Vor- und Zuname: 1st Lt. Robert M. Sloane
Gefangenennummer: Not Allotted
Lager Bezeichnung: M.-Stammlager Luft 3
Deutschland (Germany)

Kriegsgefangenenlager

Dear Grandmother — When you receive this, send word to the folks in case they have no news of me. My crew was shot down the 14th of Oct. I'm in good health and intend to be home soon. Hope you and Uncle Phil are in good health. It is beginning to get cold here and makes me think of the warm climate of Santa Ana. Write me as soon as possible. Lots of Love, Bob

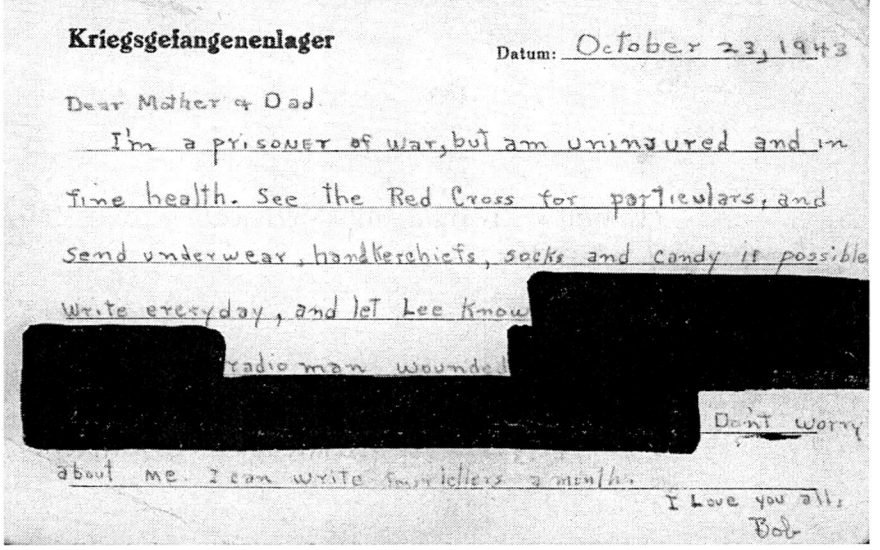

The "X" Committee

At Stalag Luft III, we were able to benefit from the experiences and subsequent disciplines initiated by senior British and American prisoners. Each "block" had an assigned 'senior officer' who was generally a Major or Lt. Col. The compound commander was a Colonel.

The senior officer in the South Compound was Col. Charles Goodrich. He had been a prisoner since September 1942 and had arrived at Stalag Luft III in March 1943. Included on his staff was an officer appointed to head the "X" activity. Members of this committee managed a myriad of activities devoted to obtaining information, planning escape activities and hiding surveillance equipment. Prisoners were not permitted to attempt to converse with or otherwise associate with any of the guards unless they had approval from the "X" committee.

The discipline and leadership of the senior American officers was reflected in all phases of life as a prisoner in the South Compound. Food distribution was organized, with each prisoner having a part to play in sharing the goods and services that were available. In each room of the blocks, the prisoners shared responsibility for clean up and cooking. A roster was utilized to assign these duties.

There was very little reference to grade or rank in my assigned room, which I'm sure was the case with the majority of the company grade officers in the compound. There was, however, a certain undefined courteous regard provided to those prisoners who had been imprisoned for a year or more. Those prisoners were generally housed in the single or double rooms in the blocks.

After several days of indoctrination and after receiving security clearance by the camp internal interrogators, we were allowed to listen to the daily "evening news," which was conveyed by special messenger to each block. Guards were posted at the entrance to the block, and when clearance was received, the appointed messenger would give his report. It was amazing to be able to hear up-to-date news about the war effort. Only those specifically cleared by the chief of the "X" activity were to relay this information, and although the source of the news was from "BBC" in England, any discussion about how or where the information was received was strictly forbidden. This activity, among others, was known only to a few and those of us not directly involved were advised not to discuss how the news was obtained.

During the first week of incarceration at Stalag Luft III, I began a daily walking program involving many circuits on a path inside the perimeter of the Stalag. The path was adjacent to a two-foot high long wooden warning rail that separated the Stalag from the outer perimeter fence. We were warned that all we had to do to get shot by a tower guard was to step across the short wooden fence in the direction of the outer double-row barbed wire fence. This warning was part of our new prisoner indoctrination program.

The second week of imprisonment, I made known my desire to participate in any activity that would provide an escape avenue. I was advised to contact Alvin "Sammy" Vogtle, an American Spitfire pilot who had been shot down in January 1943. Vogtle, who occupied the single room at the entrance to block 136, was a representative of the "X" activity and could provide me with advice concerning any escape plans. When I visited Sammy, I explained that I would be a volunteer "digger" or helper in any tunnel activity. I expressed to him my desire to escape by any means possible. Sammy advised me that my help would be welcomed but that even if I worked on a tunnel, I would not be permitted to escape if and when the tunnel was utilized as an escape vehicle. He explained that it was the policy of the escape "committee" to utilize escape resources only for those specially designated persons who could speak German or a European language. Priority would also go to those who had been prisoners the longest. As a relatively new prisoner with no foreign language capability, I was not the type of candidate eligible for a tunnel escape.

Based on this information, I withdrew my commitment to assist in any tunnel work. I could understand why the escape materials should be prioritized; however, I firmly believed that anyone who participated in risky tunnel digging should not be denied the opportunity to escape after the "priority" people had departed through the tunnel.

   I was discouraged by the information I had just received, but there still remained the option to seek approval of a plan not involving escape through an underground tunnel. I felt it imperative to find someone who felt as I did – one who would be willing to take the time to work on a plan that might merit approval and support from the "Escape Committee" or the "X activity." I wasn't certain of the procedures for approval but knew that any escape attempt would involve obtaining equipment that could cut through the mass of barbed wire in the two fences surrounding the compound. None of my nine roommates were ready to commit to participation in an escape attempt, but I had their assurances that if I ever came up with an approved plan, I would have their support in obtaining needed escape equipment.

Letter from Mrs. Harvey dated 5 December, 1943

Dec. 5th

Braisworth Hall
Tannington
Woodbridge
Suffolk. Eng.

Dear Mr & Mrs Slane,

We were sorry indeed to get the sad news that your son is missing. We seemed almost to know him, from the few hours he spent with us, the night he made that forced landing in our field.

I have often thought of him these last weeks, he seemed such a nice lad, I felt so sure we should see – or hear – from him again.

We were only too pleased to offer any hospitality our home could afford to these brave lads, who are risking their lives for us, & I do trust that your son is only missing, & that you may hear of – or from – him again soon.

Our place is almost 100 miles from where your son was stationed, so I don't know any of the other lads from there –

but I will write to the Commanding Officer of that drome, asking him to send me any information he can.

Do try to remember that there are many airmen who bale out quite safely, & very often quite away from Germany & I think your son was quite a skilful pilot, judging by the way he landed here, & well able to gain safety for himself & crew if it was at all possible.

In the meantime don't give up hope if my next letter is a long time coming, as write you again I surely will if I can get the least bit of news of your son.

I recieved your letter Dec 2nd & am writing this Dec 5th. It was the very day the "Fortress" was flown away, it has been here ever since that night your son came to us.

With sincere hope's, for the best of news from us all. Yours — Mr & Mrs Harvey.

Settling In

As the weeks slowly passed by, prison life became routine, occasionally interrupted by short periods of fear, excitement, anticipation, despair or boredom. My ever-persistent thoughts of escape were tempered by the grudging acknowledgement that I wasn't ready to attempt an escape without the moral and physical support of an accomplice.

Daily physical activity was one way to combat the boredom so I resolved to try and stay as physically active as possible. I helped Chester Lott plant tomato seeds in a small garden adjacent to our block. He had received the seeds in a letter from home. Thomas Decaro, a B-17 navigator, was the chief "tinsmith" in our room. He made most of the cooking pans and plates used by members of Room 4. He decided to make a set of "weights" for members of our room to use for exercise. I became his "first assistant." The weights were made from Klim Cans (Powdered milk cans) all fastened together and then tightly rolled. A hickory broomstick, stolen from the cookhouse, served as our weight bar. Three of us in the room utilized the weights for twice-daily exercise. Dale Perkins, a bombardier, was the third so-called "weight lifter."

Dale Perkins had an extraordinary experience the day his aircraft was downed. The pilot of his B-17 had directed him to place the arming pins back in the bombs in anticipation of a possible crash landing. The crash landing took place while Dale was still in the bomb bay holding a hand-full of arming pins. He survived the crash landing without injury.

Robert Webster, the co-pilot on Tom Decaro's crew, was also assigned to Room 4, Block 136. He and Tom Decaro were the only survivors of their combat crew. Webster was captured on land near the coastal docks at Kiel, Germany. A German patrol boat in the North Sea picked up Decaro. To their knowledge, they were the only survivors of their ten-man B-17 crew. It is interesting to note that the five crew members representing three different aircraft were all on the same mission to bomb the docks at Kiel, Germany on June 13th, 1943.

Two other prisoners assigned to Room 4, Block 136 were also B-17 crew members on the same aircraft. Navigator, Lawrence Connors and bombardier, Edward Goulz — prisoners since July 25, 1943 — were shot down by enemy FW190's and flak.

Larry Connors was the accepted Room 4 "boss." This thirty-year-old small Irishman had a great sense of honor and humor and was a mature and serious man with a deeply religious outlook on life. Shot down on August 12, 1943, Walter Fegersen, was the eighth prisoner assigned to Room 4, Block 136, prior to my arrival with the group of new prisoners that included Joe Johnson and Bill Runner. Walter was a bookworm and spent hours reading and studying the game of chess. He was nicknamed the "Birdman" for some unknown reason.

The individual barracks (blocks) were single-story prefabricated wooden structures. The interiors had never been finished, with the wooden building studs still exposed on the inside walls. There were rooms on either side of a middle corridor. Each building had an indoor latrine, a washroom with several basins and a small communal kitchen with a cook stove. The indoor latrine was for use only at night after the doors at both ends of the barracks had been closed and barred shut from the outside. During the day, the prison population used latrine buildings called the "Abort." Small rooms at both ends of the building housed one or two prisoners. One of the occupants, generally a senior officer, was considered the "block commander," sometimes jokingly referred to as the "Fuhrer." Each room contained a large window that had functional shutters. Each barrack had about thirteen rooms including the smaller two man rooms. It was within the confines of one of these rooms that a prisoner would spend a major part of every day. The need for tolerance, understanding and a good sense of humor was essential for peaceful co-existence. We all knew this, and with the "fatherly guidance" exercised by Larry

Connors, there were very few misunderstandings in Room 4, Block 136, South Compound.

With the colder months of winter approaching, it was evident that we needed to "winterize" our room area with whatever was available. There was a small pot-bellied stove in each room; however, the charcoal bricks the Germans issued were not sufficient to keep the rooms warm. Each room had a daily scheduled time to utilize the cook stove located in the community kitchen. We elected to use our limited supply of charcoal for cooking purposes.

Newspapers or paper of any sort were prized commodities and never discarded. I managed to sew newspapers between my two blankets. We used newspaper for filling cracks in the inside walls of the barracks. We were all grateful to the Red Cross for providing basic items like tooth brushes and needles and thread. Those prisoners fortunate enough to have arrived in prison with their flying jackets were able to sew layers of paper inside the linings of their jackets.

A band and choral group was formed within the South Compound, thanks to the YMCA, which provided the musical instruments. Bill Runner, an accomplished trumpet player, joined with the band whenever possible.

Christmas 1943 arrived and we were rewarded with additional Christmas food parcels. It was a relatively festive time for some, and John (Moose) Moss, a B-17 pilot from Des Moines, New Mexico, invited me to his room for a taste of raisin home brew. In the course of our conversation, John stated that we would "probably be doing this same celebration in Stalag Luft III in 1944." I couldn't accept even the thought of being a prisoner for another year. We made a fifty dollar bet, witnessed by other brew-tasters in Room 3, the room adjacent to ours.

Christmas festivities would cease early in Block 136. On the night of December 27th, we heard the air raid signals. All electricity to the barracks was shut off. Larry Connors was in one of the end rooms playing bridge with a foursome when suddenly we were all startled by two loud gunshots. The sound was deafening. We thought the shots were made in our room. We heard shouts in the corridor, and when we opened the door, we saw someone rushing down the corridor with a flaming newspaper torch. The torch was quickly extinguished when another voice shouted a warning that the light could cause further gunfire. The shots had been fired into the end room where the card playing was continuing by candlelight after the electricity had been turned off. Lt. Col. John Stevenson had been shot in both legs, and bone had been shattered in one leg. There was much confusion and delay before the Germans arrived at the scene and transported Stevenson to a hospital. There was little sleep in Block 136 that night.

Escape activity was a continuing occupation for many of the prisoners, but most of the work involved tunnel preparation. Except for awareness that such activity was taking place, those of us not directly involved had no knowledge when or where the underground work was being accomplished. It was rumored that the Germans were aware of specific areas where tunnel activity was taking place but would wait until the tunnel work had progressed to near completion before suddenly arriving with a tunnel destruct team. The purpose for the delay in destroying the tunnel was to further demoralize the prisoners who had spent months preparing a tunnel for escape only to have their work destroyed in a less than an hour. No one had escaped by tunnel in the South Compound since it had been opened for occupation in September 1943.

One morning we were awakened by a flurry of activity in the room adjacent to ours (Room- 3). It seemed that one of its occupants, John Lewis, a P-39 pilot, had participated in an escape. Shot down by an enemy Me-109 pilot, John was captured in North Africa and had been a prisoner at Stalag Luft III since April, 1943. John and another prisoner had spent months making a hinged ladder. This ladder had been hidden in the attic in Block 136 and placed in a position where it appeared to be part of the roof structure.

On the night of the escape, we had a severe thunderstorm and there was a power outage. John and his friend were dressed in black clothing as they made a run to the perimeter fences. The hinged ladder served its purpose; the first section reached the top of the inside fence and the hinged portion went over the top, covering the space between the two fences. John's friend made it across the double fence, dropped down over the outside fence and disappeared in the adjacent forest. John was not so fortunate. As he attempted to cross over the top of the two fences, the ladder broke and he fell into the mass of barbed wire between the two fences.

Discovered by the guards, John was forced to remain in the location between the two fences until daybreak. When the power was restored, the tower guards on either side of his location kept their searchlights focused on him. Since the ladder pieces had also fallen into the area where he was trapped, John could clearly see that the ladder had previously been cut by a saw. Only a small section was left uncut. The cut area had been filled in with some sort of putty. It was obvious that the Germen "Ferrets" had previously discovered the ladder and left it in place to foil any escape attempt. What the Germans didn't count on was one escapee making it over the fences before the ladder collapsed. John was extricated from the fence area at daybreak with many cuts and bruises. He was then escorted to the "cooler" where he served time in solitary confinement. His companion was free for several days before being captured at a border crossing.

One other prisoner succeeded in escaping from the South Compound prior to March 1944. I never knew the details except that he was somehow able to exit the compound by hiding in an area under the horse-drawn vehicle ("Honey Wagon") used to siphon waste materials from the latrines. This prisoner was also captured and returned to prisoner status.

On March 26th, 1944, we awakened to news that there had been a mass breakout of British prisoners from the adjacent North Compound. Eighty-eight prisoners were reported as having escaped. The news generated excitement and joy throughout the prison population. With this news, there was also a change in the mood and demeanor of our captors. For the next three days after the escape, we were subjected to sudden no-notice Appells or prisoner body counts. Prisoners were forced out of their barracks while the Germans conducted numerous searches in each block. The "Ferrets" crawled under the floors, probing the ground with long screwdrivers. The walls in every room were checked in an effort to find hidden items that could be used in an escape attempt. The attics received special attention.

On the second day of the no-notice prisoner counts, each block commander in the South Compound passed the word that we were to disrupt the count with a slow movement to the parade ground. After straggling into the parade ground, we all meandered around, shifting position in the columns, thus making an accurate count impossible. The German officer conducting the count finally gave up and departed the parade grounds. A second count was initiated a short time later with the same results. A conversation between the German Commandant and Col. Goodrich, our senior officer was indiscernible but some members of our block heard the words "We will be back."

It was later in the afternoon that we witnessed several weapon-carrying vehicles passing through the gates and proceeding on to the parade ground. Ground-mounted machine guns were placed at four locations surrounding the area where the prisoner count was to be conducted. Two soldiers manned each gun. As this action was taking place on the ground, we noticed that every guard tower was being reinforced with an additional occupant and the weather cover that normally protected their machine guns had been removed. Each guard in the tower had also been equipped with a rifle. All weapons were pointed in our direction. It was a chilling, sobering experience. We received word from Col. Goodrich that the "passive resistance" was over. The directive did not require repeating. The German commandant had clearly made his point. The prisoner count and subsequent prisoner counts were conducted in an orderly manner.

It wasn't until the first week in April 1944, that we were informed that the majority of the escapees from the North Compound had been captured and that fifty men had been murdered on orders from the German High Command. Many of those shot had been prisoners for several years, having been captured early in the war. This unpredictable action by the Germans was devastating news. There was no easy way to overcome the profound effect the deaths of these men had on their close friends and the rest of the prison population.

An air-raid warning sounded shortly afternoon on Easter Sunday, April 9, 1944. Some prisoners had just returned from a church service. The murder of the British prisoners was still the main topic of discussion. I had been walking the perimeter circuit when the siren sounded. I scurried back to Block 136. The German guards wanted us inside a building anytime there was indication of an air attack in the vicinity. I had just entered the building and was in the corridor when someone shouted, "Look out for a Goon with a gun." The warning was in reference to a perimeter guard. This particular guard had his rifle resting on the outside perimeter fence and was aiming at a target within the compound. I darted into our washroom and looked out the window. There he was, calmly sighting his rifle at some object within the compound. Fearing he might turn his sights on me, I dropped out of sight and raced to the front entrance of our block where I could see where he was aiming.

When I arrived at the entrance to our building, I looked in the direction it appeared he was aiming and saw a man leaning against the doorjamb of the cookhouse. I heard the shot and watched in shock as the man in the doorway suddenly grabbed his throat, stumbled forward out of the doorway, took two steps and fell face downward. I had just witnessed a cold-blooded murder. Part of the horror of this murder was that no one could go forward to provide assistance.

When the "all-clear" sounded, I was one of the first to reach the body of the dead soldier. I didn't know his name but I recognized him as one of the enlisted prisoners who had volunteered to work in the "communal" kitchen. His name was Corporal C.C. Miles and he was an infantry soldier. Cpl Miles had been captured by Arabs and turned over to the Germans in February 1943. He was buried in the POW cemetery at Sagan, Germany. I will never forget him or the way he died.

Adjusting to Prison Life

One of my best days in prison was April 19, 1944 when I received my first letters from home. Joe Johnson and Bill Runner had been receiving mail since the latter part of February so I knew my mother had been in contact with their families. Six months was a long time to wait for direct word from home, but arrival of six letters at one time erased all my anxiety. I had been mailing four postcards and three letters monthly to loved ones at home since my arrival at Stalag Luft III. At long last, I was receiving mail - it was a day to celebrate!

Up until that time, physical adjustment to living conditions as a prisoner had not been too difficult. I had enlisted at age eighteen as a private and had maintained enlisted status while in pilot training. Prior to and during most of my time in flight training, I had lived in an open bay in the barracks where there was little privacy. To some degree, I had been preconditioned to communal living. During the daylight hours, I tried to keep as active as possible. Located near Block 137 was a set of wooden parallel bars. My daily circuits around the perimeter included a stop to do a short workout on the bars. The workouts with the weights in combination with the parallel bars and the walking had kept me in relatively good shape. The major physical discomfort we had to contend with was a constant, gnawing hunger. We had all lost weight, but fortunately the occupants of our barracks (136) were in relatively good health.

Mental adjustment to prison life was an entirely different matter for me. Sometimes in the mornings just as I was awakening, I wouldn't allow my mind to accept the fact that I was a prisoner. I would keep my eyes closed and conjure up visions of distant places, hopeful that when I opened my eyes I would be home or anyplace other than in a prison. I battled with recurring thoughts of what might have happened if the enemy had not captured us.

I relived the events that occurred on the day my crew was lost to enemy action. "If I had ordered crew bailout earlier, would Sgt. Smith be alive today? If I had immediately descended to the "deck" after loss of two engines, would we have had a better chance to return to England?" But most of all I thought and dreamed of escape. I just had to find a way to escape.

In the days before the North and South Compounds were built, the majority of the Allied flying officers in German prisons flew for Great Britain. Some of the officers from various nationalities had been imprisoned since 1939. I was fascinated by the story about two Czech pilots who had escaped from the East Compound. The escape from the prison compound was successful and they made their way to the airfield located near the city of Sagan. They were also successful in gaining access to a German aircraft and starting the aircraft engine. The problem they encountered was an inadvertent retraction of the landing gear while taxiing out for takeoff. This story fueled my daydreams of escape. I spent a good deal of my time conjuring up all sorts of "Mr. Middy" situations where a fantastic heroic escape was accomplished.

We were all aware of a pending Allied invasion several months before it occurred, but it had little meaning for us until it actually took place on June 6, 1944. For most prisoners, news of the invasion was the greatest morale booster since being incarcerated. A map room in one of the blocks was utilized to post the latest available information on the two fronts - the Russian eastern front and the new western front in Normandy. These maps and supporting data reflected only information that was made available to us by our captors. We continued to receive secret briefings based on information received through the prisoner "X" Activity program. Protecting the source of this information required the vigilance of all prisoners.

A new prison compound adjacent to our compound was opened in late Spring 1944. Separating the North and South Compounds and the newly opened West Compound was a roadway that extended from a gate opening between two guard towers on the south and continuing on to the German occupied "Vorlager" located north of the West and North Compounds.

During the summer months of 1944, the prison population was rapidly increasing. The majority of the prisoners (self-named "kriegies") participated in one or more of the sport activities sponsored by individual barracks. A "kriegie"-built theater was nearing completion and Bill Runner was a member of a band called the "Luftbandsters." I worked on a sketchbook that depicted scenes from our room and the outside gun towers known as "Goon boxes."

Decaro, Perkins and I continued our weight-lifting program despite the fact that we had lost all visible body fat. During the warm days of early summer, we did our weight-lifting exercises outside our room window. The weights and bench were stored in the room and the open window made it easy to quickly return our equipment to the room in the event of an air-raid warning. Others who were interested in making their own weights or who just wanted to participate in an exercise program sometimes joined us. One participant was Major David Jones, a pilot and survivor of the famed "Tokyo Raid." Major Jones, holder of two Distinguished Flying Crosses, had been piloting a B-26 light bomber when his aircraft was hit by flak and he was forced to crash-land in Tunisia, North Africa. His date of capture was April 12, 1942. His quiet manner, quick humor and unique ability to communicate had gained him the respect of all those with whom he came in contact.

Regardless of the activity in which we were engaged, the main topic of discussion always centered on the progress of the invasion. We were all hopeful the war would be over before the winter months arrived.

South Compound, Stalag Luft III. Our Bombardier,
Bill "Dusty" Runner leads the band on July 4th, 1944

Left to right: Lt/Col. Clark, Lt/Col. Klocko, Col. Goodrich,
Wings Commander Day. Col. Goodrich is the Senior Officer
imprisoned in the South Compound at Stalag Luft III

Escape Plan

On August 5, 1944, I celebrated my 21st birthday. August marked my tenth month as a prisoner of war. We had just received word that for the immediate future the weekly issue of Red Cross food packages would be reduced by 50%. Instead of a parcel per man each week, the issue would be only one parcel for two men each week. It wouldn't be long before the effects of the food reduction would become very apparent. Although our captors provided bread and some vegetables to prepare a daily soup in the communal kitchen, food from the Red Cross parcels was still our main means of sustenance.

It was late August when I finally found a man who was willing to take the risks involved in a direct escape route through the perimeter fences. Glenn Oster resided in Room 3, the room adjacent to Room 4 in our same barracks. During an "Appell" Glenn was standing in front of me and had heard me say, "I've got to get the hell out of this place." After the prison count, he turned to me and said, "You've got yourself a partner." Glenn's crew was downed on October 10th, 1943 and he had arrived at Sagan about the same time I did. He had been free for two days before being captured in Holland. He said that he had been aware for some time that I was looking for an escape partner and that he had finally decided he had "had enough of life as a prisoner."

I wasted no time after Oster had made his commitment to accompany me in an escape attempt. The first step was to outline the basic plan and then seek a meeting with Lt/Col. Clark, the chief of the mysterious "X" committee. Colonel Clark was one of the most prominent prisoners in the compound and the first American fighter pilot to be captured and imprisoned by the Germans. He had been flying a British Spitfire when he was forced to bail out near the coast of France. A prisoner since July 1942, he had gained superior knowledge and first hand experience in matters pertaining to covert activities while being held with British prisoners in both the East and North compounds. He was admired and respected by the entire prisoner population of the South Compound.

I explained our plan to Lt/Col. Clark. It was a direct 'crawl' to the perimeter fence mid-way between two guard towers. The location for entry would be just to the west of Block 137. The criteria included a severe thunderstorm at night, preferably after midnight and hopefully during one of the power outages that often occurred during a thunderstorm. We would dress in black and have blackened faces. We would need assistance with wire cutters, maps and any other items that the "X" committee might suggest.

Colonel Clark listened patiently. While he was generally receptive to our need for assistance, he had serious doubts about our chances for success and indicated that the senior Camp Commander would in all probability not approve the plan. I was once again the spokesman when we visited the Compound Commander, an experienced, highly respected senior officer. Colonel Goodrich was brief and very frank in his total disapproval of my plan. He pointed out that since the escape in the North Compound, the German Commandant, Colonel von Lindeiner, had informed the senior Allied officer in each compound that any prisoner who escaped could no longer be guaranteed return to a P.O.W. camp, and that escapees could be considered saboteurs or criminals and would be shot or sent to a concentration camp. He also reminded us that any prisoner found in the twenty-foot area (no man's land) between the short wooden guardrail and the perimeter fence, albeit confined within the prison compound, would probably be "shot on sight." He evaluated my straight 'crawl to the wire' plan as suicidal. He emphasized that resources to support escape activities were limited and should be reserved for those individuals who spoke fluent German and perhaps a second European language. Qualified escapees could then be supplied with forged documents and credentials that would give them a chance to make it back to a neutral country.

Although somewhat chastised and disheartened by the interview and the decision of the senior commander, I was determined to continue planning my escape. Lt/Col. Clark recommended we delay any escape attempt but encouraged us to continue studying maps of the local area, the airfield near the prison complex and the German language, concentrating on road signs and common terminology. Most important was a program to learn the German "start-engine" sequence for several types of German aircraft.

True to his word, Colonel Clark's "X" Committee provided an unbelievable amount of data regarding German aircraft. In the adjoining North compound were English pilots who had flown the Me-109, Hinkle-111 and several other German aircraft types. Glenn Oster and I continued to study this information, having given up on the original idea of trying to escape in a heavy rainstorm at night. We decided we would have a better chance for survival if we planned an escape during a heavy snowstorm.

The conversation with our senior camp commander had left us with additional doubts about my original 'crawl to the wire' plan. Escape plans were generally limited to 'over the wire,' 'through the wire' or 'under the wire.' Other more sophisticated plans such as impersonation or riding out in a vehicle wouldn't be supported by the "X" activity unless our knowledge of the German language had vastly improved.

Since March, when the British had tunneled out of the North compound, no escapes had been attempted from either the North or South compounds. Tunnel activity continued but there had been no change in the policy limiting the escape route to those who were fluent in German or a European language.

As previously mentioned, for those who lacked the credentials to qualify for tunnel escape, the alternatives for escape were generally limited to 'over, under or through' the perimeter fences. Our plan was still 'through the perimeter fence' and it was essential that we consider the security forces we may encounter. Ten-foot high, double-row barriers of barbed wire fencing enclosed the outer perimeter of all compounds. Spacing was eight feet between the two parallel fences. Rolls of barbed wire were placed in the area between the two fences. High guard towers with mounted light machine guns and searchlights were spaced at intervals around the entire perimeter of each prison compound. Tower guards were equipped with high-powered rifles as well as binoculars. Armed guards patrolled the area outside the compounds, further reinforcing the security of the outer perimeter. Armed guards, one or two with trained German Shepherds, patrolled all areas within the compound grounds. These special patrols were brought into the compound after lock-up at night and they remained there until morning. Every night at 9 PM, crossbars were placed on the outside entrance doors at both ends of all prison Blocks. Prisoners were forbidden to be outside their Blocks after closure, and at least one bed check was conducted nightly.

Letters from Home

The summer of '44 passed slowly. Except for the addition of new prisoners, there were few changes in the prison living conditions. The arrival of new prisoners provided confirmation of war news. It appeared the German air capability was considerably less since our fighter escort range had improved.

I was receiving news from home, but the letters I received had been written between two and three months earlier. I received many letters from a beautiful little student nurse that I had met during B-17 phase training in Boise, Idaho. Her name was Mary Lee Valentine and she had captured my heart at first sight. After leaving phase training in Boise, I had written her a letter from Pendleton, Oregon asking her to marry me. Strangely, in her next letter she never mentioned or acknowledged receiving a proposal that I had considered one of the most momentous decisions in my life. She was only eighteen and happily engrossed in life and her training. Her lack of response was probably best for both of us. So many men had received "Dear John" letters that I didn't dare hope that she would still be single when or if I ever returned home.

Like most prisoners, I read and reread every letter I received. Joe Johnson's wife had given birth to twin boys and Glenn Foster's wife, a baby girl. My mother had attempted to make contact with the families of the other crew members, and through her help, I received a letter from S/Sgt Groth's sister. Charles Groth was imprisoned in another camp for aircrew members but was doing well. She reported he was also with Louis Brown. Glenn Foster's wife was able to tell my mother that Glenn was interned in a neutral country. The people at home confirmed Sgt Claud Smith's death. Finally, after almost a year, all my crew members had been accounted for.

Kriegsgefangenenlager   Datum: Oct 17th 1944

Dear Folks – Mail is still good. In fact I have three Sept. letters. They are coming through in a month. A lot of parcels are in, but haven't been distributed. Johnson and I should have at least two, because we haven't rec'd our March parcels yet. Everything here is the same. I haven't been sick since I've been here. Write the War Dept. and tell me definitely when my 1st was dated. Love, Bob

Kriegsgefangenenlager   Datum: Oct. 20th 1944

Dear Mother, Dad & Bill, – Mail is still fairly good – more letters from Lee. All the personal parcels haven't been distributed yet. I'll write again in a few days if I receive a parcel and let you know. In the parcels please send only food with socks, underwear, and dental equipment. I can obtain other clothing here. Let me know who plays on Trinidad's football team this year. Love, Bob

One day I was surprised to receive a food parcel from a family in England (the Harveys from Tannington.) As I previously mentioned, on October 10th, 1943, I had crash-landed a B-17 in a farmer's beet field in East Anglia. We were out of fuel and I had made the landing on a fog-shrouded afternoon. Two local families had provided food and housing for my crew until transportation had arrived from our base unit, the 91st Bomb Group. Somehow, this family had received word that my crew hadn't returned from the combat mission flown four days later to Schweinfurt, Germany and that I was a prisoner in Stalag Luft III. Receipt of this unexpected package created a remarkable and emotional day for me.

The summer months had passed and fall weather was about to give way to winter. The war news was encouraging and the driving urge to escape was lessoned. I just couldn't make myself believe that we would be forced to spend another Christmas as prisoners.

Kriegsgefangenenlager   Datum: Oct. 29, TK, 1944

Dear Folks, New parcel list just went up and at last my name is on it. It will make number 3. I hope it is the March parcel. I expect to receive a couple more in the next two weeks. The July cig. parcel arrived yesterday. Everything is the same here. I'll write a letter in a few days when the new letter forms are given out. Love, Bob

A New Plan

Late in November, a major change in compound security took place. All of the guards had been removed from the guard towers located between the new West compound and the South and North compounds. This reduction was probably made to conserve manpower. To me, it represented a new route to freedom. Removal of the guards meant that undetected access to the corridor road between prison compounds was now possible. After access to the corridor road was accomplished, the escape route in the corridor road would not present a direct visual line to the corner tower guards because their primary area of interest and responsibility would or should be within their respective compounds. The corridor road between the compounds was German territory. The north end of the road terminated at the German "Lager" and living quarters. The south end terminated at a gate between two guard towers. This unmanned gate was used as access for delivering utility items. The waste disposal wagon (Honey Wagon) used this gate for access to the corridor road before entering the gate at the entrance to the South Compound. The long covered coal shed in the south end of the corridor road was empty, as the supply of coal had been depleted.

Concurrent with removal of the guards from these towers, I prepared a new route of escape and then briefed Lt/Col Clark and selected members of his committee on the changes. The committee endorsed the new plan. I was told that Colonel Goodrich had been advised of the committee recommendation for approval and had offered no objection to the plan. Col. Goodrich still advised delay of any escape attempt in view of the favorable war news.

Motivated by the news that the escape plan had been approved, Glenn Oster and I spent hours re-studying the maps of the local area. We began to collect the additional clothing we would need for the cold weather. White hoods were needed as well as white cloth covers for our feet and hands. I gave Joe Johnson a $50 IOU for his leather A-2 jacket. Other roommates provided oversized long johns to be worn over our clothing.

Two new prisoners to Room 4 were particularly helpful, providing me with gloves and long johns. Horace Mockett, a B-17 pilot, had been shot down in August 1944 but had been hospitalized with a flak wound in his knee. He didn't arrive in Stalag Luft III until October 29th, two months later. Andrew Poggi, a B-24 bombardier flying out of a base in Italy, went down on his last scheduled combat mission. He had been assigned to Room 4 since mid June 1944. By the end of November 1944, there were fourteen prisoners in Room 4.

In mid December, the "Battle of the Bulge" brought depressing news. The German media was loudly proclaiming a "great victory" for their forces. For most of us, it just meant further delay before our eventual release.

It was during this period, just a few days before Christmas, that I noticed a change in the appearance of the gate area at the south entrance to the corridor road located between the two guard towers. Probably as a matter of convenience to permit easier access, the inner gates had been left open and the barbed wire barricades normally placed between the two gates had been removed and repositioned beside the open inner gates. Now, only one single-strand fence prevented access from the corridor road to the outer perimeter road. A wooded forest area was located just across the outer perimeter road.

I contacted Oster and told him that I was going to seek final approval for an escape based on the weather conditions. I received assurance from Lt/Col. Clark that the escape had been fully approved and that cutting materials would be provided just prior to our departure from a designated barracks near the corridor road fence. The route from this barracks would provide us maximum distance from the guard tower searchlights during the first critical phase of the escape plan. All that was needed was a good snowstorm.

Christmas Eve was quieter than normal. Unlike the Christmas of 1943, there was little celebrating. We had all hoped for a promised "double issue" of Christmas parcels, but there had been a delay. I went by "Moose" Moss's room and gave him the $50 IOU. I had lost the bet we made last Christmas. My good friend, Chester Lott, gave me his most prized possession — a small, penny-sized "escape" compass. I couldn't have received a better gift.

It snowed Christmas Day and for a while I was sure it was going to be "the day." By late afternoon it had stopped snowing, so there was nothing to do but be patient. I wrote a letter to my parents, sealed it and gave it to Chester Lott. He assured me that he would deliver it in person if I were unable to make it home. I just wanted them to know that I loved them and I was aware of the risks, but that I was doing something I just had to do.

The Escape

It was late in the afternoon on January 17, 1945. I was walking the perimeter when the snow first began to fall. A light dusting of snow from a previous snowfall already covered the ground. I felt a surge of excitement and fear. My adrenalin level surged to a new high. The escape night had finally arrived!

The plan was simple: Cross the clearing from the barracks to the wooden warning rail. Crawl under the guardrail and continue on to the double roll of fence at a location next to the shadow of one of the abandoned guard towers. Cut through the wire on the first fence. Crawl into the area between the two fences and cut through the center barrier of barbed wire. Cut the outside fence. Crawl through the outer fence. Splice the fence together so the openings were not obvious. Cross the corridor road to a shallow ditch on the opposite of the road. Crawl south along the corridor road for about one hundred and fifty feet and carefully pass the guard at the main entrance to the South compound. With the heavy snowfall and cold weather, the guard (if past practice was followed) will frequently take shelter in the one-man guardhouse. In so doing, he will face the South compound, away from the corridor road. Once past the main gate guard, slow down and continue crawling toward the gate at the end of the corridor that was located between the two compounds and their respective guard towers. Use the shadow of the empty coal shed whenever possible. Stop all movement whenever the click of the searchlight is heard. Start again when the light is switched off. Pray that both guards in the towers are concentrating on their respective compounds. Check for the location of the outside perimeter guard to ensure he has passed by the gate area before departing from the shadow area of the coal shed. Crawl the last critical thirty feet to the gate fence centered between the two towers. Use the out-of-place "barbed-roll" barricades for partial coverage. While making the last two or three cuts in the remaining single fence (gate), pack snow around the wire cutters before each cut to soften the sound. Go through the outer fence, crawl across the perimeter road and take cover in the road ditch. Check for the perimeter guard. If clear, crawl about one hundred and fifty feet to the forest and then disappear into the woods.

By 8:00 PM, we were dressed—layers of white underwear over heavy clothing; white hoods over stocking caps; white socks covering shoes and white mittens, plus two spares made from white socks. Food was limited to two "D" bars of chocolate. We had one general area map. We were briefed that small diversion activities would be initiated by members of the "X" committee to hold the attention of guards in the end towers adjacent to our escape route.

Several senior officers were in our scheduled departure barracks to assist where possible. Lt/Col. Clark was there, providing last minute advice and checking our clothing. Lt/Col Melvin McNickle provided the side cutters and the area map. I had a warm feeling towards these men, as they were the ones who had surfaced as leaders in an environment that had placed heavy demands on those who served their fellow prisoners.

At about 8:15 PM., we departed through the north door of the barracks equipped with three side-cutters—a large pair and a smaller set with attached long hickory handles and an emergency hand-made cutter made from a pair of ice skates. It was snowing quite heavily. Glenn Oster, who had wrists as thick as the average man's ankle, would do the cutting. I would pack snow over the cutters to subdue the sound. Guards would be at each barracks at 9:00 PM. so it was imperative that we get through the first double row fence and, if possible, past the stationary guard at the main gate before nine o'clock. We crawled on our bellies toward the warning fence, freezing our positions each time a tower searchlight came on.

Oster was leading the first time the tower light came on. This was the initial test. Would the lights be as bright as we had been led to believe, making it difficult for the guards to identify objects during a heavy snowfall? The first light remained on us for what seemed like a long time. I could almost feel the impact of a bullet. Then the light shifted and was finally turned off. We had passed the first test!

Oster was at the perimeter fence and made the first cut as I was crawling through the area between the guardrail and the fence. The cut sounded exactly like a rifle shot. Oster had made the first mistake—cutting without waiting to pack snow over the cutter head. We both froze in position for a minute or so. Oster waited until I reached the fence. We agreed that there would be no further cuts without using the packed snow technique.

The large side cutters would not work after the first cut. They were dull and required too much additional leverage to be effective. The small lineman's pliers with the hickory handle attachments turned out to be the best tool. Three cuts and Oster was inside between the two fences. I worked from outside the first fence, reaching in to pack snow over each wire cut. After entering the area between the two fences, my job was to twist the severed wires back together to cover any obvious hole in the fence material. We kept a close watch on the guard at the main gate to the South compound since he was fairly close to the area where we were making the wire cuts.

Oster made it through the second fence and on to the corridor road and was crawling into the ditch alongside the road when the guard at the gate suddenly started down the fence line in our direction. I had just started to exit from the outside fence. The guard would have stepped on me if I had remained in that position. I scrambled back between the two fences, pulled the severed wires together and froze in a face down position. The guard passed my location, continued on to the corner of the South Camp compound and then reversed direction, walking back up the fence line to his main gate position. Twice, the guard had walked by me within three feet, and he'd failed to see Glenn who was lying in the shallow ditch opposite my location. Our plan had passed a second critical but totally unanticipated test.

After the guard returned to his station at the main gate, I crawled back through the outer fence, spliced the wires together and joined Oster in the shallow ditch on the opposite side of the corridor road. We were out of our compound and so far on schedule!

The next critical step was to crawl up the road toward the gate. When the guard sought shelter in the one-man gatehouse, we would pass his location on the opposite side of the road. By the time we reached the position where we would wait for clearance of a path that would take us past the guard at the main gate, the snowfall had decreased. For some reason, the guard wouldn't take shelter in his guardhouse. It was freezing cold, but this guard, unlike most, simply wasn't ready to use the shelter. We hoped he might take another trip down the fence line, but he maintained his position at the gate. To attempt to crawl past him while he remained stationed outside at the gate would be too risky since we would pass within ten feet of his location and the lights at the gate would make us fully visible if he should glance our way.

We waited and waited, shivering in the snow, shifting positions. Ice was beginning to form on us, making the outer white underwear stiff and creaky. A ring of ice formed on the face of our hoods from our rapid breathing. Glenn, who was a body length ahead of me, finally pushed back beside me. We discussed losing time and the increased chance of being caught in a guard change. When we had finally decided to move up closer to the guard position, I heard a sound behind us on the roadway. Looking back, I saw a group of guards coming up the road. We had delayed too long! Oster had moved ahead of me, not having heard any thing. I grabbed his ankle, jerked on it and pointed behind me. We both scrunched down as low as space permitted. Glenn Oster's body looked as big as a whale. My heart was pounding so hard I was sure it could be heard. We lay as still as possible, hardly daring to breathe.

The first three guards passed by quietly. The next three were talking and laughing. One lone guard was trailing behind the other six. He came by more slowly, but did not glance our way. I thought we were in the clear but when I looked back, I saw a German shepherd coming up the roadway, lagging about thirty feet behind its master. He passed our positions. Then he suddenly stopped, turned to look in our direction and then came back toward us. In a playful gesture, it spread its front feet in front of me and barked twice. By this time, the guard was already at the gate talking to the gate guard and preparing to enter the compound. He whistled and the dog turned back, ran to the gate and entered the compound with his master. We couldn't believe our luck! I crawled up next to Glenn. As cold and scared as we were, we elbow-punched each other with joy.

Our good fortune was soon dampened by the reluctance of the gate guard to enter his shelter. He was continually turning to look back into the West camp compound and taking short trips along the perimeter road, stopping just short of our position in the corridor. It had stopped snowing and the searchlights seemed brighter than before. We continued to wait for about another hour. We had begun to fear that we would be caught in another guard change. Oster kept insisting that we needed to continue past the guard and take our chances that the guard wouldn't hear us or glance in our direction. I felt it was too risky, that we had to wait.

Finally, after more time had passed, we both agreed that the guard was never going to enter the shelter. We would just have to attempt to crawl past him – within ten feet in a lighted area. We had moved to perhaps fifteen feet of the gate-guard's position when the guard suddenly turned and entered the shelter. The shelter faced the entrance gate to the South compound so the guard had no visibility in our direction. It took us no more than three minutes to crawl past the main gate guard area and enter the shadows cast by the poles supporting the roof of the long, empty coal shed. It had taken us over two hours to cross an area that we had planned to cover in less than thirty minutes, but we had finally overcome the third major obstacle placed in our path.

The remainder of the route meant crawling even closer to the guard towers and the searchlights, so we had to be extremely cautious. This meant crawling when the searchlights were off and remaining completely immobile when the lights clicked on. We were now close enough to the towers to see the bundled-up figures of the tower guards and hear the clicks of the switches as the searchlights were turned off and on. We found ourselves laying still for as long as three or four minutes when a search light from one of the towers was on; however, as we had hoped, the primary beam of the lights was generally focused on areas within the two compounds. Unfortunately, the heavy snowfall we had hoped for had ceased altogether.

Finally, after what seemed an eternity, we arrived at the south end of the coal shed. We were less than thirty feet from the two guard towers and had twenty feet to go to reach the shadows produced by the barricades that had been removed from the area between the gates. The inner gates were still wide open. We had estimated that if we had only the outer gate to cut through, only two cuts would be required.

Another wait—this time for the outside perimeter guard to make his rounds. After this guard had passed the towers, we would have about ten minutes before he would pass by again. The perimeter guard finally passed by the two towers, calling up greetings to the two tower guards.

With Glenn Oster one body length ahead of me, we began the last stretch to the gate. If a tower guard were to look straight down next to his tower, we would be in his line of sight. Even the slightest movement could be detected. Since it was bitter cold, nearly all the guards had their overcoat collars turned up. Some were wearing earmuffs. Hopefully, these two guards would be in the latter category.

We were more than halfway between the coal shed and the fence. About eight feet ahead of us we would have shadow coverage beside the rolled up barricades. I suddenly became aware of a dog growling. I stopped, looked back and saw a blur of animal leaping at my face. I put up my left arm and the dog grabbed it. The guard with the dog let out a scream of terror and shouted as he tried to get his gloves off so he could use his rifle. I managed to get to my feet with the dog hanging on my arm. I shook the dog off and raised my hands, asking the guards loudly in German not to shoot. The dog continued to lunge at me, shredding my frozen outer clothing. Glenn Oster was on his feet now. The guards in the towers had their searchlights on us, their machine guns uncovered and ready to fire. The fence—so close—was still a barrier to freedom. There was nowhere to escape!

What turn of fate had caused the guard to exit the South compound and enter the corridor? He had certainly not expected to find us. His rifle was still strapped in place on his shoulder and his scream was one of surprised fright.

It was well after midnight when we were captured. We were stiff with cold; a sheet of ice covered our chests and legs. With just five more minutes, maybe even less, we would have been through the last barrier, across the perimeter road and into the forest. Then again, in that same period perhaps a tower guard might have sighted us and opened fire.

Even though our escape attempt did not have the desired outcome, I was thankful. During all the planning, I had not dared to ask God to spare my life. I had asked him only to give me the courage to do what I had to do when the time came, regardless of the fear I might have. That prayer had been answered.

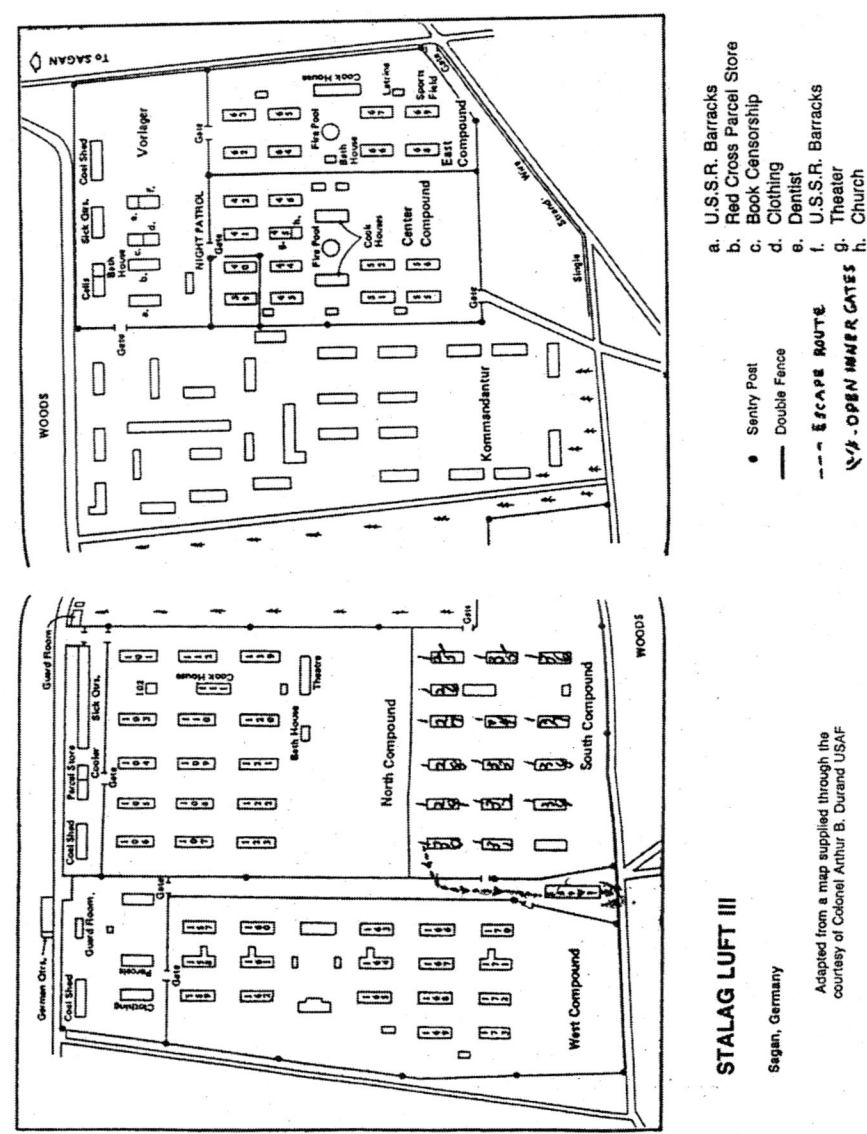

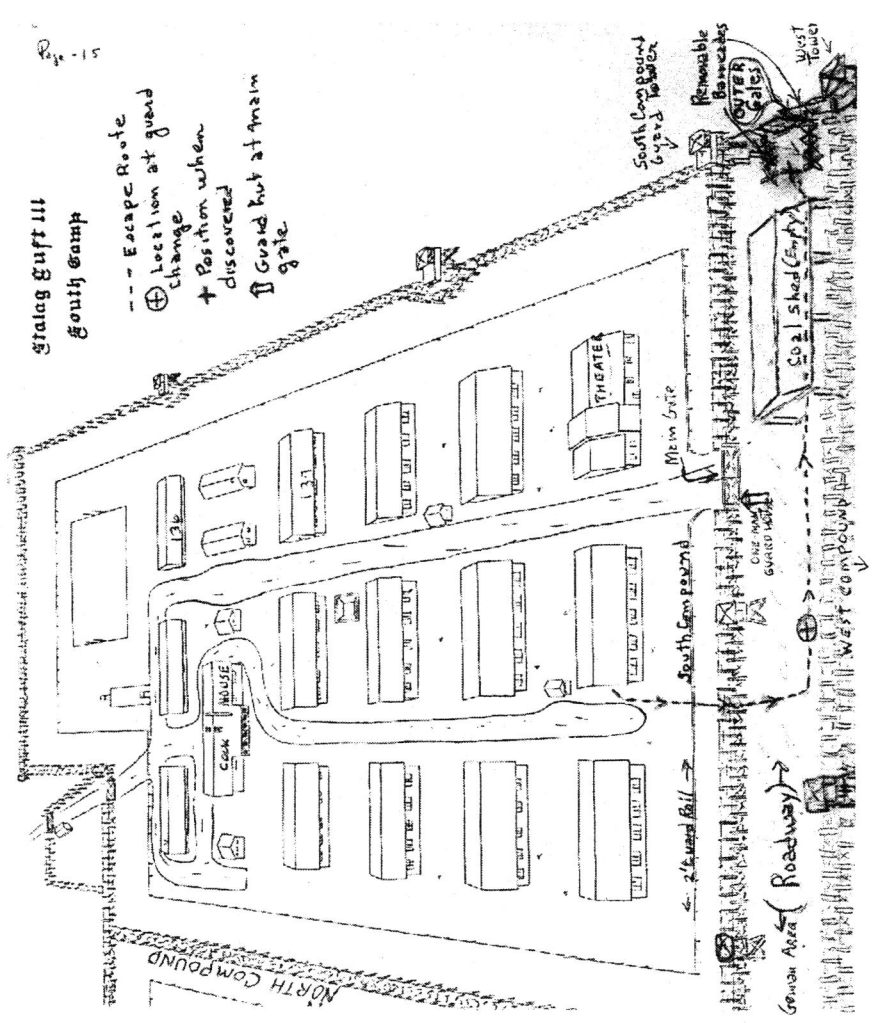

PART III

THE WAR MARCHES ON

Interrogation

Glenn and I stood with arms raised in the glare of the tower searchlights for several minutes before additional guard reinforcements arrived. Then we began the long walk back down the corridor road to the German "Vorlager" where the prison cells were located. The German Shepard dog made frequent leaps at our shredded long johns, but fortunately we had on so much layered clothing, the dog's teeth didn't penetrate to the skin.

Upon our arrival at the prison location, we were taken into an office and told to undress. We were stiff and shaking from the cold so it was difficult to remove the frozen clothing. One guard, a short stocky man, was irritated by my slow progress in removing the outer clothing and demonstrated his displeasure by frequently shoving me. His defiant look dared me to strike back. The only way I could show resistance was to stiffen my body each time he shoved me, which seemed to further irritate him. I glanced at Glenn while this passive resistance was taking place. He had a sly smile on his face. The guard never touched Glenn, who was much heavier and had a stocky, muscular build. Finally, another guard intervened and I was permitted to continue removing my clothing.

After we had removed all our clothing, we had a long wait while the guards searched every item. We were handed blankets for cover. As we huddled in one corner of the room, I watched as my outer trousers were searched. I was relieved when my escape compass, that I had placed in the watch pocket, was not discovered. The Germans don't have watch pockets near the waistbands of their trousers, so they wouldn't have thought to search there.

When the search was complete, we were permitted to dress under the watchful eyes of the two guards. We were not allowed to layer the clothing and were limited to one item of each type. I didn't have a chance to transfer the compass to my new O.D.

trousers, so I chose the old threadbare outer trousers that had been issued upon arrival at Stalag Luft III. Our stocking caps and gloves were also confiscated. I was able to retain the A-2 jacket.

After we dressed, we were taken into an adjacent corridor where the prison cells for solitary confinement were located. The south sidewall of this corridor contained windows. The prison cells were on the north side of the corridor facing the wall with the windows. There wasn't enough light to determine the length of the corridor.

I was the first to be placed in a cell. As my cell door closed, it sounded like the guards opened the adjacent cell and that Glenn was being placed in the cell next to mine. I waited for several minutes after the activity in the corridor had ceased before knocking on the wall separating the cells. I heard a dull knock in response. It was reassuring to know that Glenn and I were close enough that there might be some way for us to communicate.

The cell was small. There was a small cutout in the solid door providing a "peephole" for the guards that could be closed or opened at their discretion. The cell contained a cot with a wood-straw mattress, two blankets and a urinal can.

For a time I feared that my fingertips and toes might be frozen. I spent the first hour or so moving my fingers and toes to improve the circulation. I remained fully clothed except for shoes. I kept my feet wrapped in the blankets. As the circulation improved, I became increasingly weary. Finally, completely exhausted, I fell asleep.

I was awakened by the sound of someone opening my cell door. It was still dark outside and I had no idea how long I had been asleep. The small dim light located in the ceiling had been turned on. Major Gustav Simoleit, the acting Commandant for Stalag Luft III, entered the prison cell. Sitting on the edge of the cot, the German officer began questioning me about the escape attempt. His primary interest was in finding out if others had used or intended to use our escape route. I told him that I had no knowledge of any other prisoner who was attempting to escape. He indicated that his greatest concern was that there might be other prisoners involved and that if they were captured outside the confines of the prison camp their lives could be in great danger. Finally, he requested that I give my word as a military officer that I was providing him with truthful information. I told Major Simoleit that he had "my word of honor as an American Officer." He thanked me, reached out to shake my hand and departed the cell.

I had the feeling that Major Simoleit's major concern was the impact another escape might have on Luftwaffe staff personnel who were assigned responsibility for the security of the prison camp. There was talk among the prisoners that the previous commander, Col von Lindeiner, had been relieved of his command after the large-scale escape of British prisoners from the adjacent North compound in March last year.

What I didn't tell Major Simoleit was that prior to our escape attempt, Lt/Col Clark, our security chief had discussed with me the possibility of a second two-man team following the same route Glenn and I planned to use during our escape. I had rejected his proposal. I felt that the plan – *my* plan — was the best way to escape through the perimeter fence and that there were enough risks involved without exposing another escape team. Furthermore, if we had been successful in our escape from the prison camp, I certainly didn't want to have the alarm sounded with the discovery of the second escape team. After I voiced this objection, Colonel Clark had not pursued the matter any further; he indicated that the decision was entirely ours and the matter was put aside.

A Solitary Life

Late in the first morning of confinement, I began to feel the physical effects of our long crawl in the snow. I couldn't raise my arms without experiencing severe muscular pain in my shoulders, stomach and upper torso. It would be several days before I could return to a normal program of push-ups and fitness exercises within the confines of my small cell. Glenn and I found that there was a small opening where the partition joined the forward wall of our cells. Our first action after the guard brought food and departed our area was to use the spoon handles to enlarge this opening. We soon had an opening of sufficient size to permit us to converse by cupping our mouths next to it.

Solitary confinement also meant that we would no longer have the benefit of food from the Red Cross parcels. "Ersatz" coffee with a single slice of bread was provided in the mornings. At mid-day, we were provided with either barley soup or something that resembled pea or bean soup. The evening meal was generally a small amount of some type of soup made with rutabagas or kohlrabies and another slice of bread with a spread of some sort. On occasion, we were served a small dish of what appeared to be little baby cabbages. I had never before tasted these delicious miniature vegetables. Glenn informed me the vegetables were "brussels sprouts" and was amazed that I had never before eaten this food and couldn't identify the vegetable.

Once a day we were released from our cells and permitted to empty our waste materials in washrooms in the same building as our cells. We were also given an opportunity to wash up and use the toilet facilities. An English-speaking guard informed us that we could send a note back to the camp to request reading material and items like tooth brushes, shaving equipment etc., and he would attempt to have the items delivered. We would also be permitted to receive mail while we were serving our prison sentences. I attempted to find out how long we were to be held in confinement, but I could never get an answer.

On the fourth day of confinement, we received the items we requested. I also received a note from Chester Lott saying that the Christmas promise of a double issue of Red Cross parcels had been fulfilled and that my roommates were holding my two parcels. We would have a big celebration "bash" when I was released back to the South compound. I also received a letter from my mother that had been written on Thanksgiving Day. She was cheerful as usual and told me about the twenty-pound turkey with bread dressing that she was cooking for their Thanksgiving dinner. In her innocence, she never realized that our food allowance was at a critical state. In my letters and cards, I had never mentioned that we were beginning to suffer from the effects of malnutrition. Any such complaints that escaped the censors would just add to the worry of loved ones who had no control over events taking place in our prison. We had hope that intelligence information concerning prisoner treatment was being passed by covert means to outside agencies and that our government was aware of conditions within the military prison camps.

During the seventh day of confinement, I was permitted to leave the cell and use an outdoor exercise area for about forty-five minutes. I was surprised to find another prisoner already in an adjacent fenced exercise area. We were closely watched, so I had little opportunity to gain information from him. By jogging along the fence line adjacent to his path, I did learn that his name was Shaw and that he was a Captain. He was from the Center compound and had been imprisoned for what I assumed was an escape attempt. He was in the exercise area for only a few minutes and I was unable to gather any additional information. Glenn and I were never in the exercise area at the same time

I spent part of each day trying to read but had a difficult time since the lighting was so poor. Once my sore muscles felt normal again, I was able to do push-ups and other exercises to try and stay fit. I would jog in place several times daily for periods of about thirty minutes.

One evening while finishing a bowl of barley soup, I happened to glance at the bottom of the bowl and noticed for the first time what appeared to be little worms. Upon closer inspection, I determined that these objects were weevils and that the barley was infested with them. Fortunately, none were moving. I immediately went to the adjacent wall and knocked to get Glenn's attention. I told him that if he hadn't eaten all of his soup to save some in the bottom of the bowl and then check it. A short time passed and he called back. He said he had saved some soup and asked, "What is the problem?" The light was so poor he evidently couldn't see the weevils. I told him to wait until the guard returned to pick up the bowls and then take another look. The light from the corridor flooded our rooms when the solid cell doors were opened.

In a few minutes, the guard appeared to pick up our spoons and the bowls. As his cell door opened, I heard Glenn curse. When the guard opened my cell door, I pointed to the weevils. The guard, ignoring my complaint, took the bowl and closed the cell door. When the guard left the area, I heard Oster growling, "Damn you, Slane." That was our "highlight" of the day.

Written while in solitary (after escape) at Stalag Luft III

Dear Folks — With nothing to write about I expect this letter will take several hours. I'm always able to fill a few lines complaining about the want of information to give you. Still no mail this month. I should have a mess of it somewhere.

This should reach you sometime before Bill graduates from high school. It's about as hard for me to realize that Bill is nearly eighteen and of draft age as it was to hear that Marian Logan was married. I wouldn't be too surprised if Ethel wasn't married by now.

I would like to leave a standing order with you for one half dozen Chocolate Eclairs the day I arrive home. I've been reading a short play "Cyrano de Bergerac" and it called to my mind that of all the pastry I've missed the Eclair Ras top honors in my imagination. The food we have here is o.k. but I'm afraid there isn't much variety.

I'm anxious to hear more news of Kuhlman and whether you are in touch with the rest of the families. I was in to see Runner a few days ago. He has some pictures taken of one of his band shows. Perhaps you will see it in a Red Cross magazine. I'm in perfect health don't worry about a thing. Lots of Love, Bob

PART III THE WAR MARCHES ON

This is one of only four letters that I received and was able to salvage while a POW. I was able to save only those letters received by me while I was in solitary at Stalag Luft III in January 1945. All of my other possessions were left behind when Stalag Luft III was evacuated.

> WRITE VERY CLEARLY WITHIN THE LINES. IN ORDER TO EXPEDITE CENSORSHIP, LETTERS SHOULD BE TYPED OR PRINTED IN BLOCK CAPITALS.
>
> Nov 11, 44
>
> Dearest Bob: I MAILED YOU A REGULAR AIR MAIL YEST-ERDAY WITH SOME SNAPS OF BETTY TAKEN AT THOREAU. HAVE YOU EVER RECEIVED THE ONES THAT WERE TAKEN HERE AT HOME IN APRIL? YOUR LAST LETTER WAS THE LEAST DEPRESSING OF ANY THAT WE HAVE RECEIVED YET. SO DARNED MUCH CAN HAPPEN IN THREE MONTHS, AND A CHEER-Y LETTER HELPS US SO MUCH. I'M LOOKING FOR MORE MAIL FROM FOSTERS AND ALSO MRS. RUNNER. I'LL TELL YOU AGAIN THAT YOU PERSONAL EFFECTS ARRIVED HERE MONDAY. THEY ARE IN GOOD SHAPE AND YOU HAVE SOME LOVELY CLOTHES. I'LL HAVE THEM ALL CLEANED AND READY FOR YOU. I'M SO THANKFUL THAT LAY BROUGHT YOUR GUN HOME. SHOULD HAVE _____ A LIST OF ALL YOUR CREW MEMBERS IN A FEW DAYS NOW. WELL THIS IS THE DAY FOR THE BIG FOOT-BALL GAME BETWEEN TRIN? & CENTENNIAL. KICK OFF AT TWO. WE ARE GOING AND GUESS THAT WILL BE THE LAST FOR SOME TIME. CHARLES LATUDA WAS HOME FOR FEW DAYS AND HE AND BILL HAVE HAD SOME REAL CHESS GAMES. DAD MIXES HIS CHESS WITH CHECKERS AND DOESNT HAVE MUCH LUCK. TICKELS BILL BECAUSE HE BEATS HIM SO BADLY. I'LL BET YOU WILL BE ABLE TO CLEAN BILL GOOD WHEN YOU GET HOME. HOPE YOU ARE A GOOD BRIDGE PLAYER TOO, FOR I'D ENJOY A GOOD GAME MYSELF. WE HAVE PLAYED ONCE WITH MAMIE AND RAY SIN-CE YOU HAVE BEEN GONE. THE WEATHER IS STILL LOVELY. NO SNOW YET AND ITS ALMOST THE MIDDLE OF NOV. ITS EIGHT 15, AND DAD WILL BE HOME FOR BREAKFAST IN A FEW MINUTES. THERE JUST ISNT ANY NEWS. BILL STILL SLEEPING. SUPPOSE HE WILL BE GOING HUNTING TOMORRO-W. PROBABLY GO TODAY BUT DOESNT WANT TO MISS THE GAME. TRINIDAD HAD A GOOD CHANCE THIS YEAR BUT

TOP PANEL

BUT SOON FIZZELED OUT. CHAS AND AG ARE SUPPOSED TO GET UP HERE ON THEIR VACATION THIS MONTH BUT DONT KNOW IF CHAS WILL BE ABLE TO GET OFF. THINGS ARE THE SAME AT THE OFFICE. NO DAY OFF YET AND THE DUMMY IS STILL HANGING AROUND DOING THE CLERKS WORK. IS'NT THAT AWFUL? THREE MONTHS NOW AND HE STILL CANT DISP. TRAINS. WE ARE SURE ANXIOUS AND INTERESTED IN YOUR PLANS WHEN YOU GET BACK. HOPE YOU ARE STILL FIGURING ON MORE SCHOOLING. PAPER RUNNING OUT. ALL OUR LOVE

MOTHER, DAD & BILL.

FROM (SENDER'S FULL NAME AND ADDRESS)

MR. & MRS. R. M. SLANE
424 COLORADO AVE
TRINIDAD, COLORADO

PRISONER OF WAR POST
KRIEGSGEFANGENENPOST
SERVICE DES PRISONNIERS DE GUERRE

BY AIR MAIL
PAR AVION

RANK AND NAME: FIRST LT. ROBERT M. SLANE
(CAPITAL LETTERS)   UNITED STATES PRISONER OF WAR.
PRISONER OF WAR No. 3201
(SEE NOTE ON FLAP)
CAMP NAME AND No. STALAG LUFT 3
SUBSIDIARY CAMP No.
12196 COUNTRY GGERMANY
U.S. CENSOR   VIA NEW YORK, N. Y.

The March Begins...

On January 27, 1945, the tenth day of confinement, we still had no information regarding the length of our sentence. Although I could sometimes evoke a response from certain guards in answer to my questions, the one question most important to us remained unanswered. It was late afternoon on this date when we became aware of unusual activity taking place in the prison area. The guards were moving back and forth in the corridor, and there were sounds of activity outside the prison walls.

It was dark outside when one of the guards brought our evening meal. When he opened the cell door, I was startled at what I saw through the window across the corridor. A column of what appeared to be prisoners was streaming down the road adjacent to the North compound. The cell door closed before I could question the guard.

As soon as the guard left our area, Glenn and I were in contact, discussing what we had seen. We knew before our escape attempt that there was a possibility that Russian forces could be nearing the area, but the idea of evacuating Stalag Luft III seemed too remote to even consider. One of the options in our escape plan had been to travel east if it had appeared impossible to gain access to a German aircraft in the Sagan area. The pressing question was: What would happen to us if, in fact, prisoners were being evacuated from the area?

Glenn suggested that I be the one to ask the questions since in his words, "that one guard acts like he kind of likes you since you are always talking to him." I had no hesitancy in questioning the guard when he returned to pick up our food dishes and spoons. I asked him if the camp was being evacuated and he nodded yes. I then asked him what was going to happen to us. He broke into a broad smile and said, "We are going to shoot you!" and closed the cell door. Glenn said nothing to the guard when he opened his cell door.

For a short period after the guard departed, all was quiet. I tapped on the prison wall partition and asked Glenn if he had overheard the conservation. He replied, "Yes." Then I said, "Now are you happy with my friend?" Glenn's response was unprintable.

For the next several hours, we nervously paced our cells wondering just what the Germans had in store for us. I suppose there was a possibility that we could be shot, but I felt certain the guard had spoken in jest in response to my question about our future.

The long wait was suddenly interrupted when a guard suddenly opened the cell doors and we were directed down the corridor hall. We were told to join the column of prisoners that was passing by the prison facility. I protested and requested that we be allowed to return to our barracks and obtain our overcoats and some of our personal possessions. I wanted to save pictures, letters and, most important, my Y.M.C.A. logbook containing notes and drawings of prison life. Without headgear, gloves and additional protective clothing, we would not be physically equipped to face the snow and freezing weather that we expected to encounter in a forced march.

Fortunately, the Unteroffizier (Sgt) accompanying us agreed, and Glenn and I started back up the corridor walking parallel to the column of departing prisoners traveling in the opposite direction. The tower searchlights were on, the glare of the lights on the snow reflecting the anxiety on the faces of the men departing for an unknown destination. We heard our names being shouted as we traveled back toward the vacated barracks, so we were certain that the prisoners passing by were from the South compound. I had a mixed feeling of excitement and disbelief. The long days of boredom were now a thing of the past and we were embarking on a new and unknown adventure. Was this the first step in our path to freedom, or were we going to be exposed to greater danger in a different environment? I chose to view the change as one that would increase my opportunity for escape.

We never made it back to our barracks. We were stopped by a German officer who shouted at us to halt. The sergeant tried to explain the reason we were headed back to the South compound but this officer wasn't interested. He directed the sergeant to either have us join the departing column of prisoners or return us to our prison cells. With that kind of choice, we had no option but to fall in line with our comrades.

After joining the departing prisoners, Glenn and I worked our way forward trying to locate the prisoners from our "Block" (136). I discovered Chester Lott backtracking in an attempt to find me. Lott had an extra stocking cap for me and Andrew Poggi gave me a pair of gloves. Lt/Col. Clark had spotted us as we were released from the "cooler," and he provided us with woolen scarves. Glenn joined his bombardier, Jack Nosser, and obtained a cap and a blanket for added protection against the cold.

During the first few hours of the march, I stayed in the general vicinity of the men who had been my roommates in the Stalag. Everyone from Room 4 had on the heavy woolen overcoats that were issued after arrival at Stalag Luft III. Had we been permitted to return to our barracks in the compound, it is doubtful that I would have found my overcoat. Chester told me that on the night of our escape, my overcoat was placed in my bunk under the blankets and that they (my roommates) had rigged the bed to look as though there was a body asleep in the bed. The ruse worked. The two guards conducting the bed check that night had flashed their lights at each bed, noticed nothing amiss and then departed the barracks. It was only later, about 3 AM, after we had been captured, that the guards came back to recheck the rooms. There had been a loud disturbance in the Block when our beds were re-checked, and Chester was certain that the guards had confiscated my overcoat.

We walked in two's and three's in a loose formation. Walking with us were German guards, some with dogs, scattered at intervals along the roadside. The guards rested from time to time in a horse-drawn wagon that traveled beside the long line of prisoners. Although the majority of the prisoners had overcoats and stocking caps, the apparel varied from blankets worn as ponchos to flight jackets with blanket material sewn into the lining to provide warmth and additional length. A few men retained their "50 mission" caps, which were generally worn over a scarf that provided additional protection for the neck, ears and shoulders.

Before leaving the compound, there had been an issue of additional Red Cross food parcels. Some men had been fortunate enough to accumulate several cartons of cigarettes. Chocolate "D" bars and cigarettes were the items most prized for trading purposes. Chester Lott indicated that they had very little advance notice to prepare for evacuation of the compound. After notification of the pending evacuation, everyone had scrambled to prepare for a forced march. Backpacks of every conceivable size and shape had been hastily put together. I noticed one prisoner carrying a Red Cross box under his arm. He had tied a rope to both ends of the food box and then extended the rope around his neck. Others had made packs by tying together the bottom of a buttoned shirt and then tying the sleeves together with a short cord. The sleeves were used as carrying handles, sometimes thrown over a shoulder or around the wearer's neck. Those men without packs often had articles stuffed inside their shirts or jackets. Blanket rolls of all shapes and sizes were common.

The difference in dress and appearance was most apparent among those prisoners who had been incarcerated the longest. Many of the American flyers who had been captured while flying with the Royal Air Force or the Royal Canadian Air Force had retained the uniforms from those Services. Col. Walter E. Arnold, who had been shot down in late August of 1944, couldn't walk and was being assisted by other senior officers. Initially they pulled him along in a makeshift sled. Lt/Col Clark was one of the officers caring for Col. Arnold. Some time later, I saw Col. Arnold aboard one of the horse-drawn wagons used by the guards to carry their supplies.

The pace of our march began to slow as darkness turned to daylight. The snow had continued for most of the night, but the real enemy had been an intermittent bitter cold wind. As the icy wind whipped around my legs, I questioned my decision to retain the threadbare trousers instead of the new trousers. We normally walked for about an hour with a ten-minute break at the end of each hour. During the short rest stops, I kept my feet moving to help maintain blood circulation.

As the morning wore on, the stops became more frequent and many prisoners began to discard items considered nonessential. I had nothing extra to carry when I had begun the evacuation so I was able to obtain bread and other food items that had been discarded. During the rest stops, it was a common sight to see men collapsing in the snow to rest their tired legs. When the march started up after a break, those of us still standing did our best to assist the fallen ones back to their feet. Some just didn't have the strength or will to move, and waved off any assistance. We could only hope that the German guards would help by permitting the weak and sick to climb aboard one of the crowded horse-drawn wagons. I was thankful that I had kept active and followed a program of endless circuits around the prison compound. There were prisoners living in our Block who to my knowledge had never made any effort to stay in good physical condition.

There were no toilet facilities. We had to find a spot by the side of the road that provided some cover and hope that the guards would understand. My first action when items were being discarded was to find a book that would be suitable for toilet use. I found a French dictionary and it remained one of my most valuable assets.

As we traveled through the small villages and farms adjacent to the roadside, prisoners began to barter with some of the villagers and farmers. The fortunate ones were those prisoners who possessed cigarettes and chocolate "D" bars. I had nothing to trade so I remained an envious onlooker.

I kept close to my friends, Chester Lott and Dale Perkins, during most of the afternoon, but I also managed to move forward through the column of prisoners to find Glenn Oster. I noticed that the guards were not as watchful as they had been at the beginning of the forced march. Most of the guards were older men with stress and fatigue reflected in their faces. I discussed with him the possibility of escape during the coming night. Glenn wasn't receptive to any discussion about an escape attempt while on the march. He said he wasn't physically able to even think of escape. I didn't question his decision and decided it would be best for me to wait. There was still the possibility that the Russians could liberate us. Being out of confinement and able to move freely within the column of prisoners gave me a sense of freedom.

We were walking in darkness again. We had been on a continuous march for almost twenty-four hours with only short hourly rest stops. There were frequent outbursts of cursing and cries of anguish. Everyone was being encouraged to assist one another. We heard that the Germans were seeking shelter for us in the next town.

We received information that certain prisoners had been designated by the Block commanders to provide assistance and encouragement to those prisoners who were having difficulty keeping pace with the body of prisoners. Lt. Warren "Rip" Collins was evidently the man designated to assist prisoners who had been assigned to Block 136. This man was everywhere in our area, offering assistance and encouraging others to provide help for their comrades. Collins was demonstrating amazing physical strength and his actions seemed to inspire others to exert greater effort to cope with their particular situation.

I had been walking shoulder to shoulder with Chester Lott when I suddenly became aware that he was no longer with me. I surged forward in the column thinking that he might have gone ahead of me but he was nowhere to be found. Perkins and I then began backtracking, fearful that he might have fallen by the wayside. We finally located Chester. He was still on his feet but trying to walk in the direction opposite to our path of travel, and he had his hands out, groping like a blind man. For some unknown reason, Chester Lott had lost his vision. With Dale's support, I was able to get Chester back on track and we continued the battle to stay in the staggering formation.

There were rumors that those prisoners who couldn't keep up would be shot but we saw no evidence of this happening. In fact, the Germans had picked up some of the men who had fallen and placed them on their over-loaded horse-drawn wagons. Dale Perkins and I sought the help of one of the guards in an effort to place Chester Lott on one of the wagons. The guard left us promising help, but he returned stating that there was just no room. Although unable to see, Chester was still on his feet and able to walk so Dale and I continued to guide him, praying that we would soon find a place to rest in the next village.

Stalag Luft III
The Forced March Begins, January 17th, 1945

Rest Stop - Forced March
Stalag Luft III January, 1945

Hiding Out in Muskau

It was several hours after midnight when we arrived at a factory containing a huge glowing furnace. Upon entering the furnace room, we were met by a welcome blast of hot air. Prisoners swarmed all over the area, seeking a place to sit or lie down and thaw out. A large spiral staircase wound around part of the furnace and terminated on an upper level. Despite the intense heat, the staircase was a coveted location for many of the prisoners. Looking around, we saw several men being administered to by their comrades. The sudden change in temperature had been too severe for some and they had fainted before becoming acclimated. Dale and I steered Chester to a level spot on the lower floor of the furnace room where we settled down to rest and sleep.

At daybreak, we left the area of the furnace and began investigating other areas within the huge factory. Lott had regained his vision — we had nothing other than extreme fatigue to account for his loss of eyesight. There was hot water available for cleanup and most of the rooms in the factory were well heated. We also discovered toilet facilities in several areas.

The German guards were in evidence at various locations in the building but they didn't pay much attention to our wandering throughout the various storage areas. They were stationed at or near the building entrances and exits. Factory workers were for the most part slave laborers from France. We were told that some of the workers had been doing forced labor for the past five years.

We stayed in the warmth of the factory all day. The Germans provided us with no food, evidently expecting us to subsist on food from the Red Cross parcels issued just prior to the evacuation from Stalag Luft III. I found myself dependent on the generosity of my former roommates who still banded together to share their food supplies. Tom DeCaro had managed to salvage one of his cooking stoves, and we gathered around the stove while he divided a can of Spam into equal shares, topping each piece of Spam with a thin slice of cheese. The meat and cheese were cooked together on a makeshift frying pan and we had our first "hot" meal in three days.

There had been rumors abound about the location of the Russian forces. One of the French workers said he expected they would be liberated within the week. I decided that I would attempt to hide in the factory when the forced march was resumed. Again, I could not interest any of my former roommates in joining me. I wandered through areas of the factory until I found a place I thought would be suitable for hiding. I approached one of the French workers who spoke good English and seemed to be in charge of the French workers. I told him about my plan to hide in the factory. He offered no objection, as he was certain the Russians would be in control of the factory within a few days.

On the second morning after arriving at the factory (which I found out was located in the city of Muskau) the South compound prisoners were ordered back on the road. I stayed hidden in the factory. Along with anticipation that the liberating force would appear at any moment, I had some misgivings.

The day after departure from the factory by prisoners from my compound, a new group of prisoners from the West compound at Stalag Luft III arrived. I don't know why I hadn't considered the possibility that other prisoners would be brought to the factory. Until the arrival of the West compound prisoners, I had been unaware that the South compound had been the first to evacuate.

At nightfall, I left my sanctuary and talked with several of the newly arrived prisoners. They had word that the Russians were not advancing as had been anticipated and it appeared that I was in for a longer period of hiding in the factory than I had anticipated. French factory workers aware of my situation had been bringing me bread, sausage and drinking water. I was somewhat fearful that one of them would report my presence to the Germans.

The West compound prisoners had departed and it was the

third day since my South compound roommates had departed. When the French worker I called "Pierre" arrived with food that evening, he appeared nervous and troubled. He told me that the Russian troops had been stopped by opposing German forces and that it could be weeks before the Russians would overrun the city of Muskau. Finally, after several minutes of discussion, Pierre informed me that several of the French workers were concerned that my presence in the hideout would be discovered by the Germans and that they would be punished for assisting me and for not reporting my activities to the proper authorities. Pierre tried to emphasize that I had his support, but after five years of "slave-labor," his workers were fearful of doing anything that would jeopardize their lives. They were all very hopeful and praying for liberation by the Russians. Pierre was "asking for my understanding" and he pointed out that there was a group of my comrades in the factory preparing to depart the factory at daybreak. The newly arrived prisoners were primarily those who were sick or had difficulty keeping up the pace of the forced march, including some of the older German guards.

  I had not been out of the general vicinity of my "hideout" since the West compound prisoners had departed and I had no knowledge that yet another group of "kriegies" were being sheltered in the factory. It appeared that I had two choices. One choice would be to attempt to leave the vicinity of the factory and try to travel east at night. The other was to give up any thought of escape for the present and join the group of sick and injured prisoners. It was obvious to me that I was not physically equipped to attempt to reach the Russian front. I had no food stockpiled and my A-2 jacket wouldn't provide sufficient warmth for the intense cold I would encounter. During the march, I had been able to tolerate the cold because we had kept moving and I could position myself behind people warmly dressed in their winter overcoats. Traveling alone, I would be unable to use the roadways and would probably spend most of my time seeking shelter and food. I decided to join the group of newly arrived prisoners and hope for another opportunity to escape during warmer weather.

The March Continues...

I waited until it was dark outside before I left my hiding place to join the new arrivals. The factory had areas where the lights were on day and night. I tried to be as casual and unassuming as possible as I made my way back through the maze of building materials stacked in various areas of the factory. No one seemed to notice as I settled down near a group of men who were administering to their sick friends. I saw one German guard near a doorway, but he showed no interest in me. I asked the man nearest me if the guards had a list of names of those prisoners present. He responded that there were no roll calls and there had been no attempt on the part of the guards to control prisoner activities or curb movement within that area of the factory.

I discovered that there were prisoners from the South compound among this group. I was surprised to find that Douglas Reid, who had shared the same room with Glenn Oster at Stalag Luft III, was in the group. He had injured one of his legs and was using a makeshift walking stick to assist in walking. He told me that he had fallen behind during the first night of the march and that he was finally placed on one of the wagons with other men who had fallen behind.

The following morning, I was part of the cadre of sick and wounded that was ordered back on the road. It was rumored that we were headed for a location where we would board trains for transport to a new prison camp. The progress of the march was understandably slow. Some men were sick with diarrhea, others had severe blisters on their feet and a few were sick with pneumonia-like symptoms aggravated by exposure and exhaustion. Sharing the roadway were a large number of refugees who were fleeing from the anticipated Russian occupation. The German guards were older men. I suspected they had been purposely assigned to this group of prisoners because they were also suffering from physical disabilities.

It was no longer snowing and the wind had died down as we continued the journey to our unknown destination. I stayed close to Douglas Reid, as he sometimes needed help getting to his feet after a rest stop. Despite his crippled condition, he had managed to continue to carry a form of bedroll stuffed with Red Cross food items. Reid gave me one of the small metal can openers that accompanied each Red Cross parcel and we shared some of his food during one of the rest stops.

The majority of prisoners in our company had been imprisoned in the West compound. They told us of an incident enroute to Muskau where a sudden loud noise had caused the prisoners to bolt for cover. Thinking the prisoners were attempting to escape, the guards had opened fire, wounding and perhaps killing some of the prisoners. Those prisoners wounded during this incident were not part of the 'sick and wounded' located in the factory.

At midday, during a rest stop, I became aware of a dull pain in the heel of my right foot. The pain became progressively worse until I could no longer put pressure on that area of my foot and was forced to walk with an exaggerated limp. I couldn't account for this sudden onset of pain, but I did recall that years ago while in Jr. High School, I had fallen from a rope while swinging over a small stream and my right foot had landed on a log in the water. I had limped around for several days with a pain similar to the one I was now enduring, but had finally recovered without ever seeing a doctor. All I could do was hope that time would once again heal my foot.

At nightfall, we arrived at the town of Spremberg and spent the night in a building the size of a gymnasium. We were served good hot soup. I found an empty Klim can and was able to get two servings of the soup. Sleep came shortly thereafter.

Boxcar Blues

The next morning we were on the road again after being offered bread and an "ersatz" coffee before leaving the city of Spremberg. The railroad yards were some distance from Spremberg. When we arrived, we joined up with another group of prisoners already in place. These men, with a few exceptions, were former West compound prisoners. We lined up along the railroad tracks and after some delay the Germans began loading prisoners in the '40 and 8' boxcars. I never knew whether the 40 and 8 was a designation of '40 men and 8 horses' or '40 men or 8 horses,' but it made little difference to the Germans who stuffed sixty-five of us into one boxcar. Those of us who boarded first could not believe the number of additional men the German guards were able to force into the boxcar after a fifty-man count was reached. We had been led to believe that fifty would be the maximum load in each boxcar. When one of the prisoners who spoke German asked why we were being overloaded, the response was that more unexpected prisoners had arrived. Before we could protest further, the boxcar door had rattled shut and we were locked in.

It was obvious that we needed to immediately establish some rules to help alleviate the panic that was beginning to surface as the boxcar door closed. Someone spoke up and said, "We don't need to panic; we need to get organized." The response was positive. We agreed that there were three or four men aboard who were too sick to stand. Those men were brought to the rear of the car where there was a small barred window on the upper level and the air was better. Friends or caretakers of these men were also moved to the area to provide assistance if needed.

The remaining prisoners aboard were still standing after this first adjustment. We knew that we could not all continue to stand in the car, so a decision was made to seat several rows of men.

The first man seated would rest his back on the wall of the boxcar and draw up his knees. The next person would rest his back on the drawn up knees of the first man. This same procedure would be followed until the row was filled. There were several rows seated in this manner until about half of the men were seated and the remainder left standing. A fluctuating time schedule was followed and those seated would rotate positions with the standing prisoners. It was the fairest system we could devise under the circumstances and no one seemed to complain.

We remained stationary in the boxcar for about an hour before the train finely got underway. I was one of those standing in the first shift and it wasn't long before I began to feel a severe pain in my injured heel. I finally moved to a position where I could lean my back against a wall of the boxcar and the pain lessoned. The real torture came several hours later. Because my worst fear was being thirsty, I had intentionally filled up with water before boarding. We had not been permitted to leave the boxcar, although the train had made several stops. We had Klim cans that could be used as urinals in an emergency, but we also had men suffering from dysentery. The smell from vomit and diarrhea was ever present.

When the train finally did stop and the boxcar door opened, there was near panic as we all rushed to get outside to relieve ourselves along the rail embankments. It was an incredible sight for us and for the civilian populous that might be watching. There was little time during these stops for us to complete the task and we had no way to properly wash before being rushed back to reboard the boxcar. The nightmare aboard the boxcar continued for two days before we arrived at our destination late the second night. We finally knew our destination. It was Nuremberg, Germany. The rumors that we were going to Munich had turned out to be false.

Prisoner At Nuremberg

The boxcar door was rolled back and we disembarked with some difficulty. It took some time to assist those who were sick and others who were having problems regaining mobility after the long hours sitting in a cramped position with legs folded. Once again, we formed up in a loose formation and waited for the order to move forward. There were no headcounts or any other effort by the guards to account for prisoners by name. During this journey through hell, our captors had treated us the same impassive way they would have treated the cattle that the French boxcars had been designed to transport.

Finally, with every boxcar unloaded, the column of prisoners began to move. It was difficult to judge the distance we covered from the railroad yards to the new prison camp, but it probably wasn't more than a couple of miles. The guards meeting the train were wearing the green uniform of the Wehrmacht — the ground or defense forces of Germany. There were more guards present than I had seen at any time since the forced march had begun. The very thought that we would now be under the control of the German ground forces had a chilling effect on all of us. A large sign arched over the main gate identified the prison camp as "Stammlager XIII B-1. Stalag or Stammlager. The words made little difference to me; they were both German names for prisons.

We passed through the gate and up a corridor road. The column of prisoners was stopped at each barracks or "block." After each block was filled, the doors were barred shut and the column of prisoners moved forward to the next barracks. Doug Reid and I were together when it was our turn to enter the barracks. There were no lights in the building and for a while there was utter chaos as we all pushed forward in the darkness. Someone with matches was finally able to light the wick in a can of margarine. Others managed to light papers to serve as temporary torches.

By dim light, we discovered we were in a barracks with open bays and a center corridor. Each bay contained a three-tiered row of wooden frames to be used as beds. There were no mattresses on the beds and not enough bed boards to allow prisoners to use the beds. It was too late and too dark to accomplish anything until morning. Most of us found a place on the floor where we could rest our weary bodies and get some sleep. At least there was more room to stretch out than we had in the boxcars.

I awakened to the sound of the door barricades opening. There were no toilet facilities in the barracks but we were located near a building that housed a latrine. Outside our barracks, between the latrine and the barracks, was a single pipe with a faucet extending up through a small concrete pad. This was the water supply for occupants of the adjacent barracks. My first action after using the latrine facility was to wash my hands and face with a small bar of soap I had taken from one of the lavatory rooms in the factory. My hands were unbelievably filthy and I shuddered to think that I had been handling bread and other food items while aboard the boxcar. I noticed that other prisoners were beginning to stir and gather up what appeared to be bedding that for some reason had been discarded outside the building. We assumed the Germans had removed the bedding from the building to air it out. I overheard a guard telling one of the prisoners that the barracks had been occupied by a group of Italian prisoners who had been relocated several days earlier in preparation for our arrival.

I lost no time in finding a new-looking burlap mattress that was stuffed with wood straw. The mattress couldn't have been outside too long as it didn't appear to have any moist areas. I set up my bed on a top outside bunk in the bay nearest the back entrance to the building. I had to search for additional bed boards as my bunk had only three boards in place. Reid was in the top bunk adjacent to me and I helped him with his mattress, which was thinner and appeared to be filled with shredded paper.

Our bay had twelve bunks on each side with a narrow corridor between the rows of beds. A cook stove and table occupied one of the center bays but there was no firewood or coal to fuel a fire. There were six double bays in our barracks. About one hundred and forty men had been assigned to occupy this space.

By nightfall, there was some semblance of order in our living quarters. Someone had started a fire in the stove and several "kriegies" (prisoners) were heating soluble coffee and cooking some unidentified food. The Germans had provided us with only two servings of bread and weak soup this day. Some prisoners who still had Red Cross package food shared their food with friends. Most important, we had been issued weak wattage light bulbs to place in the empty ceiling light sockets. The lights would normally be available at night until nine o'clock

Since the start of the forced march we had been sleeping fully clothed. Tonight would be different! I undressed down to my long johns, as did most of the prisoners. We had all been issued two blankets. Some prisoners had additional blankets that they had carried with them on the forced march. Most had retained the heavy G.I. overcoats issued by the Red Cross at Stalag Luft III. Lights were out at nine o'clock and the doors barred shut. I settled down to sleep in the first bed since leaving the cell where I had been held in solitary at Sagan.

Don't Let the Bedbugs Bite

I don't know what time I awakened, but I was suddenly aware of a burning itch all along my left leg. I had been lying on my left side facing away from Reid. As I turned over, something dropped onto my face. I also felt an insect crawling on my head. It took me a few minutes to realize that I was being eaten alive by fleas and some kind of moving bugs. I sat up in bed, my head almost touching the ceiling, and again felt some type of insect fall onto my face.

It was obvious that I could not stay in bed. I grabbed my trousers and A-2 jacket and climbed out of the upper bunk bed. I didn't know how many of the bugs were still on me or in my long johns so I immediately removed both my underwear and socks. It was too dark to see if the fleas were still in the clothing so I fumbled my way to the bay where the chairs were located. Finally seated, I slowly and carefully went over my underwear with my hands, attempting to locate any flea or bed bug that might have remained on my clothing. I could feel fleas that were imbedded in the legs of the long johns and I picked at them until they were dislodged.

It was an hour or so before I put my long johns back on and returned to the bay where my bed was located. There was no returning to bed, however, as I had itchy welts on every part of my body. After shaking the A-2 jacket and feeling for bugs, I put the jacket back on. Both legs were on fire but the left leg and hip had received the most bites. I had been lying on my left side, thus providing quick access for the fleas and bed bugs that had been hibernating in the mattress. My legs were covered with bug bites. I pulled up the left pant leg of my long johns and slowly and methodically counted the number of bites on that leg. There were two hundred and forty welts on my left leg; covering just the area from my toes to my knee. The bed bugs that were falling on my face and head were coming out of cracks in the ceiling. There were several lumps on my face and neck. One eyelid was swollen.

I was desperate and near panic as I sat there itching and counting the number of bites on my leg. For the first time since becoming a prisoner, I had doubts that I would survive. I had great difficulty in controlling my emotions the day we were shot down and when I learned that Claud Smith had not survived. This was the first time since that day that I could not stop the flow of tears. I was thankful it was dark and hoped no one could hear me. I finally asked for God's help. Praying seemed to help. There was no sleep for me that night, but I still had hope that tomorrow everything would be better.

At daylight, the sound of the outside barriers to the barracks doors being removed was my signal to get busy and try to get some relief from the constant itching on my legs. I soaked a cloth in the cold water from the outside spigot. The icy water seemed to provide some relief from the persistent irritation.

I noticed that prisoners from adjacent barracks were already disposing of their mattresses. I was the first in our barracks to carry out my mattress and place it in the center of a growing pile of bedding. Later in the day, with permission from the German guards, these mattresses were burned.

Our problems with fleas and bed bugs were not restricted to just the mattresses. The bed bugs also hid in cracks in the wooden bed frames, the walls and in the ceiling boards. The fleas were unlike any I had ever seen. They were red and when we exposed them to sunlight, their bodies glistened. One way to help rid the area of bed bugs was to light a torch and hold it adjacent to their hiding areas. We tried this in our bay and killed hundreds of bed bugs in this manner but finally gave up when we ran out of fuel for the torch. It wasn't the best or safest way to rid ourselves of these blood-sucking pests but we'd reduced the number of potential attackers. For some strange reason, a few of the prisoners didn't suffer from bites, and other than the sensation of the insects crawling on their bodies, they seemed to be immune from the discomfort the rest of us suffered.

Adding to the problem of controlling the vermin were those few men who wanted to retain their vermin-infected mattresses. Not bothered by the fleas or bedbugs, they were understandably reluctant to give up the only comfort that these living conditions could afford them. Those of us without mattresses were scrambling to find additional bed boards. Sleeping on bed boards with only a blanket or heavy overcoat as a fill-in for a mattress posed an additional physical hardship. Despite our requests for assistance from the Germans, we were not provided spray solutions or ingredients to kill the pests.

Following my initial nightmare encounter with the fleas and bedbugs, I established a routine procedure that I followed in an effort to defend myself from the pests. During the day, I took my blankets outside, placed them across the wire fence adjacent to the center roadway that ran through the camp and then methodically searched for and killed any fleas imbedded in the blanket. Before lights out in the evenings, I would undress and check each item of clothing, one by one, before putting it back on. After I was fully dressed, I tied shoestrings around my lower pant legs to seal off any openings and then tied string around the cuffs of my sleeves. I wrapped my scarf snugly around my neck and zipped my A-2 jacket up as far as possible. My stocking cap was worn over a section of newspaper that I first placed on my head. With gloves on, I was now prepared to face the "enemy" for the rest of the night.

Hunger Pains

When I joined the group of prisoners at Muskau, it had been my hope that our destination would be where the South Compound men were being held. I missed the friendship of my comrades from Block 136 at Stalag Luft III; adjusting to a new location among strangers had proven to be more difficult than I had anticipated.

It was customary for several prisoners to pool their resources for food preparation, cooking, clean up, etc. Doug Reid had invited me to join his group. Unfortunately, I had no food to contribute to this group and I could feel some resentment from two or three members of the food pool. The resentment had some merit. The Red Cross food supplies carried by men on the forced march were being depleted and our lives were now primarily dependent on the meager supply of bug-infested soup and bread provided by the Germans. I dropped out of the food pool after a few days as it was apparent the Red Cross food would soon be no more. There was a growing feeling among some of the prisoners that it was "every man for himself." We were all, to varying degrees, approaching the road that eventually leads to starvation. The pangs of hunger became a part of my life. The hunger was comparatively mild in the mornings, seemed to increase throughout the day and by evening was difficult to manage. Sleep was often the only source of relief.

The forced march and relocation to the prison camp at Nuremberg had resulted in a temporary disruption of the news service we had become accustomed to at Stalag Luft III. For several weeks, our German captors provided the only news available. Because this news was transmitted in German over a loud speaker, it had to be translated. Without a reliable news source, we were exposed to all sorts of rumors. The British had taught us the terms to identify and quantify the news. If it was thought to be from a reliable source, it was labeled as "Pukka Gin." If the news or rumor was considered suspect or unreliable, it was classified as "Duff Gin."

Air Raids

We were very much aware that the prison compound was located near the rail center for the city of Nuremberg and that the camp location was, in fact, on the outskirts of the city itself. The previous prisoners at our location had started to dig trenches outside the barracks for protection in the event of an air raid, but we were advised not to use these trenches during night raids. The Germans feared escape attempts might be made during periods when the prison compound lights were shut off. Heavy anti-aircraft batteries surrounded the camp, and it wasn't long before we were exposed to the dangers of being struck by falling metal debris from the exploding 88mm shells fired at aircraft flying in the vicinity of the prison camp.

One night we heard the distinctive sound of a low flying British Mosquito bomber, followed shortly thereafter by a tremendous explosion that shook every building in the compound. We weren't certain of the location of the bomb but it had apparently been a delayed fused bomb dropped by the Mosquito bomber somewhere on or near the railroad complex in Nuremberg.

During February, there were several daylight air raids on targets in and around the industrial areas at Nuremberg and we could only hope that the crews had been briefed on the existence of our prison. During the raids, we removed shutters from the windows and raced to the trenches, using the shutters for protection from falling shrapnel as the antiaircraft shells exploded overhead.

One day in mid February, a formation of American B-17's with fighter escort flew near our location. It was a clear day, thus providing us with an unrestricted view of the formation. Of particular note was one aircraft that was trailing dark smoke and obviously in trouble. It was positioned below the formation, making a slow turn in our direction. It flew directly over the prison camp and as we continued to watch, two parachutes blossomed out. We could see the airmen as they drifted over the camp and disappeared from view. The aircraft continued its flight until it, too, was out of sight.

Air raid sirens, the boom of the antiaircraft guns, searchlights and the sounds of attacking aircraft became a routine part of our existence.

Bomb Attacks

It was early March 1945 and finally showing signs of an early spring. I am back to walking for exercise. The pain in my right heel had finally been reduced to the point that I could put full weight on my foot without wincing. I still had no idea what had caused the sudden pain during the forced march. I was just thankful that I could again walk normally. Unlike the perimeter pathway along the inside perimeter of the prison grounds at Stalag Luft III, my new walking area was a roadway that appeared to run through the middle of the prison camp.

The "good news" was that we were finally receiving daily news reports from the British broadcasting agency (BBC.) It appeared that the Allied forces in the west and the Russians on the eastern front were making rapid advances. The radio parts, secretly hidden and carried at considerable risk by "kriegies" during the forced march, had evidently been reassembled and were now in use. The hope that freedom may be near and that we would soon be liberated provided us with renewed strength to survive each day.

The "bad news" continued to be the uncertainty of our situation, the vermin problem, inadequate food and an increasing number of prisoners sick with severe diarrhea and other symptoms of dysentery. The bed bug, flea and lice problem continued with several men now hospitalized with serious infections. Burning the infected mattresses and a limited issue of flea powder had been of invaluable help in the battle to reduce the vermin population.

Also, because I was separated from the South Compound prisoners, it was unlikely that I would receive any mail that was addressed to me at the Stalag Luft III address. I considered that to be a self-inflicted wound.

A night bombing raid in mid March 1945 by British aircraft provided us with sights and sounds that will probably remain etched forever in the minds of all who witnessed the events of that night. It was a quiet warm evening and a few wispy clouds were still visible overhead when we first heard the sounds of several low flying aircraft approaching from the west. Mosquito bombers were sighted flying past the prison compound as they moved on to drop locations around and within the city of Nuremberg. These relatively fast fighter-bombers were marking targets in advance for the larger bomber force that was to follow. It appeared that flare markers were also identifying the prison camp — at least that was our hope.

The Mosquito bombers had arrived so unexpectedly that it was some time before we heard the sound of counter anti-aircraft gunfire. The sky was suddenly alive with bursting shells from the barrage of anti-aircraft guns. The German guard in the nearest tower left his position in the tower and raced to the nearest trench for protection. His movement seemed to be the catalyst that motivated the prisoners from my barracks to also seek safety in the nearest trench. I was huddled with two other men under a shutter we had removed from the barracks. The shutter quickly proved its worth as jagged fragments of the exploding shells began falling around us. The German guards made no effort to force us back indoors.

A surrealistic scene began to unfold before our eyes. The first heavy bombers began their entry into the target area, dropping not only bombs but also yellow flares to mark the flight corridor as well as red and green flares probably intended to further define the target area. The earth-shaking sound and huge fires from bombs, the eerie glow created by the strings of falling colors from the flares, the search lights on the ground reaching upward through the wispy clouds, and the red glitter of fire from the bursting anti-aircraft shells combined to provide us with a terrifying vision of hell. The bomber aircraft appeared to be approaching in single file. We were witness to the life and death struggle taking place as the searchlights captured an aircraft in its glare and flak bursts appeared to engulf the aircraft. Some of the bombers escaped using evasive action; others continued on their flight path, often accompanied by a trail of fire.

We watched in fear as one bomber received a fatal wound. Instead of continuing forward flight, this aircraft started to fall straight down and we saw a huge explosion in the air. Then, after a few seconds, we heard the sound of the aircraft as it was falling through the maze of flares and searchlights. The bomber was on fire. Now, looking more like a huge boxcar than an aircraft, it began to emit wailing sounds that sent chills down my back. We all feared it would crash close to our trench.

After what seemed an eternity, the aircraft struck the ground and the sounds of agony were silenced. It had fallen just outside the prison compound. The raid was finally over but the fires from the bombing still rages and the acrid smell of smoke would remain in the air for days. We had been front row witnesses to the horrors of war.

Journey Out of Nuremberg

Another Easter arrived and I vividly recalled the brutal murder of Corporal Miles only a year ago while we had been imprisoned at Stalag Luft III. It was difficult to accept the fact that I was still a prisoner, but I was grateful that I was alive.

The main topic of discussion was the location of American forces that could possibly be in a position to liberate our prison camp. We had just been notified by the German guards that we would be evacuating Stalag 13B the following morning. The news was received with mixed emotions. We were excited, but hopeful that we would be liberated without any further "forced marches" or transport by rail in the dreaded 40 & 8 boxcars.

We received a partial issue from Red Cross food parcels. Each parcel was to be divided among four men. My share of the food included a box of prunes, a tin of biscuits and half a package of processed cheese. I traded my share of the cigarettes for a package of sugar cubes and a small bar of soap. This parcel did not contain the usual issue of Spam. A special issue of bread was the major food contribution made by our captors.

We were on the road by mid-morning on April 4th, 1945. One by one the barracks of prisoners marched out the main gate to begin yet another journey into the unknown. Prisoners from my barracks were among the first to depart the prison compound. We weren't far from the head of the column. It was a beautiful clear day in contrast to the weather we had faced when we had departed the prison compound at Stalag Luft III back in January.

Our fear that we would be placed in boxcars was lessoned as we walked past the rail complex in Nuremberg where we had debarked in February. Our journey out of the Nuremberg complex continued in a southerly direction.

Looking back, I could see the column of prisoners trailing far in the distance. I was walking with two Lieutenants with whom I had become acquainted after I had arrived at the prison compound in Nuremberg. I knew them only by their last names — Feldman and English. I had previously told them that if we were ever exposed to another forced march, I had every intention of escaping. Feldman indicated that he would join me if conditions permitted. I told him that I wanted to wait until we were out of the Nuremberg area before even considering an escape attempt.

We had been on the road for about two hours when I decided to open my box of prunes. I had eaten only a couple when I became aware of a guard walking near me in the roadway. He was older than most and he looked tired. He had been watching me as I ate the prunes and I knew he was hungry. I handed him the box and indicated for him to take some. He thanked me, took only one prune and handed the box back to me. I shook out a handful of prunes and handed them to the old guard and he accepted them. His gratitude was reflected in his low words of thanks spoken in German. It was apparent during this forced march that many of the guards knew it was only a matter of time before Germany would have to acknowledge defeat. It would be dangerous, though, to assume that the German guards would fail to carry out their duties because of the circumstances of the war.

A flight of P-47's flew overhead and the column of prisoners suddenly came to a halt. The aircraft continued flight toward Nuremberg until they reached the small town we had just passed through. Suddenly the P-47's turned left and started a dive-bombing attack on what I thought was a railroad trestle. We had passed under this trestle while traveling through a small town named Fuecht. The line of prisoners appeared to trail as far back as the trestle and we were close enough to hear the bomb explosions. We could only watch in helpless fear as the two P-47 fighters made their diving attacks.

Suddenly the attack was over and the German guards were shouting at us to continue on our way. Concurrent with the appearance of the aircraft, a white bed sheet that had large POW letters painted on its surface had been unfurled. Several prisoners at the head of the column had used this method to warn Allied aircraft of our presence. The German horse-drawn wagons also had large cloth covers with Red Cross symbols painted on them. At the sound of aircraft, these painted covers were exposed. The P-47 pilots may not have seen these symbols of peace, but they had made no attempt to strafe our column of prisoners. I assumed they were targeting the rail trestle. We could only hope and pray that the prisoner column had already cleared the area where the bombs fell.

   The pace of travel began to slow with frequent stops required for those prisoners who were sick and had diarrhea. I told Feldman and English that at the first opportunity, I intended to escape by feigning a need to urinate while we were stopped to wait for prisoners with diarrhea to complete their business.

A Taste of Freedom

We were passing through the outskirts of a small village when the column suddenly stopped to allow several prisoners with severe diarrhea to seek relief. A slight down slope with tall grass and weeds provided the men with some degree of privacy. On the opposite side of the road was a small fence and what appeared to be an open storage area for building materials. There were stacks of tile, concrete pipe and concrete blocks that would provide an ideal hiding area; however, there was a guard on that side of the road.

After a few minutes of waiting, the guards became concerned that the prisoners were taking too long. Several prisoners had moved farther down the slope. The guard on our side of the road crossed over to the other side and went part way down the slope to assist two other guards in getting the prisoners back in line. This was the opportunity I had been waiting for!

I stepped out of line on the right side of the column and walked over to the fence. Looking around, I saw that the guards were still occupied on the other side of the column. I stepped over the fence and continued walking toward a stack of building material. Out of the corner of my eye, I saw Feldman and English step over the fence and walk to my left. I found an opening in the stacked tiles. After looking around and seeing no guard, I positioned myself in a small area between two stacks of building materials. I was able to peer through an opening in the stack of tiles and saw Feldman and English disappear behind layers of concrete pipe. I also noticed a woman looking out of a window in a house some distance from our location but adjacent to the area where the building materials were stacked. She appeared to be looking at the column of prisoners, but I wasn't certain.

I had been in my hiding position for only a few minutes when I was startled to see Lt. English suddenly stand up and walk back to the fence, step over the fence and join the column of prisoners. The column had started moving when Lt. Feldman also decided to leave his hiding spot and join the formation. I don't know why they took the risk of attempting to hide and then decided to return to their prisoner status. Perhaps they felt that the woman looking out the window had spotted them as they sought cover among the building materials. I had emphasized to both of them that if any of us escaped during daylight we should seek a hiding location and remain hidden until nightfall.

The long line of prisoners disappeared down the road and I was satisfied that the actions by English and Feldman had not compromised my location. It was my intention to wait until dark and then began traveling in a westerly direction. I still had my prized compass and on clear nights I could use the stars to guide me in the right direction. I ate a few more prunes, hoping they wouldn't cause the diarrhea to kick in.

Some time in the early afternoon, I heard the sound of high-flying aircraft. Before long, a large formation of B-17's flew directly overhead. I was amazed that most of the aircraft were silver-skinned and not the drab olive color that had been on all the aircraft during the period when my crew was shot down. I was thankful to still be alive, but I longed to be free and was envious of those airmen above who were still flying and would hopefully return safely to their home bases. I often wondered what my fate would have been had our aircraft been able to return to our home base on the day of the Schweinfurt mission. I know I would have continued flying combat until I had completed my missions. My desire to fly combat in fighter aircraft had not lessoned. The sight of our B-17 force seemed to awaken thoughts that I had tried to bury during the months in captivity.

I was lying on my back half asleep waiting for nightfall when I suddenly become aware of a face staring down at me. That face had an amazing resemblance to that of the man who was in German custody the day I was shot down. He had the same broad face, straight blond hair, blue eyes and facial structure that I remembered. I was startled by his sudden appearance, but all he did was stare at me. I put my finger to my mouth, signaling for quiet. The man looked at me intently without saying a word and then suddenly disappeared as quietly as he had arrived. No words had been spoken between us. It was still daylight so I didn't dare try to relocate my hiding spot. The man had been dressed in workman's clothing and since he had sounded no alarm, I hoped he might have been a refugee or perhaps a slave laborer from Poland. All I could do at that point was pray that he would remain quiet and not divulge my location to anyone.

Twenty or thirty minutes passed and still no one had sounded an alarm. I began to believe that this man would not report my presence to anyone. I knew I would be traveling all night so I decided to try and sleep. I had no sooner closed my eyes than I heard a shuffling noise. This time when I looked up, I was staring at a small silver, automatic handgun. The holder of the gun was a tall, well-dressed, distinguished looking man. He ordered me to stand up and raise my arms. Standing nearby was the man with the Slavic features. I had the sensation that this was a repeat of the day I had initially been captured after crash-landing the B-17. My freedom this time had lasted only about six hours.

Escape with a Friend

I was taken to an office about a mile from my roadside hiding place. The man with the Slavic features wandered away from the area where I had been captured without ever speaking a word. The small office where I was detained had a comfortable couch where I was permitted to rest while waiting for transport. I was offered water and told that I would be returned to my "comrades."

After about a thirty-minute wait, a horse-drawn open carriage pulled up in front of the building. I was told that this would be my transport. Seated in this carriage was a middle-aged, well-dressed woman. As soon as I had boarded the carriage, the woman announced that she was Hungarian and that she was fleeing from the Russian Communists. The carriage was loaded with her personal belongings. Evidentially she had been provided German guard escort. A young German soldier held the horses reins and another very young German guard was seated behind the woman. I had fully expected to be placed in a prison cell in the village so I was surprised and a little skeptical about the turn of events.

I was seated in the front on the same bench with the driver and had a unobstructed view of the traffic on the roadway. We passed wagons loaded with family possessions. It seemed everyone was headed in the same southerly direction either on foot or in some type of vehicle. I was startled to see three familiar looking figures walking along the roadside but traveling in the opposite direction. Two of the men were dressed in what appeared to be new G.I. uniforms, A-2 leather aviator jackets and OD trousers. The two young officers had their military ranks displayed on their shirt collars. Their companion was in military khakis and had on a wide-brimmed fatigue hat. A barracks bag was slung over his shoulder. They were very obviously American military men, and seeing them in broad daylight on a congested highway was unbelievable.

We had already passed the trio when one of the guards suddenly seemed to comprehend the situation. The carriage jolted to a halt. The guard seated in the rear of the carriage leaped out, raced back down the road and apprehended the three musketeers. After some adjustment of the lady's suitcases, the two 2nd Lieutenants were seated at the back of the carriage. The other passenger was directed to sit in the front of the carriage next to me.

As soon as he was seated, my new seatmate extended his hand and announced in a firm voice, "Sergeant Olson, Chicago." I shook his hand and told him my name. After looking me over he said, "You been a prisoner a long time?" It was more of a statement of fact than a question. I nodded, not ready for a long conversation. Sgt. Olson, however, was full of nervous enthusiasm and needed to talk. He had been a prisoner for only a short time. He had only just met the two lieutenants on the road. I didn't try to get an explanation as to why they had had the audacity to travel on a roadway in broad daylight when it was obvious they would be caught. Sgt. Olson did say that they had been traveling for several hours on this roadway and had not been previously stopped.

A short time after gaining our new passengers, the guards stopped for a short rest period. The driver left his seat and joined his comrade on the ground at the rear of the carriage. Noting that the guards were not within hearing distance, Olson turned to me and said in a low voice, "Let's take them. There are four of us and only two of them." I was alarmed. It would be foolish to attempt to disarm the two guards in broad daylight and in full view of the other travelers, and I wasn't interested in doing anything that would further jeopardize my life. I told Olson that we should wait until nightfall. If, in fact, we were returning to join the column of prisoners, there should be an opportunity to escape without attempting to overpower any of the guards. Sgt. Olson finally accepted my advice after I assured him that I fully intended to escape with him later in the evening. I had no discussion with the other two captives as they were seated too far back in the carriage for conversation.

Late in the evening, we arrived at a temporary stopping place for the men from our prison compound. The two guards from the carriage left the four of us in the custody of one of the German Unterofficers guarding the roadway. This guard apparently had no idea what to do with us. He first peered into Sgt. Olson's barracks bag. When he was satisfied that there was no weapon, he handed the bag back to Olson. He called for another guard and with his help, each of us was subjected to a brief search. Once the search was completed, we were placed with a group of prisoners who were standing in line for an issue of bread and soup. The guard had not even bothered to take our names. Both guards then sauntered off, evidently satisfied that we were just misplaced prisoners.

The soup line was reasonably short as most of the men had already been served. I had no container for the soup but was able to borrow a canteen cup from a man who said he had been through the soup line twice. The rich, thick barley soup was flavored just right and was the best soup I had ever tasted. Olson and I ate the first helping and got back in line for seconds. The two lieutenants were in the soup line just ahead of us. After eating, I obtained drinking water from an outside faucet and was able to rinse out the canteen and return it to the owner. This man gave me an empty food can for my future use. My new friend, Sgt Olson, put the can in his barracks bag.

It was now time to attempt another escape. It appeared that we wouldn't have too much difficulty avoiding the guards. Prisoners were wandering all over the area and the guards didn't seem to pay much attention to their activities. The prisoners had been told that they would be spending the night at this location and some guards were assisting them to find shelter in barns and buildings adjacent to the roadway. We were in what appeared to be the outskirts of a small village in an area surrounded by houses.

I asked Olson to check with his two travel mates to see if they were interested in joining us. The two lieutenants indicated they would follow my lead and accompany us. I provided only brief, sketchy instructions to the other three intended escapees. I told them to act casual and, if stopped, to say that we were simply looking for shelter. Under no circumstances were we to resist if stopped — just act like poor bewildered prisoners seeking help. It was agreed that I would do the talking for the four of us if we were challenged by any of the guards. There was no great master plan for this escape attempt; I simply wanted us to wander to the outer fringes of the areas where the prisoners were attempting to bed down. If a guard didn't stop us, one by one we would take cover behind one of the houses and then wait until all four of us were safely assembled behind the house. We would then regroup and continue walking until we were out of town. I had the compass and would lead the way.

Sgt. Olson, barracks bag and all, was the first to suddenly disappear. I followed Olson. We had almost given up on the two Lieutenants when they finally appeared together behind an adjacent house. We left as a foursome and began our travel down a side street in a westerly direction. We had reached the edge of town when a man suddenly stepped out of the cover of a porch and told us to "halt" and we immediately halted. This man appeared to be one of our guards. He had a flashlight and used it to examine each one of us. I explained that we were seeking "drinkwasser" (water). The guard opened the door of the house and called out to a woman. After a short discussion with the guard, she brought out a tray containing a pitcher of water and four mugs. When she opened the door, she also turned on a porch light. The guard was now in plain view and I suddenly recognized him as the same guard who had shared my box of prunes earlier in the day. We drank the water and handed back our cups. As the guard gave the tray back to the woman, he looked directly at me. We were still offering thanks when the guard abruptly said goodnight. He turned and followed the woman into the house, closing the door as he departed from our view. We had just been given a clear signal that this guard would not take any action to prevent our leaving the area.

We had been moving silently in a grassy meadow for about an hour when we came to a river or large canal. It was too dark to determine the depth of the river but there was sufficient light to see the opposite bank. After a short discussion, we decided to continue traveling adjacent to the river, hoping to find a bridge.

After traveling only a short distance on the bank of the river, we discovered a railroad trestle. We crouched down on the railroad embankment and remained that way for about fifteen minutes, looking for any sound or sight of a guard. I could see over to the opposite side of the trestle; if there had been a guard, he would have been visible. I told Olson that we should chance a crossing and he agreed. I was in the lead as we started crawling across the trestle. I stopped after traveling about fifteen feet. Looking back, I was surprised to see that only Sgt. Olson was following me. I told Olson to hold his position and I crawled back to where the two officers were still hiding on the bank of the river. I asked them if they were with us or if they had decided to travel alone. They acknowledged that they wanted to continue to accompany Sgt. Olson and me. I told them that if they were serious about staying with us, they could start by sharing the same risks. I angrily told them that it appeared they had been waiting in position to see if Sgt Olsen and I had been challenged or perhaps shot at before exposing themselves to any risk. I turned and began my crawl back to where Olson was waiting. The two lieutenants followed me.

The four of us finally made it safely across the railroad trestle only to find a small ditch with about a foot of water paralleling the riverbank. We decided to continue walking on the riverbank hoping to find a place where we could cross the small stream without getting wet. It looked like there was a trail along the riverbank with high weeds on either side that would provide good cover.

I was in the lead following the trail when a sound ahead of us forced us to stop and listen. All was quiet for a moment and then off in the distance we heard someone shout, "Halt!" in a very loud voice. I crouched down and quietly crawled on my stomach to gain cover in the grass on the outside slope of the riverbank.

Olson followed me, turning to the other two men behind him and whispering for them to get down. We lay quietly for a few minutes and all was still. Suddenly there was another shout closer to our position. The person who heard us was calling for help. Sgt. Olson crawled up next to me and I said, "We'd better get out of here fast!"

I continued crawling down the embankment and into the small stream of water. Olson was right beside me. We crawled through the water and continued on a perpendicular path away from the riverbank. Our next obstacle was a fence. Olson was still dragging his barracks bag of goodies, which made it difficult to get through the fence. Once we were finally clear of the fence, we continued to crawl on our bellies for a considerable distance. The two lieutenants evidently had not followed us, choosing instead to remain hidden in the bushes adjacent to the riverbank. Olson and I continued to crawl on our bellies until we were near exhaustion. Finally, we were far enough out that we felt safe enough to stand and run toward a distant dark area that appeared to be a grove of trees.

We had no sooner started running than we were shocked to hear two gunshots back in the area where we had been hiding. About the same time as the gunshots came a horrible scream mixed with loud shouting. A third shot was fired and the screaming was renewed. Olson and I stood in silent shock for a few minutes. When the screaming stopped, we continued to hear shouting. I didn't even know the names of the two lieutenants. We could only say a silent prayer for their safety.

The screams continued to haunt us as we continued our journey on a path that we hoped would lead to freedom. Arriving at the tree line, we stopped briefly to rest and evaluate our future actions. We were both soaked to the skin but didn't notice the cold. The intensity of our physical activity, coupled with the emotional events that had just occurred, had drowned out any thoughts of physical discomfort. A light rain had begun falling and we sought cover under a tree.

Olson lit up a cigarette while I searched for my compass. I remembered placing the compass in my watch pocket before crossing the railroad trestle, but now that pocket was empty. After a methodical search of all my pockets, the compass was still nowhere to be found. We used up several precious matches searching the ground where I had been standing in case the small compass had fallen to the ground when I had first checked the watch pocket. The search was futile; the compass was lost.

Travel at night or even in daylight would be difficult during periods when the sky was overcast and the sun or stars were not visible. To further complicate the problem, neither of us had a map of the area. I felt badly about losing the compass, but we both agreed that the lack of a compass would not deter us from continuing our travels.

After a short rest, we decided to walk adjacent to a dirt road that we felt was headed in a westerly direction. The rain was increasing and travel became more difficult. Olson had poor night vision and, out of necessity, walked behind me most of the time. We had walked for about an hour in the steady drizzle before we acknowledged that we were just too tired to continue. We weren't certain that we were traveling in the right direction so the obvious thing to do was to seek shelter of some type and try to rest until morning.

We found a large tree that provided some relief from the rain. Olsen reached into his barracks bag and pulled out a rain poncho. We sat back to back under the poncho. My thoughts drifted back to the two lieutenants. Why had they not followed us as we crawled out of danger? The sound of the gunshots and screams kept racing through my mind. I could tell by the sound of his breathing that Olsen was asleep. Then I, too, fell asleep until daybreak.

The sound of a creaking noise awakened me. Approaching us down the roadway was a man in a wagon being pulled by oxen. The strange noise was the sound of the wheels turning. I shook Olsen to wake him. If we stayed in our present location, we would surely be seen. We scurried back behind a group of trees, not sure if we had been noticed. The driver was alone and gave no indication that he was aware of our presence as he passed our location.

The rain had stopped and there were breaks in the clouds, indicating the weather was clearing. We needed to hide in a remote location during the day as we intended to continue traveling at night. Unfortunately, most of the forested areas had been cleared of brush and debris, making it difficult to find a place suitable for hiding. We finally found an area in the woods where the tall grass hadn't been cut. By tromping on the grass, we were able to stake out a resting place where we could remain hidden and still have an open area for the sun to dry out our clothing.

Sgt. Olson was a smoker. Once he was settled in our new hideout, he relaxed by chain smoking. I ordinarily didn't smoke but to save on his limited supply of matches and to give him a brief rest from smoking, I would sometimes light one up from the fire of his nearly depleted cigarette. We had to be especially careful that the smoke did not alert anyone to our location.

As the weather warmed and the sun came out, we removed our outer clothes and hung them in the sunlight to dry. Olson checked the cigarettes and food items from his barracks bag. The carrying bag was made from the same waterproof material as his poncho and the water had not damaged any of his "goodies." Olson had been fortunate in that during the distribution of food before the forced march began, he had been able to save several cartons of cigarettes. He had also acquired food from two or three Red Cross food parcels. Only a man with Olson's strength, endurance and determination could have survived his experiences while lugging a large heavy sack over his shoulders. I was fortunate to have him as a traveling companion. He had willingly shared his food with me and his courage was never in doubt.

The day was one of rest and we both slept for several hours. I found no sign of fleas or bugs in my clothing. I hoped I was completely rid of the vermin that had plagued me at the Stalag in Nuremberg. By late afternoon, the clothing was mostly dried out and it was time to get ready for the night's travel.

The sun provided us with the initial direction to take for a westerly heading and if the night sky remained clear, there would be no problems continuing westward. We had obtained water from a small stream. I had drunk so much that I was nearly bloated but I didn't want to get dehydrated while traveling at night. Olsen had a full canteen of water attached to his belt.

We started walking at dusk in a forested area and moved into open fields when it was safe to travel without being seen. I had to lead the way as Olson continued to have difficulty with night vision. We shared the workload by sharing the responsibility for carrying the barracks bag. Olson frequently rested one hand on my shoulder to insure that he didn't run into an obstacle in the dark.

We had been walking in the darkness for several hours and I was encouraged at our progress; however, at the end of a rest period, Sgt. Olson suddenly made the request that I continue without him. He told me that he was unable to see in the dark and he had decided it was best if he traveled during the day. His major concern was that he was slowing me down, thus reducing my chances of reaching friendly forces.

I considered Olson my friend and I did not relish the thought of traveling alone. During the ensuing discussion, I told Olson that we should stay together for our own safety and well being. We agreed to rest the remainder of the night and get a fresh start in the morning. The plan was to travel in wooded areas wherever possible and to bypass any villages. There was always the chance that we would spot an American military unit in the area. The previous day we had heard booming sounds that sounded like bombs or heavy artillery, and for all we knew we could already be in an area that was under Allied control. We were both trying to keep a positive outlook.

At daybreak, we made our way through a heavily forested area, occasionally deviating from our proposed westward track to avoid villages and farms. The area was hilly and most of the houses and farms were in the valleys. We made frequent rest stops and when the sun was overhead, we stopped to eat some bread and a can of Vienna sausage. We drank from a small stream and filled Olson's water canteen.

In the early afternoon, we ran into a major obstacle. In the valley below us was a roadway that ran in a north-south direction. On the opposite side of the valley were forested hills — a continuation of the forest that had been providing us with protective cover. We had to cross the roadway if we were to continue in a westerly direction. We walked down the hillside until we reached the edge of the trees. Ahead of us was a grassy area on either side of the roadway. Our objective was to cross this area and re-enter the forest on the opposite side of the road without being seen. Finally, after a long wait, the roadway was clear and we began to casually walk across this open area and re-entered the forest.

Our relief in crossing without being seen was short-lived. We hadn't counted on anyone already being in the forest. As we struggled up the hill, I became aware of two boys looking intently in our direction. They were standing about thirty feet from our location. As soon as they realized that I had seen them, they darted behind the trees. I grabbed Olson's arm and pointed in the direction where I had seen the two boys, but they had already disappeared. We stopped for a few minutes, checking in all directions for any sound or sign that we were being followed. Not seeing or hearing anything unusual, we continued traveling up the hilly incline, hopeful that the boys would not sound an alarm.

Twenty or thirty minutes passed before we became aware of a group of boys walking parallel to us. They were keeping a reasonable distance away, but it was obvious we were being tracked. When we stopped, they also stopped. We couldn't move fast enough to outrun them and they seemed content to keep their distance. It wasn't long before larger boys joined this group, some carrying clubs. When a man with a long-barreled rifle joined the group, we finally had to acknowledge that further travel was futile. We stopped and the group of eight or ten young men and the man with the gun began closing in on us. We were surrounded, and after a brief search we were instructed to follow them back down the hill to the roadway. We were walked down the roadway for about a mile to a small town where we were turned over to the local police.

Search for Freedom

Our time in the local jail was short. After waiting for about an hour, we were ordered to climb into the back of a truck with two civilian guards. The truck had a canvas cover so it was difficult to determine the direction we were taking, but after about a two-hour drive we were on the outskirts of another small village. Once again, we were turned over to military guards assigned to Stalag 13B. We were back with the tail end of the marching prisoners. The guards and prisoners were in the process of finding suitable locations to bed down for the night. We were released to join the other prisoners, grateful that we had not been punished or further restricted.

There were no familiar faces in the group of prisoners as the main body of prisoners had already passed through the town. We inquired about food and received information that the Germans were permitting the prisoners to barter for food with the villagers. Although water was made available, the German guards had not issued any food at this location. We still had German bread. Olson opened a can of corned beef and we ate half of the contents with the bread.

It appeared that the guards were paying only token attention to the activities of the prisoners. I suggested to Olson that we should just slip away in the dark and continue on our way. His response wasn't immediate but it was obvious to me that he just wasn't ready to try another escape. He explained that if we left now we would once again be traveling in darkness and he just couldn't travel at night. I felt it was too dangerous to wait until daylight for an escape attempt. I was reluctant to try another escape alone, but I just couldn't pass up what might be my last opportunity to remain free. The future was still very uncertain for those who remained incarcerated and there were rumors that Hitler or the German high command might decide that we should be housed in a concentration camp or, if need be, eliminated. I knew only too well the risks and problems in attempting an escape while imprisoned in a Stalag. The decision was made. I was going to attempt to escape again while I still had the opportunity.

Olson provided me with several canned food items from his barracks bag. Despite two escapes and subsequent recapture, he had been permitted to retain the food and cigarettes he had carried in the barracks bag. His generosity had given me the additional strength and energy I needed to continue my search for freedom. Olson stood watch as I edged ever closer to a fence that bordered the roadway. When he gave me the 'all clear' signal, I dropped down and rolled under the fence. Once clear of the fence, I crawled on my hands and knees until I found cover behind a tree.

Satisfied that I had not been seen, I stood up and walked across a grassy meadow. There was no moon but the stars were out and I had a clear view of Polaris. I continued traveling in a westerly direction, avoiding areas where there were lights. I followed a path running along a fence line until it turned in a southerly direction, avoiding the forested areas where deep shadows from the trees restricted my vision. I continued walking for several miles before I began to tire and was forced to make frequent stops.

It wasn't until I realized that I was starting to sleep walk that I finally stopped and decided I could go no further. I had been following a path on a hillside. The area adjacent to this path appeared to be covered with grass. I stepped off the path and lay down. Using my arm as a pillow, I closed my eyes. Sleep must have been instantaneous, as I remembered nothing for the rest of the night.

When I opened my eyes, the sun was shining on my face and for a few moments I remained very still, confused as to where I was and why I was lying on the ground. The distant sound of a barking dog helped me recover from my lethargy.

The trail along the edge of a wooded area appeared to be well traveled. If I continued on this path in daylight, I would soon be discovered. I headed for a wooded area north of the trail and soon found a location among some large boulders and trees where I could remain hidden for the day. If I attempted daylight travel in a westerly direction from this position, I would surely be discovered. Night travel was my only option. I spent the day attempting to rest but a nagging thirst kept me awake. Water from the recent rain had accumulated in depressions on some of the larger boulders and I sipped water from these areas. The water had a strange taste but I continued to drink until I was no longer thirsty.

Late in the afternoon, I began to have severe stomach cramps followed by diarrhea. I was sure the water had been tainted and I attempted to vomit but had no success. I was thankful that in my packet of belongings I still had the French/German dictionary that had been discarded by someone on the march out of Stalag Luft III. I also had a thin bar of soap. The only food I attempted to eat that day was from a tin of hard biscuits.

The stomach pains had lessened by nightfall and although I felt somewhat weak, I began my nightly travel. I stayed on the border of the wooded area and headed in a northwesterly direction until I felt it was safe to travel in the open fields. It was another cloudless night and I felt reasonably certain that I was following a westerly direction. I could only guess at the time since I had no watch, but I stopped to rest at intervals that approximated an hour. My night vision was surprisingly good but I had an uneasy, scary feeling about traveling alone at night. I missed my friend, Olson. His fearless presence had strengthened my own resolve not to be afraid and to believe that anything was possible. It was his misfortune and mine that he had no vision in the darkness of night.

It was probably two or three o'clock in the morning when I suddenly became aware of a rustling noise somewhere along my route. When I first heard the noise, I could feel the hair on the back of my neck rising. I stopped to listen. Sure enough, there was something moving in the brush behind me. I stood still for a minute or two longer and heard nothing further. I rationalized that I had probably scared some type of animal and it had run off to safety. I continued walking through this wooded area and was startled to hear additional rustling noises ahead of me and to one side. After a moment, I stopped. The noise of something going through the brush continued for a moment and then the noise stopped. I had the feeling that several animals were stalking me. I thought I saw movement in the brush behind me so I leaped forward in that direction and yelled at in an effort to frighten whatever was stalking me. For the first time, I got a glimpse of two closely set eyes just before the animal disappeared in the darkness. I thought it might have been a wolf but the animal appeared to be too small and I had always envisioned wolves as snarling, growling stalkers. Could it have been wild dogs? Again, I didn't think dogs would be noiseless stalkers. It could have been a fox or foxes, but whatever animal it might have been, I was convinced there was more than one and that I was being stalked.

I knew I couldn't continue this cat and mouse game any longer. I looked around for the largest tree I could find and somehow, supercharged with fear, was able to climb the tree to a level where I felt secure. The tree had a large branch high enough off the ground that I was safe from a non tree-climbing animal. Shortly after climbing the tree, I thought I heard animal movement, but my own heavy breathing made it difficult to hear anything else. What few belongings I had been carrying were still wrapped in a burlap bag at the base of the tree.

Once settled in the tree and reasonably confident that I was not going to be attacked by night stalkers, my main challenge was to stay awake and not fall off the branch. I removed my belt and looped it around a smaller branch near my shoulder. I put my left arm through the loop to provide me with additional support should I start to slip off the branch. This second night of travel was again terminated early. I would remain in the tree until there was enough light for better vision.

At first sign of daybreak I was out of the tree and on my way again. The burlap bag lay untouched at the bottom of the tree. There was no sign of an animal or animals, but I was convinced I had had company earlier in the night. I walked only a short distance in this wooded area before stopping to rest. I needed sleep in a place where I would feel relatively secure.

At the edge of the wooded area, I saw a barn some distance from a farmhouse. The barn evidently housed a large wagon or farm appliance because a hole had been cut in the doors to permit the tongue or pole of the wagon to protrude outside the barn. It was still too early for the farmers to be out and about. I scanned the area before deciding to risk approaching the barn. The barn doors were locked, but the hole for the wagon tongue was large enough for me to squeeze through. I entered the barn, frightening some chickens that were roosting on the wagon. The barn had a loft and it appeared to be about half full of hay. I climbed the ladder to the loft and made a bed in an area in the back of the barn. Even if someone were to climb into the loft, I couldn't be seen unless they went around a huge pile of hay. I couldn't remember ever being so tired, but also so comfortable. Completely exhausted, I fell into a deep sleep.

At some period during my sleep, I was awakened by the sound of voices. Someone had entered the barn and was talking to a woman who must have been outside the barn. After a few minutes, the sound of voices drifted away and I returned to sleep. I had intended to wait until darkness had set in before departing, but I had been so exhausted I had slept through the night. I finally left the barn just before daybreak. I had been in the barn for almost twenty-four hours.

I was able to clear the area and enter the woods again without being seen. It was going to be a beautiful spring day and except for the pangs of hunger, I felt refreshed. Before leaving the barn, I had knelt in the loft asking for help and strength to continue my journey to freedom. At least part of that prayer was answered in that I was still free and physically able to travel. I ate the last of a can of beef. Except for a partial loaf of bread and some sugar cubes, I was out of food.

Eichstatt

I had no idea how far I had traveled since dawn, but the sun was overhead so I estimated that I had been on the move for at least six hours. I walked in a wooded area parallel to a highway. This highway appeared to run in an east-west direction and hopefully would be utilized by any advancing Allied forces. I periodically heard the distant sounds of bombs or heavy artillery so I felt certain I was headed in the right direction. Since the edge of the forest terminated at the roadway and there was very little undergrowth, I had to be especially careful not to be seen by anyone traveling on the adjacent highway.

I was suddenly startled by the sound of a low flying aircraft and a burst of gunfire. The aircraft was evidently strafing a target somewhere on the highway. A few minutes after hearing the gunfire, a P-47 flying near ground level flew directly overhead. I once again heard a burst of gunfire in close proximity to my position.

I was stopped, standing still and listening to the sounds of the aircraft when, without warning, five young German soldiers came into view and headed directly toward me. They had dismounted and were pushing their bicycles into the protective cover of the forest. I was caught, flatfooted and in the open. I stood frozen in position as the cyclists continued in my direction.

They were very excited and talking among themselves as they suddenly stopped about twenty feet from where I was standing. Placing their bicycles down on the forest floor, they then proceeded to open up their knapsacks and have lunch. Unbelievably, I had not been seen although I had been standing in full view of all five men. The nearest cover was about six feet away but I knew that any movement I made would be detected. Finally, after what seemed an eternity, a soldier glanced my way. He hesitated, stared at me in disbelief, then shouted something and reached for his holstered gun. I was a prisoner again.

I raised my arms in surrender as the five young soldiers converged on me. Seeing that I was unarmed and posed no threat, they holstered their pistols and began questioning me. Two of the men had evidently studied English and were anxious to test their knowledge by talking to me. They wanted to know if I was an American. Was I an aviator? What aircraft did I pilot? From what prison camp had I escaped? The questions came so fast that I had difficulty trying to respond. I did explain that I had been a prisoner for a long time and that I was a P-38 pilot and had been shot down by an Me109 while flying combat in North Africa. I told them that my only desire was to go home. I didn't tell them that I was a Bomber pilot and that I had been shot down while on a bombing mission. As the war continued and the bombing of targets in cities became more concentrated, we had been receiving increased reports of downed bomber crew airmen being beaten or killed by irate citizens.

During the questioning, one of the soldiers asked me if I was hungry. I gave an affirmative nod and indicated that I needed water. There was no hesitancy as several men offered me water from their canteens. One solder said that he had bread and after folding the bread over a slice of some kind of meat, he handed it to me. With a broad grin he proudly asked, "America sandwich?" I replied, "Yes, American sandwich."

Finished with their lunch, the soldiers indicated that they would take me into the next town. They started back on the road without mounting their bicycles. They were staying alert, ready to plunge back into the forest at the first sound of an aircraft. I was walking at a slow pace surrounded by my escorts, who were not trying to hurry me.

We traveled back in an easterly direction for perhaps two miles before stopping to rest. During this time, one of the English-speaking soldiers suddenly shocked me by saying, "Your President is 'kaput.'" I couldn't disguise my feelings as I tried to respond. When I asked how or what had caused his death, the first thought I had was that President Roosevelt might have been assassinated. The soldiers didn't know what had caused his death but they claimed he had died the previous day and that he had not been assassinated. The days since the evacuation of the prison camp at Nuremberg were a blur and I had no firm recollection of the day of the month. The soldiers told me that the President had died on April 12th. Today's date was either the 13th or 14th of April. My only accomplishment appeared to be that I had known freedom for most of the time during the past ten-day period. And, although emaciated and weak, by God's Grace I was still alive.

We approached the outskirts of Eichstatt, Germany. Visible to the left of the highway and located on a grassy hillside was a large red brick building that appeared to be a school or some type of municipal building. There were uniformed men on the grounds of this building. As we drew closer, we could see that they all had the distinctive emblems and uniforms worn by the dreaded SS (Storm Troopers.) The thought of being turned over to the SS was frightening. I asked my guard escort if that was to be my fate. I was told that the building was a hospital for amputees.

As we passed by the building, the large Red Cross sign associated with a hospital was very visible. The men sitting and walking on the hospital grounds were close enough to be fully identified. I didn't see a single man who had not suffered from the loss of an arm or leg. It was a sobering experience, especially when they were all dressed in full military uniform.

The escort dispersed as we entered the main part of the city. I remained in the custody of two of the young soldiers and was taken into some form of municipal building with barred windows. The two soldiers turned me over to the custody of the local police.

I was immediately placed in a cell with three other American prisoners who were busy trying to loosen the bars on a small window that was located about ten feet above the floor. Two of the men hoisted the third man up on their shoulders. The object was to chisel away the material holding the bars in place. This activity must have been going on for some time, as there was a pile of concrete dust in one corner of the room. The prisoners were from another Stalag. They had escaped during a forced march and had been recaptured several days earlier.

Oflag VIIB

I had less than an hour to get acquainted with my new cellmates before I was taken from the cell and escorted outside where an automobile was waiting to take me to a new unknown destination. I was fearful that I might receive the same fate as the fifty British prisoners of Stalag Luft III who were shot to death upon being recaptured after escaping from their prison compound. These prisoners had been murdered by the German Gestapo while being "escorted" by automobile back to the prison camp at Stalag Luft III.

My trip was a short automobile ride to another prison camp located only a few miles from Eichstatt. A gate sign announced the location as Oflag VIIB. Oflag identified it as a Ground Force officers' prisoner camp. A shocking, ghastly sight greeted me as I embarked from the car. A row of bodies covered with sheets had been placed adjacent to the roadway just inside the prison gates. Further on were scattered groups of bodies, some lying on the ground, others laying on cots or beds inside the prison grounds. My first horrible thought was that the Germans had killed those whose identity was hidden under the sheets and shot the prisoners who were still alive on the ground suffering from serious wounds. Blood was in evidence everywhere — on the sheets, on the ground and on many of the prisoners who were apparently trying to administer to their fellow comrades. The scene was a nightmare of shock and horror.

My questions were met by a stony silence from the two guards who had delivered me to the prison camp. After a few minutes of waiting inside the prison entrance, I was placed in the custody of a German Hauptman (Captain.) It was then that I was informed that the prison Commandant wanted to talk to me. Enroute to the Commandant's office, I noticed that all the prisoners were dressed in light brown, short-waisted jackets and trousers – the uniform worn by British Officers of the Ground Forces.

The German Commandant was a tall, distinguished Colonel, much younger than Colonel von Linder who had been our Commandant at Stalag Luft III. As he spoke, his face and voice revealed the agony he was attempting to control. In excellent English, he first queried me about my status. When he was satisfied that I was a former prisoner at Stalag Luft III and part of the prisoner force that had evacuated Stalag XIIIB at Nuremberg, he then concentrated on questions about what precautions had been made to insure that we were not subjected to attack by Allied aircraft while on the forced march. I explained that because I had been with the prisoner column from Nuremberg only on the first day of the evacuation, I would not be aware of any attack that might have occured after my departure.

I informed him of the overpass bombing the first day of our evacuation from Nuremberg, but emphasized that I had no knowledge of whether or not any of my fellow prisoners had been located in the vicinity of the highway where the bomb attack had occurred. I advised him that all the German wagons had large Red Cross sheets that had been displayed at the sound of an aircraft. Also, I was aware that a large sheet at the head of the column had P.O.W. painted on its surface, and if an aircraft had been encountered, this sheet would have been unfurled and positioned over the heads of the group of prisoners who were leading the column of prisoners.

It was only after this discussion that the German Colonel, with tears welling in his eyes, informed me that the British prisoners of Oflag VIIB had just left the prison grounds to begin their forced march when the marching column had been strafed by two American aircraft. While he asked his questions, I realized that this probably explained the dead and injured prisoners that I had encountered at the entrance to the prison compound.

I felt it was important to mention one more factor to be considered by the Commandant. He had explained that the Oflag VIIB prisoners were "marching" on the highway. I told him that two major differences existed between his prisoner force and the American prisoners. His prisoner force was dressed very much alike in their military uniforms and if they were actually "marching," they could very likely be mistaken for a military unit. By contrast, our prisoner force had no matching uniforms and although we walked on the roadway in a column, we did not "march" line abreast. Our forces were considerably less disciplined with respect to staying in any type of military formation, which could be to our advantage when sighted by an aircraft intent on destroying enemy troops.

The Commandant thanked me, and the discussion was terminated. I was taken to a room in an outer office where I was offered a cup of coffee. I requested and was provided with water. After a few minutes, an orderly brought in some sort of sausage and bread. I didn't hesitate to accept the food. I tried to act casual as I gulped it down, but there was no disguising the fact that I was very hungry.

A German guard arrived to take me back to the prison compound where I was to remain in one of the barracks for the remainder of the afternoon. I was finally able to determine the details of the strafing attack and the events preceding the attack. The first shocking news was that this particular prison housed the majority of the British Officers captured early in the war. In addition to prisoners who had been captured in early 1940 by the Germans at Dunkerque in the first battle of the war, there were also prisoners who had been captured during the German parachute invasion of the island of Crete and in Libya, South Africa in 1941. The survivors of the Dieppe massacre, almost all Canadians, were also incarcerated at Oflag VIIB. The majority of these men had been prisoners for four or five long years.

With respect to the strafing attack, I was told the following:

"The prisoners had evacuated the compound in an orderly fashion and were maintaining fairly good formation when their group was sighted by an American P-38. The aircraft circled the formation at low altitude and when flying overhead, one of the German guards fired his rifle at the aircraft. There was no confirmation that the pilot was aware that his aircraft had been fired upon. The P-38 departed the area only to return in a few minutes, this time accompanied by two P-47s. The pilots of the P-47s made one strafing run on the column of prisoners. The strafing pattern was made at a forty-five degree angle to the formation. Despite the fears of many, the aircraft did not return for additional strafing runs. The casualties from just the one attack were severe."

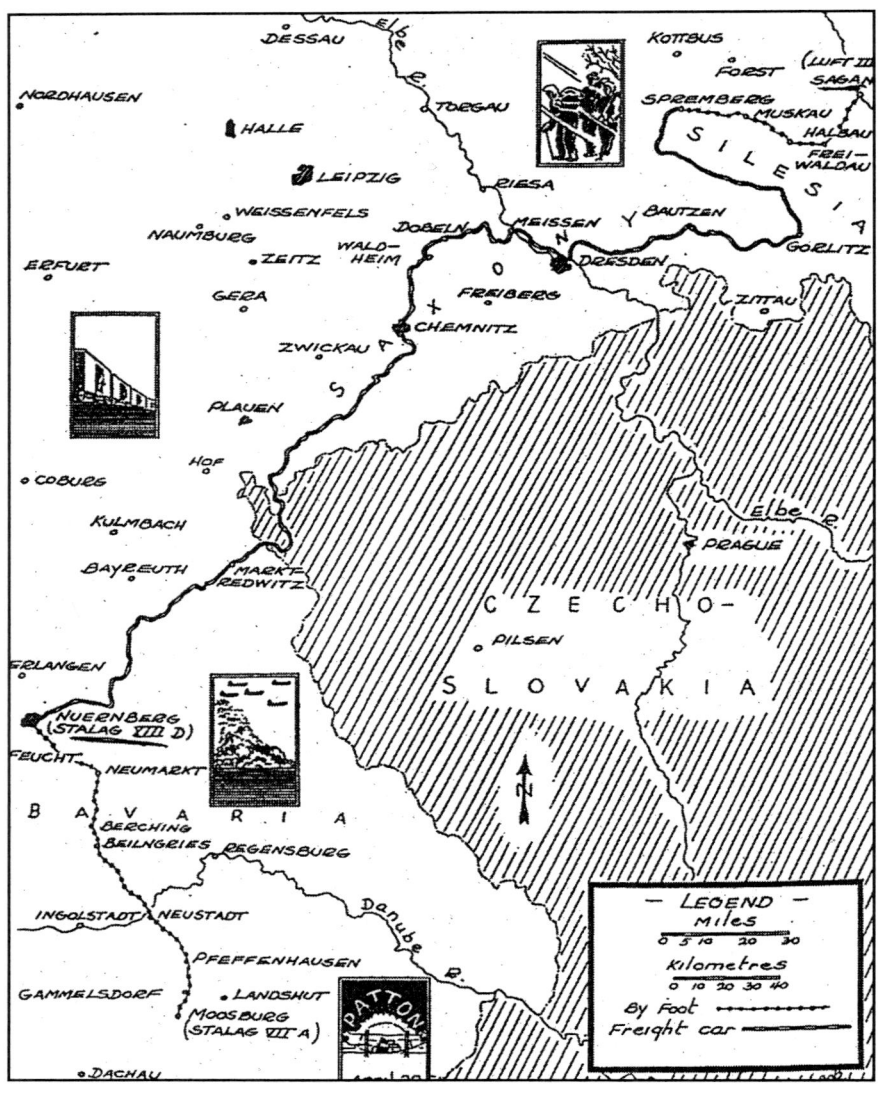

Evacuation Routes as prisoners from Stalag Luft III were moved from Sagan to Nurenberg and Moosburg

Stalag VIIA

For the safety of the prisoner force and to administer to the dead and wounded, the Commandant ordered the prisoners to be returned to the compound. Those prisoners who were wounded, but not needing hospitalization, would be evacuated by vehicle at nightfall. The rest of the prisoners would continue their march by foot as soon as possible.

I don't know whether it was the Germans or the British Senior officers who made the decision for me to travel in one of the trucks, but it was obvious to some that I was not in the best condition for further travel by foot. I didn't object to this decision; I knew I didn't have the physical strength to attempt any further escapes.

I was the last one to board a truck. In addition to prisoners, the truck was packed with highly valued personal items saved over the years. Although somewhat crowded, it wasn't an uncomfortable ride. We appeared to be traveling on a main highway. The headlights were shaded and I admired the ability of the drivers as they drove in the darkness. I slept most of the way and awakened when we arrived in the city of Moosburg. It was daylight when we entered a large prison compound. We had arrived at Stalag VIIA.

I stayed with the British prisoner force as we were taken to a barracks area that had evidently been made available for occupation by the British Officers. The barracks were not partitioned and contained long rows of double-deck beds that extended the length of the building. It was not as crowded as the barracks at Nuremberg. I had a top bunk and a British Flying officer from South Africa occupied the lower bunk. The mattresses appeared to be new, but after my experiences with fleas and bedbugs at Nuremberg, I was very skeptical of using a mattress. Fortunately, I hadn't encountered any vermin since departing the prison at

Nuremberg, and that in itself was a form of freedom.

I don't know how many prisoners occupied this Stalag, but the most quoted "rumor" was 27,000, its supposed limit. Some prisoners were in tents, so the prison must have been housing many more prisoners that its' designed capacity.

There were a myriad of different compounds with representatives from every nation and nationality in the Allied forces. The Russian compound was adjacent to the American compound. There was a separate compound for the enlisted prisoners. Tents had been set up in many sections of the compounds as prisoners from all over the Reich poured into this crater of human misery. Food from the Red Cross parcels was supposedly available. I was told some prisoners had been receiving a parcel a week, but I still didn't believe it.

I was anxious to see if I could find my old roommates from Stalag Luft III. We had been told that the South Compound prisoners had been transported here in 40 and 8 boxcars last January when I was separated from my prisoner roommates.

I had just decided to rest on my bunk before attempting to leave the area in search of my friends when the British Officer in the lower bunk introduced himself. His name was Mueller. He was tall with dark hair and eyes. I commented that he didn't look like someone who would have a German name. His response was that he owed his life to the name "Mueller." He thus began a story that will be embedded in my memory the rest of my life.

Mueller was one of the participants in the "Great Escape" from the North Compound at Stalag Luft III on March 26th, 1944. I have previously discussed the events of this escape, as well as the murder of fifty of the escapees by order of Hitler. Mueller was one of the seventy-five or so who were able to get clear of the area after escaping through the tunnel in the North compound. The German High Command took immediate steps to alert all areas to be on the lookout for these escapees, and within a few days all but two or three had been apprehended.

The recaptured prisoners were not immediately returned to the prison camp at Sagan (Stalag Luft III.) Gorlitz, a town located less than forty miles south of Stalag Luft III, was the collecting point for all the recaptured prisoners. After being apprehended, the prisoners were told they would be returned to Stalag Luft III when transportation plans had been completed. When the transportation arrived, the men who were to escort them were dressed in civilian suits. There were a few men in military uniform but none in the uniform of the Luftwaffe (Air Force.) The men were loaded into the vehicles, apparently on their way back to the prison camp. Enroute, the caravan stopped and the prisoners were told that it was a rest stop where the men could relieve themselves. After all the vehicles had stopped and the prisoners were milling about, they were required to line up and a roll call was taken. As each prisoner's name was called, he was to step out and form with a new group. Mueller's name was called. As he stepped forward, the man calling the names beckoned him to approach. When he did, the man asked, "Your name is Mueller?" Mueller replied in the affirmative. The caller then said, "*My* name is Mueller! You will long remember this day!" He then paused and told Mueller to return to his previous position. The men whose names had not been called, including Mueller, were returned to their vehicles and transported to Stalag Luft III. The other fifty men who responded when their names were called were never delivered to the Stalag. They were all murdered in an area near the roadway. The instructions by Hitler had been carried out. Flight Lieutenant Mueller was spared because of his name. A chilling true story!

The day after arrival at Moosburg I finally located my friends and roommates from Stalag Luft III. It was a joyous reunion. There had been much conjecture among them about whether or not I had escaped and reached freedom. Lott was afraid I might have been captured and that I hadn't survived. He was still carrying the sealed letter I had written to my parents prior to the escape attempt in January. He said that one of his greatest fears was that he might have had to deliver the letter as promised. It was an emotional moment for both of us when he returned the sealed letter to me.

I joined the food pool that Dale Perkins, Tom DeCaro and Chester Lott had formed after arriving at Moosburg. I continued to sleep in the barracks where I was fortunate enough to have a bunk, but I shared all the food I received with the other three good friends.

Seeking my escape partner, Glenn Oster, I discovered that he had joined up with his crew bombardier, Jack Nosser, and they had exchanged their "dog tag" identities with two enlisted prisoners. Both men had departed the prison camp and were part of a "work" party with other enlisted prisoners who were scheduled to do farm work in a location near Munich, Germany. The purpose of the exchange of identity was based on the premise that there would be more opportunities for escape while on a work party. The bombardier on my crew, Bill (Dusty) Runner, was in the prison hospital and it was reported that he had pneumonia but was recovering.

I had no knowledge of where or how we were receiving news reports, but there was every indication that Allied Army forces were moving in our direction. Along with the "good" news were the rumors that the Germans were going to force us to evacuate the prison camp at Moosburg and begin another forced march to the south. It is difficult to believe that they would attempt to move us in the face of reports that some elements of the 3rd Army were already closing in on our location.

New prisoners evacuated from other locations continued to pour into this Stalag. The tents already in place when I arrived contained a mass of humanity. There were not enough beds in some of the compounds, forcing some prisoners to sleep outside on the ground.

Most of the cooking was done on the grounds outside the barracks and the tents. Bed boards, barracks wall siding, wood stripped out of the attics and even the wooden supports for the bomb trenches were fair game for the cook stoves. The outside cook stoves were mostly constructed from "Klim" cans, the powdered milk containers in the Red Cross food parcels.

The faces and bodies of my friends had changed considerably since the days at Stalag Luft III. All had lost considerable weight. Their faces were sallow and their eyes seemed to have grown larger. With the exception of Bill Runner, none of my close friends had a serious illness, but it was obvious that we were slowly starving. As bad as the conditions seemed to be at Moosburg, this place was still an improvement over the prison camp at Nuremberg.

Main Road of Stalag VIIA with a checkpoint.
(Photo: Moosburg Communal Archives)

Freedom at Last!

It was the last week of April 1945 and the sounds of artillery fire had been moving closer each day. Low flying Me-109's (Messerschmitts) and FW-190's (Focke Wulfs) flew a path over the prison compound, causing a mixture of excitement and fear to permeate our very existence. Sleep was difficult as we dreamed day and night about the future.

On April 28th, we become aware that American forces were in the vicinity. The rumor was that the Germans had agreed to declare the prison camp neutral territory. We didn't know how such an agreement would affect us.

Late that evening, I was in Chester Lott's barracks. Shortly after my arrival, we were told that there would be some type of negotiations taking place in his barracks. Suddenly, there was a commotion at the entrance to the barracks and someone called "Attention!" All discussion ceased as two German Officers entered the building and started down the center aisle of the barracks. An American Colonel in khaki uniform followed the two Germans. Following the Colonel was a tall blond American Major with a holstered Army "45" hanging at his waist. They walked rapidly down the corridor. As the Major grew nearer, I recognized him. As he passed my position, I spontaneously called out his name. "Whitfield." The major slowed and looked back but had no time to linger and continued down the corridor. He had urgent business and it was doubtful that he had recognized me in the dim light. I was only one in a sea of prisoner faces. I fought back the urge to follow him.

It was rumored that a meeting to decide what ground rules could be negotiated with respect to protecting the prisoners was taking place in the barracks. It was approaching the time for "lights out" and I needed to return to my own barracks. I had no opportunity to see Whitfield again.

Seeing Whitfield under those circumstances had been unbelievable. My first assignment after completing basic training in the Army Air Corps in 1941 was to be an apprentice aircraft mechanic on BT-13's (aircraft basic trainers) at Bakersfield, California. I was a Private assigned to S/Sgt Whitfield's aircraft maintenance crew. I applied for Enlisted Pilot Training, as did Sergeant Whitfield. My application was delayed but Whitfield left Bakersfield and reported to a primary flight school. He returned a short time later when it was discovered that he was colorblind. Whitfield then applied for Officer's Candidate school and was accepted. He departed for Ft. Benning, Georgia, about the time I left Bakersfield to begin my pilot training. I had not had any contact with Whitfield since early 1942, when we both departed to begin training in our respective schools.

I could hardly contain my emotions as I made my way back to the barracks. I had difficulty trying to sleep that night. The excitement of seeing my friend, Whitfield, and the realization that American Army forces were possibly in a position to liberate the entire prison population had caused a maelstrom of mixed thoughts to race through my mind.

On Sunday, April 29th, I awakened to the distant sound of bombs or artillery fire. We were greeted with the news that the Germans had not agreed to withdraw their forces from the area surrounding the prison compound. Apparently, the American Officer who represented the Allied forces had informed the German negotiators that American forces would forcibly take control of the prison camp and surrounding area that morning.

I raced over to the barracks where Chester Lott and Dale Perkins were heating coffee for breakfast. They had received the same information about the status of the camp, and the word was being passed from barracks to barracks that we should remain inside the barracks in the event we heard gunfire. There had already been reports that several tanks had been sighted outside the prison, but they had been identified as German.

I was outside the barracks when a P-51 flew at low altitude over the campsite. The prisoners who witnessed the flyover gave out a thunderous roar. When a German guard in one of the towers fired at the P-51, the aircraft made a rapid climbing turn back in our direction. Then the P-51 unleashed a volley of fire from its guns and the tower crumpled in a mass of twisted lumber. We didn't have time to see if the guard survived because we heard gunshots and the whine of bullets coming from an unidentified direction. We scrambled back into our barracks.

Scared and excited, we waited anxiously for word that the battle might be over. We received information that all the prison guards were leaving their posts and departing the area of the prison compound. Peering out the window, someone sighted what he thought was an American tank. The tank disappeared from view and we could hear the muffled sound of explosions somewhere near the prison compound. These new sounds were rumored to be mortars, but it was difficult to determine exactly what targets were under attack. We had not heard any explosions within the prison complex other than small arms fire and the damage done by the P-51. One prisoner was reported to have been shot. He had been running across the road between the barracks when a ricocheting bullet struck him in the leg.

The sounds of distant combat went on for about two hours before they gradually abated. Quiet returned as the battle forces moved on to the east. I left the barracks area and headed toward the prison main gate. We were all milling about, wondering what would happen next when we heard the sound of an approaching tank. I climbed to the roof of a barracks close to the gate entrance. Chester Lott was with me, as were several other prisoners who were seeking a better view of the activities outside our prison. Suddenly a huge tank appeared on the road headed in the direction of the main gate. Our fears gave way to shouts of joy when we saw the most beautiful flag in the world unfurl from the tank turret. The tank kept coming directly toward the main gate and didn't stop. It crumpled the gate and kept right on moving. It came to a complete stop only when it was in the prison compound and further movement would have endangered the lives of the joyous prisoners who were surrounding the tank.

It was the moment we had all hoped and dreamed would someday come true. I stood there with my friend, Chester Lott, listening to the laughter and shouts of joy. I wanted to shout with joy too, but all I could do was stand there, not daring to believe that it was over, that I was free, that all of us were free. I could feel the emotion taking hold and I suddenly wanted to be alone. I choked back tears. I looked over at Chester. He was grinning at me. Suddenly we were both laughing and crying and life was very good indeed.

Back on the ground, I stayed in the background waiting and watching as our liberators passed rations from the monstrous tank to the prisoners surrounding the adjacent area. Lt/ Col Clark and several other officers climbed aboard the tank and someone took pictures of the event. There were frequent shouts as soldiers from the 14th Armored Division called out names of prisoners, hoping that a brother or friend of the past might be found among the thousands of cheering faces.

Someone called out Dale Perkins' name and Dale was shocked to discover that a soldier from his hometown — Struthers, Ohio — was one of our liberators. I was with Dale when his high school classmate found him. The soldier was an infantryman and a platoon leader assigned to a tank battalion. After a brief meeting with Perkins, his friend departed with the promise that he would be back at eight o'clock the next morning with a jeep to take Perkins with him to the house where most of his platoon was to be temporarily quartered. At my request, Perkins asked that I be included in this outing. Happily, the response was "yes."

It was sometime later when I became aware of additional activity at the main gate. General Patton, 3rd Army Commander, had arrived. His jeep looked factory fresh with flags attached to both sides of the windshield. The General stood tall and resplendent in his uniform; his two pearl-handed revolvers could not be overlooked. He had on jodhpur riding breeches and highly polished boots. I was standing too far back to hear his words as he spoke to those around him, but the cheers gave credence to the fact that his words were appropriate for the occasion. Suddenly he was gone, but his presence and his words were an inspiration to all who had been close enough to see and hear him.

There was little sleep that night. Excitement intermingled with confusion had taken control. The euphoria was mixed with feelings of uncertainty as each prisoner tried to visualize a future that promised a new way of life.

For our protection, our prison camp leaders requested that we not attempt to leave the prison compounds unless escorted by our liberators. There were already rumors that the majority of the Russian prisoners had left the confines of their compound and were entering the town of Moosburg. Russian prisoners were also intermingling with prisoners from other compounds, exchanging greetings and trading items they had obtained from outside the prison.

My thoughts kept reverting back to the letter I had written to Mary Lee Valentine, wherein I had made a written commitment expressing my desire to marry her. That letter had been written over two years ago, just before my overseas deployment. Although she had faithfully written to me while I was imprisoned at Stalag Luft III, she had never acknowledged receiving that letter. I hadn't heard from her in the past six months. Was it possible that she could still be waiting for me? Or had she grown tired of waiting and found someone else? My feelings toward her remained unchanged, and I had a queasy feeling in the pit of my stomach when I thought that I might have lost her forever. Those kinds of thoughts had to be controlled or, in the words of the English prisoners, you would "go around the bend." For me, prayer was the best antidote.

Liberation Day
29 April 1945

Lt/Col. Clark
X-Activity Chief

Lt/Col Stillman   Lt Schrupp

Stalag VII, Moosburg, Germany. Main Corridor Road

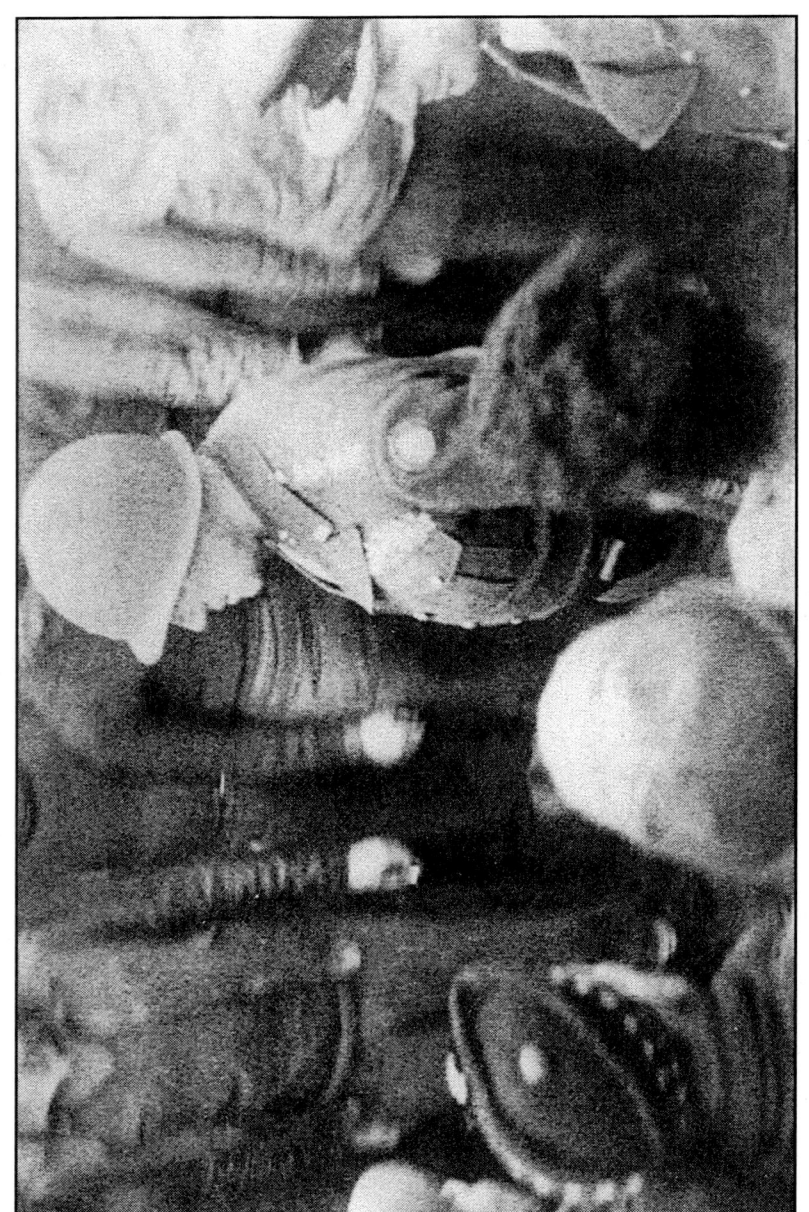

General Patton at Stalg VIIA. His forces, the 14th Armoured Division, liberated the prisoners at Moosburg, Germany

PART III THE WAR MARCHES ON

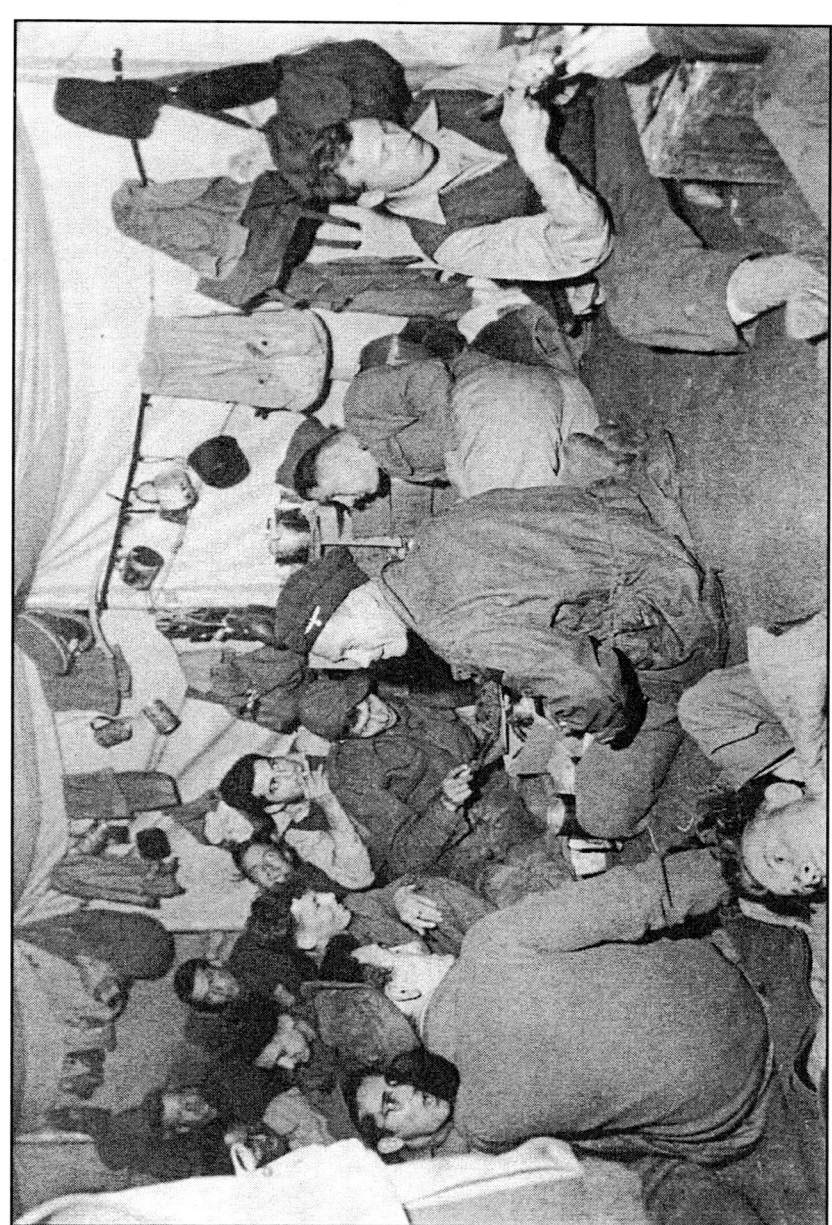

Tent City at Moosburg, liberated prisoners waiting to be evacuated to Camp Lucky Strike, LaHavre, France

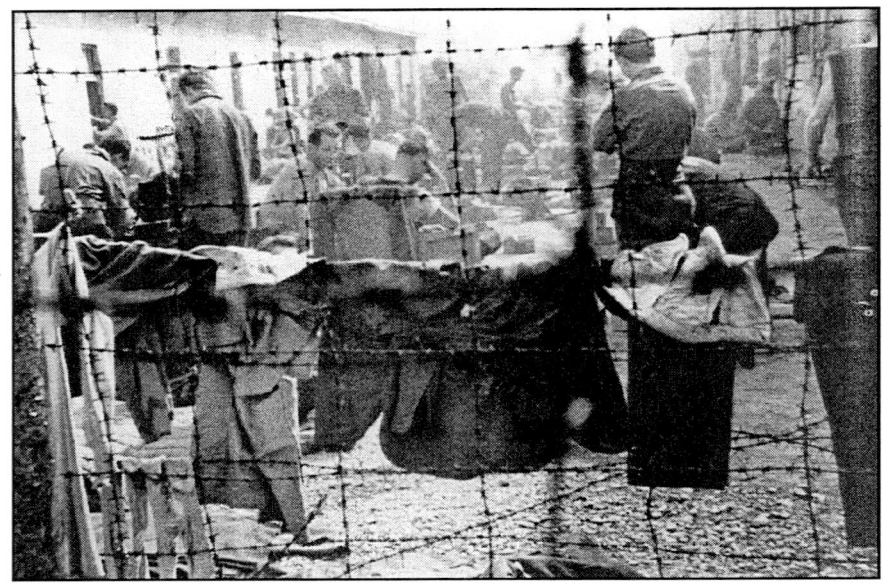
Chaos at Moosburg

Moosburg Hilton

Moosburg Library

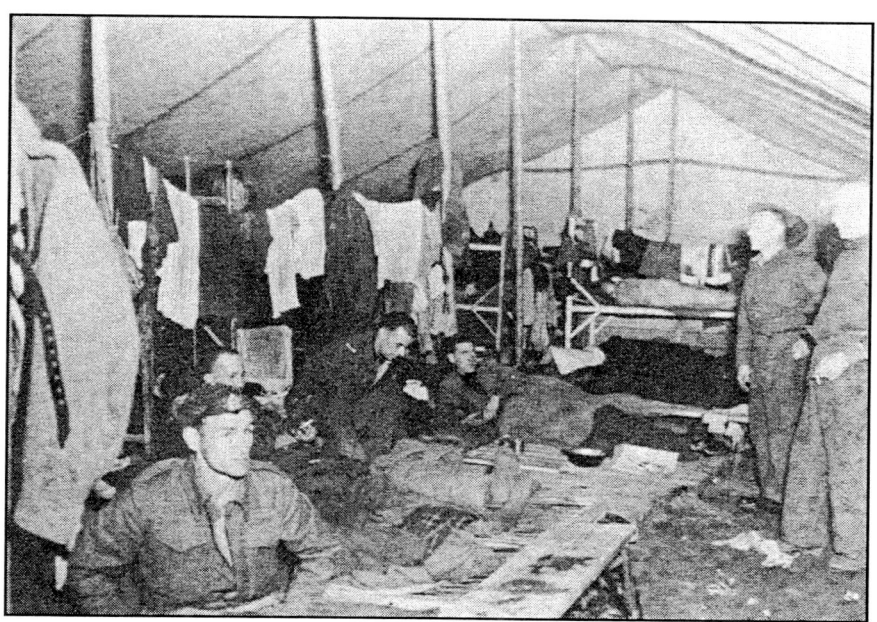
Moosburg Hilton Annex

Moosburg Hilton Annex

Moosburg Chefs, above right - Dale Perkins

PART III THE WAR MARCHES ON 225

LIBERATION ! April 29, 1945

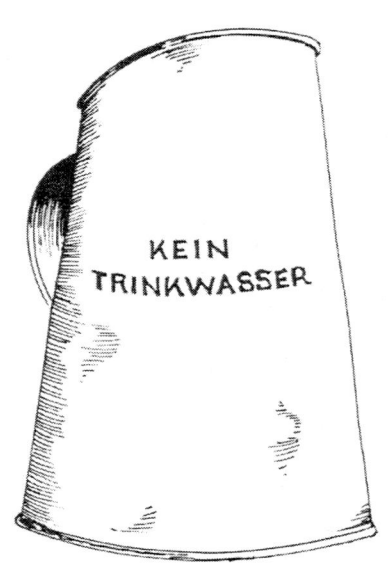

A New World Begins

It was the morning of April 30th, 1945. As I left my barracks, I could hardly contain my excitement. As promised, Dale Perkins' friend had sent a jeep and a driver. We had no problems leaving the prison compound. The first stop was a house that a squad of infantrymen had taken over for their temporary quarters. The driver informed us that the first order of business was breakfast. A young rifleman was cooking eggs in a large flat-bottomed pan. He asked us how many scrambled eggs we wanted. Before we had a chance to respond, he said, "How about a dozen apiece?" We smilingly agreed. I ate my eggs with some "hardtack" biscuits. Dale was unable to finish his eggs, so I volunteered to help him out.

Members of this infantry platoon had been on the move for several days without any rest. During the short stay at Moosburg they had a chance to catch up on their sleep. One by one, the young men came down from the upstairs bedrooms to have breakfast. We stayed about an hour at this location. As we left, the men were either cleaning their rifles or gathering up their gear in preparation for moving out. Dale and I watched them as they prepared to leave. We thanked them for our freedom. These young men risked death every day to save our lives. It was a sobering departure for all of us.

Our assigned escort drove us into the middle of the town of Moosburg where there was more evidence of looting than a battle. We ran into a group of former Russian prisoners who greeted us with hugs and handshakes. One Russian had four or five swords, one of which he handed to me. I placed it in the jeep.

We drove around the central city area and then into a residential section of the city. A woman standing in her backyard motioned us to come closer. She spoke English and wanted to know if we would protect her from the Russians. She said that her neighbors were all in hiding because they feared the Russians. Our driver tried to reassure her that the American soldiers would insure that she was not harmed. We left knowing full well that unless an American force was near her home, there was little that could be done to protect her.

Shortly after noon, the driver dropped us off at a Tank Destroyer outfit. He said that this unit had regular cooks and that the infantry riflemen often went there for food when circumstances permitted. We were welcomed into their "chow" line and filled our metal trays with food. This was the first time that we had tasted white bread. I thought it tasted just like Angel Food cake. Dale didn't argue as he ate a huge chunk of the bread. We ate and talked with personnel from this unit. We marveled at the size of the guns that were utilized to destroy tanks. I hadn't known there were guns designed to disable tanks.

It was late in the afternoon when we stopped by the house where the infantrymen had been staying. The platoon had moved out but the house and goods in the house had been left intact. I found a basket and filled it full of eggs. The eggs were packed in a large center-divided wooden box. When filled, this box was identical to what we called a "case of eggs" back home.

It was approaching darkness when we returned to the prison compound. I delivered the eggs to Chester Lott for the following morning. Lott, De Caro, and several other former roommates at Stalag Luft III had pooled their food for a celebration "bash." A big cake had been baked and our friends were waiting for Perkins and me to return before beginning the feast.

I was able to eat only a small piece of the cake before I began to feel the nauseous effects of overeating. My stomach began to swell and I had to leave the celebrants and return to my barracks. The next few hours were spent in agony as I tried to rid myself of the food that was bloating my stomach. Lt. Mueller was sympathetic and tried to help, but it was several hours before I had vomited enough to relieve the stomach pain. My painful groans were loud enough to awaken the entire barracks so I spent most of the night sitting on a log between the barracks and the latrine.

Mueller stayed with me part of the time. He obtained some tooth powder from a friend. It contained baking soda, which helped relieve some of the gastric pain.

All in all, I had a miserable night, but by morning, I was almost back to normal. I drank only fluids for the remainder of the day. I had also decided to leave the compound the following morning.

Knowing that I would soon be leaving, I attempted to find Bill Runner, but in the confusion was unable to locate him. He had been in the hospital but I was told our liberators had removed the patients. The hospital was located in the same Lager where the Germans had maintained our records. Bill had somehow obtained Joe Johnson's and my personnel records. Another prisoner had given the records to Joe while I was out of the prison compound. My picture was missing from my record but Joe's record was intact.

It was perhaps too early to complete plans to evacuate thousands of prisoners, but once I was free, I couldn't continue to live in the squalor of the prison compound. While visiting with soldiers from the Tank Destroyer unit, I had inquired about the nearest hospital where dental care could be provided. I had lost a cap on a tooth and suspected I also had several cavities that needed filling. I was told that the nearest large Allied hospital was located in Epinal, France. Epinal was near the German border and, most important, was on the main supply route used by Allied forces. With this knowledge and with Epinal being my destination, I informed Chester Lott and the rest of my former roommates that I was going to leave the prison compound the following day. I invited anyone who so desired to join me. Chester Lott and Dale Perkins indicated their willingness to make the trip with me. I gave the newly acquired sword to Joe Johnson, my co-pilot. Joe was a patient man and he had elected to wait in the prison compound until the promised air transportation had arrived.

Preparation for departure was simple. My belongings consisted of the clothes I was wearing, dog tags, my pilot wings, lieutenant bars and the personnel card — minus my picture. We encountered no problems while leaving the prison compound. Early in the morning on May 2nd, 1945, we simply walked over an area where the fence had been knocked down, disappeared in the woods and then walked to a nearby main highway where we flagged down the first GI truck we sighted that was traveling in a westerly direction. I told the driver that our destination was the hospital at Epinal, France. After a short discussion with the driver, we were invited to climb aboard and in a few minutes, we were out of the city of Moosburg and on our way to France. Truly, this was the first day of real freedom.

The truck driver had a re-supply schedule to meet and he drove without stopping for several hours. The route he followed started in a northeasterly direction, passing through the outskirts of the German city of Wurzburg. This city had been totally destroyed. We saw no signs of life and there was not one building left standing. The scene exemplified the horror and tragedy of war. What we viewed had a sobering effect on the three of us and for a short time, the elation over our freedom was subdued. I gave silent thanks to our Lord for our freedom and a prayer for those who at one time had lived a peaceful existence in this city.

Departing Wurzburg, we followed a roadway in a southeasterly direction. The devastation effects of warfare were evident in all directions. We arrived in Epinal, France in the afternoon. The young truck driver knew exactly where the hospital was located and he delivered us to the entrance. After we had answered questions about our status, we were accepted as patients. The first order of business was to take a delousing shower. With the exception of the A-2 leather jacket, all my clothing was taken away to be destroyed. Lott and Perkins were given the same treatment. We were assigned beds, but were considered ambulatory patients. I was scheduled to see a dentist the following morning and the three of us were to receive physicals. New clothing would be issued after the physicals. There were no complaints about the hospital food that was served after the showers, but we were cautioned to eat small amounts of food and were offered frequent snacks. I was already very familiar with the problems associated with overeating.

We were provided with stationary and in the evening I wrote to my mother and father. The last letter I had received from home had been written by my mother on Thanksgiving Day in 1944. A German guard had given the letter to me in January 1945 while I was still in solitary confinement at Stalag Luft III. I had received no mail or word from home for the past five months.

The added bonus for this day was a bed with a pillow and clean, vermin-free sheets and bedding.

The next three days brought about a flurry of activity. The dental work was completed and the three of us had complete physical examinations. Chester and Dale completed their physicals while I was in the dental chair. The physical was comprehensive, the biggest concern expressed by the examining doctor being "extreme malnutrition." My weight had dropped to one hundred and three pounds. I had weighed one hundred and forty-eight pounds prior to being captured nineteen months earlier. Except for malnutrition, there were no other physical problems reported.

We were issued new clothing and introduced to the new Eisenhower jackets with matching trousers. What a great feeling it was to feel clean and to know that there was no vermin hiding in your clothing! My A-2 jacket had been taken somewhere for cleaning and it was returned to me.

Now, as far as I was concerned, we were all set to continue on our way. When we first arrived in Epinal, I had informed the Hospital Adjutant of our intention to continue traveling to Le Havre, France where prisoners of war were being processed for shipment back to the United States. I was not prepared for the news that I was to be the "Troop Commander" for a mixed cadre of seventy-seven patients who were being discharged from the hospital and transported by rail to camp "Lucky Strike" in the port city of Le Havre. Dale Perkins and Chester Lott were on the same orders, so at least we would continue to travel together. Interestingly, the former patients were a composite group representing the United States, United Kingdom, Canada, Australia and New Zealand. I was provided with the medical records for several of the men who were scheduled to continue medical treatment at their new destination. I had been reminded very early after release from prison that responsibility is a part of the framework of freedom.

The train departed Epinal, France at 17:45 on May 8th, 1945 and we were all aboard.

Epinal Hospital

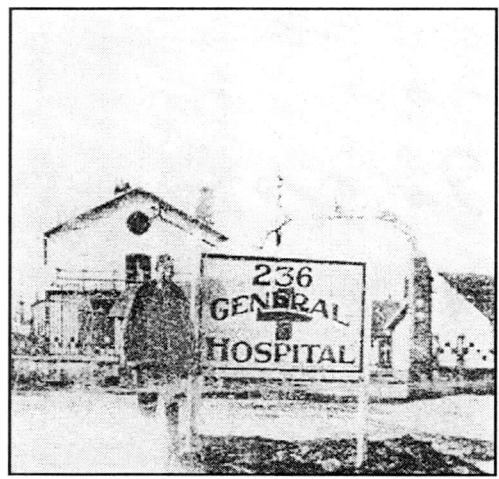

PART IV

AFTER LIBERATION

Camp Lucky Strike

Prior to leaving camp "Lucky Strike," the melting pot for repatriated Allied Prisoners of War located at Le Havre, France, I was able to very briefly visit with three former members of my crew who had been imprisoned in Stalag 17B located at Krems, Poland.

Stalag 17B was one of the main prison camps the Germans had designated to imprison Allied air crew, Non-Commissioned Officers. I met with Sherman Sly, the engineer and top turret gunner, Louis Brown, the asst. engineer - ball turret gunner, and Robert Soloman, the left waist gunner. All were in good spirits having survived their ordeal without apparent physical injury; however the long marches and lack of food had taken a toll as their faces were drawn and their bodies were thin.

I was unable to locate Charles Groth during the three days that I was in the camp, but I was assured by the other crew members that he had arrived at Camp Lucky strike and was in reasonably good health. Bill Runner was still in a hospital recovering from pneumonia. He had been one of the first prisoners evacuated from the prison camp at Moosburg (Stalag 7A) and was probably going to return to the United States by air.

I remained at Le Havre for three days after being informed that it might be as long as three weeks before ocean going transportation would be available to send us back to the United States. I was impatient and had no desire to spend the next several weeks in the crowded confinement of a tent while awaiting transportation.

Thomas DeCaro, Dale Perkins and I went to the train station at Le Havre one evening and just before a train bound for Paris departed, we jumped aboard. After arrival in Paris, we managed to spend the remainder of the night in a place operated by the Red Cross.

There was a huge Allied Officers' mess located in downtown Paris and after receiving partial payments we decided to stay at a nearby hotel and eat as often as possible at this dining hall from "Paradise."

We had been in Paris for about a week when we had the good fortune to dine with an Army Major who worked in Military Transportation. He wanted to help us and did so by providing us with train orders to the city of Nice, on the French Riviera. Nice was the R&R (rest and recuperation) center for Allied airmen. We had a deluxe compartment. Champagne along with a dinner was served to us as we viewed the passing countryside and enjoyed the luxury of our newly found freedom.

The first day at the Riviera, Tom DeCaro, claiming to be an expert "sail boater," sailed the three of us out into the beautiful Mediterranean. We had been in the water for over an hour when we decided it was time to return to shore. Unfortunately, the wind was suddenly completely calm and the sail simply drooped like a broken wing. The sun rays were intense so we stayed in the water and tried to push the boat toward the shore. It was another hour before the wind picked up enough so that we could use the sail and proceed back to the safety of dry land.

We were all three badly sun burned and went to an Aid Station to get help. For the next two days we were unable to do much sight seeing and we were also running out of money. We had used up our authorized partial payments and in fact, by going to two different pay stations, we had already received double the authorized amount of payment. We were broke and anxious to go home.

As fortune would have it, there was a Saturday night dance at the Officers Club and we were greeted by a B-17 pilot who had just flown in a group of R & R troops stationed in Italy. He was departing the next day for Caserta Army Air Base located near Naples, Italy. I told him that we were Ex-Pows' and that we were seeking a way to be airlifted home. Caserta was the staging base for airlift for that area and he promised us that he would make room for us aboard his B-17, but that we were on our own to explain our presence at Caserta.

It was a Sunday when we arrived at Caserta so it wasn't until the next morning that we reported in to a Major and attempted to explain our presence in Italy. When it was disclosed that we were not prisoners in Italy or the Baltic, there was considerable consternation displayed and lengthy discussion regarding our status. There was even the possibility that we would be returned to Camp Lucky Strike at Le Havre. We were told that the Military Police in Paris were rounding up all of the ex-prisoners that had migrated to Paris and that we could be considered as "Absent without Leave." We kept silent except for repeating that we were now under Allied control and that we were just seeking a faster route home.

Finally, it was decided that the easiest solution to the problem would be to just put us on orders and get rid of us by sending us home - by air. Our goal had been accomplished!

Tent City at Camp Lucky Strike. LaHavre, France

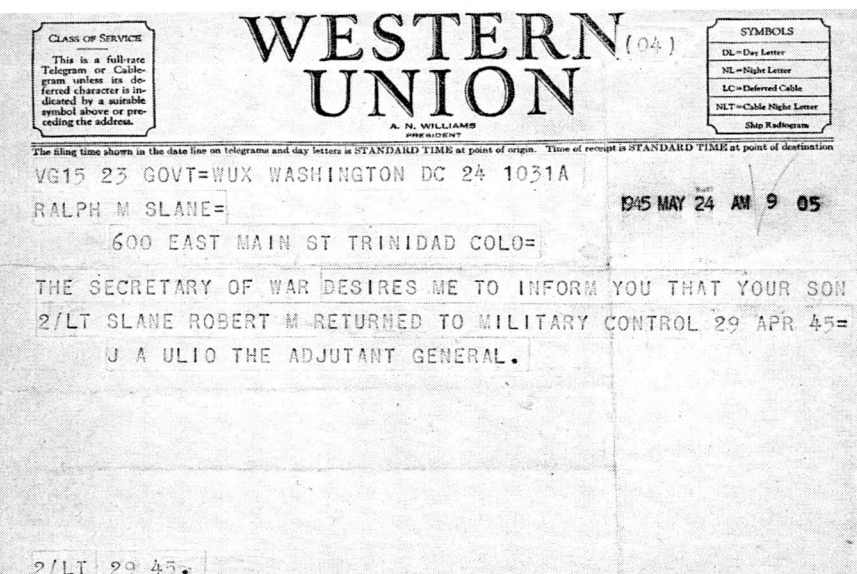

24 May 1945

23 June 1945

Home At Last

We had a few days to wait but finally the day came for departure. Dale was on the first plane to depart and I was on one that followed. Tom DeCaro missed his flight.

The flight home was via Casa Blanca, the Azores and then direct to New York. Upon arrival at New York I discovered that air transportation was not possible. The trains could offer no assurance of ready transport to a location where I could obtain a flight home. After obtaining another partial payment of about $250, I found my way to a trucking firm and was offered a ride out of the city. This truck was going on to the south so I thanked the driver and started hitchhiking on the Pennsylvania turnpike. I hitchhiked from New York to Chicago and was able to purchase an airline ticket in Chicago for a flight to Denver, Colorado.

During a waiting period in Denver I placed a phone call to the student nurses' home (St. Margaret's Hall) in Boise, Idaho. I was hoping to contact Mary Lee Valentine. I was informed that she was "no longer at St. Luke's hospital" and that she was in Salem, Oregon. There was no further explanation provided and I was reluctant to ask any further questions for fear the answer would be that she had perhaps found someone else. My last letter from her had been written in October of 1944 - nine months earlier. On the train trip from Denver to my home in Trinidad, Colorado, I kept recalling the stories of fellow prisoners who had received "dear John" letters and I had a feeling of dread that seemed to be centered in the pit of my stomach.

My despair was short lived. My mother had been in contact with Mary Lee and she quickly put my mind at ease when she told me that Lee was in Salem as part of her training to become a nurse. I wasted no time! I called her, asked her to marry me - she said "yes" and with permission of her Director of Nurses' at St. Luke's hospital she was granted a 10 day leave of absence. I married my "Valentine" on the 3rd of July, 1945. Since she had two more months of training to complete before graduation and the rules at the time were that a student nurse must be single, our marriage was more or less a "secret." After graduation from nurses' training she joined me at my new assignment in New Mexico.

Life Begins Anew

When we departed the camp at La Havre, France and finally returned to the United States, we, (my former combat crew members) went our separate ways. With the exception of Glenn Foster, the navigator and Bill Runner, the bombardier, it was many long years before I spoke to or made contact with other members of my combat crew.

During the period when I was a prisoner my mother had corresponded regularly with Glenn Foster's wife as well as Bill Runner's mother and it was partly because of her diligence in writing that I kept up with both Glenn and Bill. The two, like me, had remained on active duty and Bill Runner was accepted for pilot training and was one of the first applicants to receive a "Regular" Officer commission. In 1947 we received word that Bill Runner had been killed in an automobile accident. I did not learn of his death for several weeks after the accident and I was late in sending my regrets to his mother. His loss, just as he was beginning a new career after spending a year and half as a prisoner of war, was doubly tragic.

As the years passed, we remained in frequent contact with Glenn and Gloria Foster. Their first child had been born while Glenn was in Switzerland. Each year there seemed to be a new baby. The final tally was 16 children.

When the atomic bombs were dropped on Hiroshima and Nagasaki in early August of 1945 I was undergoing re-qualification training in the B-17. After the Japanese surrender agreement was signed, our re-training program dissolved. The B-17 bombers at Hobbs Army Air Base, New Mexico were flown to an airfield at Walnut Ridge, Arkansas where these valiant warriors were systematically destroyed. The closure of air bases and de-mobilization of military units was taking place so rapidly that life for a military family was pure chaos for the next several years.

The base at Hobbs, New Mexico was closed and we were transferred to the air base at Big Spring, Texas. Big Spring was deactivated and we were reassigned to Midland Air Base. At Midland my job, I was now a Captain, was to take a truck load of former flying officers, all Lieutenants, and proceed to the bombing range where our duties were to "clean the bomb range" by loading all of the old practice bomb casings in a truck and depositing them in a rail car. We were advised on a daily basis that if we did not care for the assignment that our requests to be relieved from active duty would readily be accepted.

The base at Midland closed and for a short period of time we were stationed at Lowry Air Base located at Denver, Colorado. While assigned at Lowry a massive reduction in force saw 147 officers involuntarily discharged at that base. I was on that discharge list, but I did not willingly accept a discharge and instead wrote a letter stating my case. I was retained in the Army Air Corps and sent to Merced Army Air Base in California. Lee and I had five different duty stations in the first year of our marriage. Our daughter, Judy, was born in the midst of all this turbulence in May of 1946. Our son, Tom, was born four years later - in 1950

We were at Sheppard Air Force Base in 1951, and I had just applied for flight training in the new jet bomber, the B-47, when a man scheduled to fill a non-flying job in Korea was suddenly withdrawn from the assignment and I was forced to fill his position. I had less than a week to settle my affairs and report to the port of debarkation in San Francisco

I was assigned to the 501st Tactical Control Group stationed in Soul, South Korea. It took me six months of letter writing and the assistance of a Congressman to have my request for a assignment to a tactical combat unit approved.

Note: This congressman was Congressman Chenowith. The same man who years earlier had written to me while I was a prisoner in Stalag Luft III, telling me that I had been promoted to 1st Lt.

Finally, I was assigned to the 3rd Bomb Wing at Kunson, South Korea. I had never flown a B-26 attack bomber, but by flying day and night for 10 days in the B-26, I was checked out, certified as combat ready, assigned a crew and scheduled to fly my first night combat mission in a B-26. That first mission was flown just 15 days after arrival at my new duty station. I completed 40 combat missions, all but one at night, before my normal one year rotation date arrived. During these missions, that often penetrated to areas near the Manchurian border, I had strapped to my body a 38 cal. Colt automatic and the standard issue Army 45 cal.- automatic. I also carried extra ammunition for each firearm. One thing was certain; I would never be a prisoner again!

I still stay in contact with my B-26 navigator, Bernard Waller. I flew the majority of my missions with Bernard; sharing with him the beauty and fear of incoming 40 mm fire streaking past our wings. His position in the glass nose of the aircraft seemed particularly vulnerable to enemy fire. Eighteen B-26 crews were lost in North Korea during the period that I was assigned to the 3rd Bomb Wing.

Upon my return to the United States from South Korea in June of 1952, I was assigned to Civil Air Patrol Headquarters at Washington, D.C. This was an assignment that I had not requested as I still had hope that my request for training in the new six engine jet bomber, the B-47, would be approved.

Although approval was finally granted to enter this program; I discovered that I was to first, before beginning check out in the B-47, complete a six month course in navigation and radar bombing. I completed this course but my request for formal B-47 aircraft commander flight training was then denied.

Since I was now navigator qualified it was determined that my training could best be utilized in the co-pilots position to provide assistance to the regular navigator by making celestial observations with a sextant. It was another year of flight as a co-pilot before I was to became a B-47 aircraft commander.

Korea, 1952. Dave Rutledge, Bernard Waller, Robert Slane

CLIMBING FROM THE COCKPIT ... of an Air Force B-26 light bomber after finishing another combat mission against the Communists in Northern Korea is Captain Robert M. Slane of Boise. Captain Slane has flown 15 combat missions with the 3rd Bomb Wing, which is attempting to cut the enemy's rail and supply lines in operation "Strangle." The captain's wife, Mrs. Mary Lee Slane, lives at 602 Village Lane, Boise.

Survivor

On 30 November, 1956, I was the aircraft commander and sole survivor of a B-47 accident in Canada that took the lives of three of my crew members. Our wing of B-47 bomber and tanker aircraft was participating in a large scale exercise that simulated an attack by an enemy force that would penetrate our northern borders and strike targets within the continental United States.

I was flying in a four ship formation of B-47's. I had a crew of three; Lt Richard Martin - co-pilot, Lt Donald Petty - navigator and another navigator, Lt. Max Workman. Max was a spare navigator along for the training. Since there was no ejection seat for more than the three primary crew members, Max would occupy a position in the aisle of the aircraft and by moving forward in the aisle he would be adjacent to and could work with the navigator. His escape exit in emergency would of necessity be through the main entrance hatch located in the aisle.

We had a long 13 hour mission scheduled. Departing from Barksdale AFB in Louisiana, the flight would fly northeast and refuel over the Atlantic after departing the eastern coast of the United States. We were to meet tanker aircraft for a second refueling as we passed near Greenland and turn to the northwest enroute to a geographic point near the Artic Circle. At the Artic Circle the flight was scheduled to turn southwest flying over Canada and then make simulated bomb runs as we penetrate the border and hit selected targets in the U.S.

During the flight our aircraft experienced multiple hydraulic problems with the power controls for the ailerons; however, the most serious consequence that we were aware of was that with complete aileron power control failure, we would be compelled to "hand fly" the aircraft without the boost from the power controls. This would mean a long and tiresome period of using additional physical strength to control the aircraft.

We were at 32,000 feet, still over Canada, when the formation made a turn movement to correct our position. The formation was loosely formed since the navigators were using radar as the primary source for maintaining our position in the formation. We were simulating weather conditions where the pilots could not fly visual formation and radar "station keeping" would provide information for corrective maneuvers.

Our main hydraulic system had given us indication of failure and we were using the emergency power control system for aileron control boost. We had been airborne for about nine hours.

I had just completed a 5 degree turn to the left and had centered the control wheel when the control wheel began a slow, steady turn to the right despite the fact that I was exerting pressure to keep the wheel centered. My co-pilot, Richard Martin, seated in an ejection seat behind me, in a tandem arrangement, suddenly asked me "why are we doing Mach .81 ?"

At the time of the co-pilot's question I had just alerted to the fact that there was something wrong with the aircraft controls. The aileron control wheel was slowly and steadily turning to the right and I could not by brute force stop the wheel turn movement. My reply to Richard's question was firm. "shut-up and get ready to get out of this thing." The only response I heard on the aircraft interphone was someone making a gasping sound, a sound of disbelief and possibly of terror.

I saw the left arm of my navigator, Lt. Petty, extend backwards, pointing to the exit in the aisle - directing the "fourth-man," Lt. Workman to go to that exit position. Max, who had no ejection seat, started scurrying back from the nose of the aircraft to this exit; located in the aisle below the pilot's position.

A series of unanticipated events occurred in a matter of seconds. The aileron control wheel continued the slow turn to the right and I called for Richard to help me hold and turn the control wheel back to center. All of the aileron power control lights were red indicating complete system failure. I was applying full left rudder and was using all of my strength to pull back and left on the control wheel - the wheel movement apparently could not be restrained.

I pulled off all power on all the engines and there was still no change in the wheel movement. I applied full power on the right wing engines – nothing changed. At this time the aircraft was in a left wing high attitude of about 60 degrees. The nose of the aircraft was positioned slightly below the horizon. During those few moments while I was trying to stop the movement of the control wheel, I had a feeling like none I had ever experienced. I knew then that unless I could stop the turn of the control wheel that we were flying a doomed aircraft. I was experiencing the horror and terror of that knowledge.

I had just given the ejection order when the aircraft very suddenly and violently rolled to the right. I called the lead aircraft and reported that we were "in bad trouble and we are ejecting." Like a sound in a dream I heard a voice asking "No.2 what is the matter,"—"what is the matter?" I recognized the voice of Lt/Col. Dayton Taylor, our squadron commander. I didn't respond, as by this time we were in the second roll of a severe spin.

Except for outlines in the glow of the red lights, I could see no instruments. After releasing the control wheel, my arms were forced against my body with such force that I had great difficulty in moving them. It took all my strength to slide them forward along my legs far enough to grab the ejection seat handles. I grasped the left handle first and was attempting to reach the right handle when the cockpit suddenly fogged up. The right handle is the one that activates the ejection process.

Finally the right handle was in my grasp and I pulled the handle up and back. I felt a sudden jolt as the seat bottomed and I saw the control column fall forward to the stowed position. The fog suddenly cleared and as I looked to my left I was looking directly at Max Workman. He had been shoved forward by the forces of the aircraft motion and was immobilized in an area next to the radio amplifiers located in the aisle. He was looking directly at me. I was also immobilized and powerless to do anything to help. I found the trigger in the right handle. I closed my eyes and squeezed the trigger.

I felt a tremendous surge or force and heard a terrific roar. I was out of the aircraft and tumbling very rapidly in a pit of darkness. I was gasping for air as I sought to straighten my body to reduce the tumbling motion. I felt a sudden release and in my confused state my immediate thought was that it was the release opening of my parachute. I was still tumbling, but not with such terrific force as before. I had the impression that my parachute had released and I kept waiting for the opening shock. The thought crossed my mind that I had a faulty parachute and that it had opened but was a streamer. I frantically reached my hands behind my back and discovered that the parachute was still in place – on my back.

I was still tugging on the "D" ring to release the parachute when the chute suddenly opened with a terrific jolt to my body. The chute opening was so severe that I thought that surely some of the shroud lines must be severed, but my first thought after the chute opened was to activate my bail-out bottle. My helmet and oxygen mask were still on but the mask was pushed away from my face. I grabbed the mask, pressing it up against my face and I could feel a strong flow of oxygen hit my face. The force of the parachute opening had activated the emergency bail-out bottle.

Shortly after parachute opening, I noticed a huge red glow directly beneath me. The glow was in a layer of clouds that covered the ground below me. I wondered if I might be drifting over a large city, but I knew there were no large cities in this area. The next time I looked down the glow had disappeared. It was only then that I realized that the glow reflected in the clouds was from an explosion as the B-47 impacted the ground.

I estimated that I was still at a very high altitude, maybe even 20,000 feet. The severity of the shock at parachute opening could be related to the high altitude. I checked all of my shroud lines and there was no apparent damage to the parachute. I was drifting in an eerie silence. I thought that Petty and Martin and possibly Workman might also be drifting in their parachutes and I hollered their names while facing different directions. There was no response. Darkness had fallen, but my eyes were adjusting to the dim light. In one direction I could see the lights of a city near what appeared to be a lake. Except for the belief that the cities were south, I was unable to get oriented as to direction. Stars were visible but I couldn't find Polaris.

During the first phase of the descent, I was aware of extreme cold. My helmet and mask prevented my face from freezing and I kept my hands tucked in my clothing. I had put the parka between the parachute and my body when I strapped the parachute on. Fortunately it had not pulled out during bail-out. My gloves, wallet, cap and most items in the zippered flying suit had been lost. One pocket containing extra socks had remained zippered.

I tried turning and several times I pulled on the risers to stop oscillations, but whatever I tried was not too successful. I had been gradually getting closer to the lower cloud cover and I had no idea how close to the ground those clouds might be. I also had to be prepared if there was water in the landing area. I would release the survival kit to dangle below me if the landing area was over water or smooth terrain, but I did not want it released if I was going into a forested area. I feared that the kit could catch on a large tree and if there was a wind it could interfere with my landing.

I entered the under cast. I could see nothing except a gray mist. I tried to assume the correct landing position. I knew or at least I felt like I was drifting backwards and I was afraid to attempt any changes for fear of collapsing the chute and not have enough altitude to recover. It seemed I was in the clouds for a long time before I finally broke through the overcast and saw a snow covered forest of tall evergreen trees. I wasn't in total darkness and as I broke out of the clouds I estimated that I was somewhere between two hundred and five hundred feet above the ground. The snow and darkness made it difficult to gauge distance. I was thankful that I was apparently over land and not water.

I was descending rapidly and was attempting to keep the proper position for landing - knees slightly bent, don't look directly down! I appeared to be drifting toward a small clearing. I kept my eyes looking ahead at the tree line near the edge of the clearing. I hit the ground feet first but sat down pretty hard on the survival kit. I rolled left and laid still for a moment. I felt no injuries so I unbuckled the parachute harness and got to my feet.

For a little while I did nothing but stand. I was trembling, partly from the cold but mostly from the shock of the experience just encountered. I knelt down and thanked God for my life and I prayed for my crew members. Mostly I prayed for Lt Workman. I knew that unless he was thrown out through an exit or there was a change in the pressure forces that he would probably have not been able to exit the aircraft. When Lt. Petty ejected there would exist another opening where the flow of air could have forced him from the plane. I knew he had on his parachute, but I was also aware of the fact that he did not have his survival pack attached.

Martin and Petty, I was certain, had ejected. I believe that the first time the cockpit fogged over, when I gave the ejection order, that Lt. Petty had gone through the first phase of his ejection procedure. I believe that the cabin depressurized before I completed my ejection sequence because the cabin fogged up just before I blew the canopy.

I expected at any time to hear their voices call out for help. I put my parka on and walked around my parachute several times. I didn't want to do a thing until I could think a little clearer. The snow in this clearing was about a foot deep and under the snow was a shallow ice pond. I had missed all of the large tall trees surrounding this ice pond and that in itself could be considered a miracle.

Leaving my survival pack and parachute, I attempted to walk to the nearest edge of the clearing. The snow drifts in this area were waist deep. I finally broke through into a slushy area of ice and water. I back tracked to the landing area. On the opposite side of the clearing the snow depth appeared level and the slope, upward from the edge of the pond, looked steeper. I made my way to the tree line breaking through into slush only once. About eight feet into the tree area the ground looked high enough to prevent water seepage; also, there were fallen trees criss-crossing each other in a manner that could provide a temporary shelter. I went back to the survival kit to gather up all the equipment. I also faced in four directions and in each direction I shouted the word "Help," with all the strength of my lungs. There was no answer.

Bending down to pick up the equipment, I noticed a sharp pain in my left chest. I first wondered if I might be having a heart attack brought on by the events that I had just survived. I was relieved when I felt what appeared to be muscle or cartilage rolling in my chest when I made certain movements. Perhaps I had pulled ligaments or had a rib jarred loose.

Despite some chest pain, I carried all of the survival gear and the parachute to the site I had decided would be my temporary camp. I scooped the snow out in an area estimated to be big enough for the life raft, but I could not find firm ground. The surface below the snow level was spongy feeling. I pulled the life raft release and after the raft was inflated, I placed it bottom side down in the scooped out area. I shook the parachute out as best I could and folded it in the bottom of the raft. The parachute harness was placed at the head of the raft and was supported by a tree to provide a wind break. The wind was light, but I felt it might increase later in the night.

I crawled in under the parachute cloth and tried to organize my thoughts. The events of the emergency and the ejection were racing through my mind and I needed to settle down for a few minutes and just rest. I had no gloves so I kept my hands inside the parka until they finally began to warm up.

I rested for a few minutes, but there was much to do and I needed to examine the contents of the survival kit. One problem was the mukluks. They are not waterproof. They were designed for use in artic regions where everything was frozen solid. If our crew had been forced to eject an hour or two earlier we would have been in an area where everything was frozen solid and that was "mukluk territory." Ordinarily I would have worn my waterproof flying boots but I was prepared for the worst weather we might encounter. "Rudder feel" was difficult enough when flying with mukluks, but mukluks over boots would have been too cumbersome. I kept thinking, "I could have brought the boots along and changed while in flight." I finally decided that I had no time to review what "could have been" and I needed to concentrate on the essentials related to helping me with survival in what appeared to be a remote wilderness.

I had the packet containing the survival equipment alongside the raft. I opened up the packet and began removing the wrapping on the items – one article at a time. I found the small URC-4 radio. I placed the battery for this radio inside my clothing next to my body. It was vital to keep this battery from freezing. After a struggle I finally got the cable connected between the battery and the radio unit. I was not sure of the correct position for the UHF/VHF switch and I left the antenna in the stowed position. The receiver background tone on the radio appeared to be o.k.

I found the knife and put the disassembled 22. Caliber Hornet together. Every item was opened inside the raft as I feared that I might drop something in the snow. I saved the wrapping paper for fire material. After considerable difficulty, I found the matches. They were all stuck together in one wad. I broke off a dozen or so and put them in various pockets. I put another group of matches in the raft at a location near my head and the remainder I wrapped up in a piece of parachute. I was afraid I might lose the matches and for that reason dispersed them in different locations.

The compass was intact but it didn't seem to be operating. The movable dial would not revolve. I was unable to locate a cap or gloves, but I did find an extra pair of socks. Any movement that required me to turn or lift my arms brought pain in that one area of the chest located just below my heart. My hands seemed to get cold after being exposed to the outside air for only a short period of time and thus my hand movements were slow and my fingers stiff. After warming my hands in the parka I finally decided to use the spare socks as gloves and wondered why I hadn't done

PART IV AFTER LIBERATION

so sooner.

I didn't know the exact time, but I had been on the ground for maybe two hours when I heard the sounds of aircraft. The sounds were those of low flying aircraft and they were fairly close. I ran out to the center of the pond with my heart pounding. I had the URC-4 radio and it was picking up voice transmissions. The conversation was related to sightings the aircraft had made and it sounded as though a survivor or survivors had been located. There was discussion about seeing lights flashing at them from the ground. I don't know how anyone aboard our aircraft had managed to retain a flash light, but it sounded as though a survivor might be signaling one of the aircraft.

We were logically the survivors that they were seeking. The aircraft were reporting their findings to some place called "Lake Head Tower." I tried transmitting using both the UHF and VHF frequencies but could not get any response. I felt that I needed to be on higher ground but I did not dare leave this camp area where I had all my gear. I tried to send an S.O.S. by keying the transmitter and I was certain someone heard part of the transmission as one voice kept complaining that the radio frequency was being blocked.

Not getting any response, I returned to the raft and built a fire. By the light of the fire I was finally able to see the radio switch positions. With the fire blazing, I hoped the flames would be seen. I continued to monitor the radio and it appeared that the people airborne were directing a ground party to a location where survivors had been discovered. My hopes were kindled by these transmissions and I thought it possible that at least two of my crew members might be together.

I attempted aircraft contact at intervals for several hours, but finally decided that I had better save my battery and at daybreak try and seek higher ground where my transmissions might be heard. I left the fire unattended for such long periods that it finally died out. The transmissions from the aircraft had ceased and I felt that there was not much I could do until daylight except try and rest and organize my thoughts. My feet were wet so I went back to the raft and changed socks. My feet stayed cold and at intervals I left the raft and stomped around to regain circulation. I would infrequently check the radio but I was no longer receiving transmission of any type.

It wasn't until I removed the mukluks and socks and wrapped my bare feet in parachute cloth that they warmed up. I needed rest but my mind refused to shut down. I kept remembering Max's eyes as he watched me go through the ejection process. I was powerless to help him as the "G" forces had us both immobilized, but that knowledge did not seem to help relieve my despair or wipe away the vision of terror that I saw in his eyes.

My thoughts were suddenly interrupted by the sounds of an owl in a nearby tree. I was reminded that I was probably not alone in this forest. I wasn't particularly concerned about wild animals as I had the 22 Hornet rifle and although it would not stop a bear the sounds of a gun-shot would scare away most predators.

Suddenly, I was aware that dawn was breaking. I had finally dozed off, but had no idea how long I had been asleep. I had the mukluks under the parachute near my body. Thankfully, they were not frozen stiff and with some effort, I finally got them back on.

I checked the .22 Hornet and loaded it with ammo. I fired four shots in the air. I received nothing in return. I was hopeful that if I was anywhere near a crew member that I might get a response. We would be widely separated if they had delayed parachute opening. I estimated that I floated in the parachute for at least 20 minutes before reaching the ground. A difference in the time of parachute deployment could result in our being miles apart. There was an automatic device on the parachute that would open the parachute at 14,000 feet if the jumper was disabled for any reason. I believe that I was well above that altitude when my parachute deployed.

I inspected the equipment again in daylight looking for flares. I found no flares and decided that the best thing I could do was build a big fire. While gathering firewood I again heard the sound of aircraft. I raced to the parachute and was cutting a red panel out of the chute when I saw a C-47 twin engine aircraft approaching at low altitude. I grabbed the radio and was busy connecting it to the battery when the aircraft flew past my location. I waved frantically but was not seen. By the time I had the radio assembled, the aircraft had disappeared behind the trees. Although the receiver seemed to be working, there was no response to my transmission.

I went back and finished cutting out the panel. I re-inspected the survival pack and made one more search for signal flares and sea marker dye. I wanted the dye to place in my footprints in the snow. The search for these two items was unsuccessful.

I had just placed the red panel in the center of the ice pond when I saw a low flying helicopter passing to one side of the clearing. I immediately made a call over the radio reporting that I was a "B-47 survivor." I received a response; however when I directed the helicopter to make an immediate right turn, it continued on in straight and level flight. When I queried the helicopter pilot about his failure to turn the reply was "I am in a right turn." It was at that moment that I saw a second helicopter and it was in a right turn!

After a couple of minutes of my providing turn directions, the second helicopter headed my way and the crew sighted me visually. I called, asking if they wanted to also recover my gear. The response was no, that he, the pilot was not going to land for fear of bogging down. I raced back to the raft and picked up my helmet. The helicopter was hovering at the edge of the clearing. Two crewmen pulled me aboard and the helicopter immediately started upward. My first words were "How many others have you found?" The response was "You are the only one." I was stunned, as I was certain from listening to the radio transmissions during the night that one or more members of my crew had been found.

The helicopter flew directly back to an airport called Lakehead at Ft William, (later re-named, "Thunder Bay") Canada. I barely had time to shake the pilot's hand and thank the crew before the helicopter was back in the air to continue the search. From the airport, I was taken directly to McKeller General Hospital in Ft William where I was admitted as a patient. I was warmly received at the hospital. The only visible damages to my body were bruises around my eyes and chest that probably resulted from the severe jolt as the parachute opening stopped my descent.

An investigating team, headed by Col. C. D. Lewis, from Barksdale AFB, Louisiana arrived in the area that evening, but I did not receive a visit from any of the team members until morning.

Early the next morning, following my rescue, I was able to call my wife, Lee, to confirm that I was ok. I tried to be as optimistic as possible with respect to finding the other crew members. Just hearing my beloved wife's voice once again buoyed my spirits.

After the call home, I was examined by a USAF medical Officer, Captain , (Dr.) Robert Hamlisch. Capt Hamlisch had flown up from Duluth Minnesota to examine me and prepare a report for the Accident Investigation Board. By evening the physical effects of the ejection were beginning to set in as every muscle in my body appeared to be stiff and every movement was painful. Dr. Hamlisch had predicted this condition and he had confirmed that I had a severe cartilage tear in my left rib cage.

While in the hospital I prepared a report that spelled out all of the problems that my crew encountered with the aileron control system and provided this information to the team of investigators that were examining the crash site.

Members of the team were very interested in the exact location where I had been recovered and they had already flown two helicopters to the general area, but had no success in locating the site. It was the third day of December and still no sign of any of my crew. I was concerned that some day my camp location would be found and perhaps leave the impression that a survivor had been there but had never been found.

When queried about finding the location I told the team members that I was certain that I could find the camp site from the air. I also informed the team members that I wanted to participate in the search for my crew members. At Lakehead airport, I boarded a U.S. built B-25 twin engine bomber that was part of the search force. The crew was Canadian and they were flying the search mission without wearing or even having a parachute aboard the aircraft. They had rescue equipment aboard but no room for parachutes. Flight without parachutes was standard procedure for the Canadians while on low level search missions. I owed my life to the ejection seat and to a parachute and I would not have thought that my next flight in a military aircraft would be without a parachute, but such was the case.

I felt confident and was at ease flying with this rescue crew. I flew in the co-pilots position. I had been checked out in the B-25 during my short assignment to the Civil Air Patrol headquarters and was familiar with the cockpit and controls. We flew on a heading to the north following the flight path provided by the helicopter crew that rescued me. We had been in flight for about 30 minutes when I sighted a large bare pine tree that was located at the edge of the clearing. Circling the site we spotted the 22 Hornet still propped against a tree near the life raft. The navigator plotted the location on his map and we continued flying for several more hours searching the area for any sign of a survivor. It was dark when we landed back at Lakehead Airport and I returned to the hospital where I was still considered a patient.

Later that evening, Major Driskill Horton a member of the investigation team brought me the bad news. The search team at the crash site had found parachutes in the wreckage on the first day of search and on this day, the third of December, the team had found the co-pilots ejection seat and further evidence that all three members were in the aircraft when it struck the ground. I had difficulty believing or accepting this information and that was because of the radio transmissions I overheard the night of the crash.

My report of the transmissions had also been investigated and the explanation was that the crash site was very near a lumber camp and following the crash and huge explosion, a group of these lumbermen were on the ground seeking to find the cause of the explosion. The aircraft observers in the area sighted the flashlights carried by the ground search party and thought the lights were possibly signals from survivors. There was logic to this explanation, but I just had a difficult time accepting the fact that I was the only one able to operate the ejection seat.

I had told the search party that I wanted to remain in Canada until my crew members were rescued; now that I knew there would be no rescue I just wanted to go home. I needed the comfort of family and I needed to see and try and explain to the loved ones of my crew why I was still alive and that it was not within my power to save them.

I was flown back to Barksdale on the 5th or 6th of December. The weather in Canada worsened and after the identification process was completed the accident investigative team left that area. Ground temperature on the 8th of December was 27 degrees below zero. Weather prohibited any further effort to obtain my survival gear.

Members of the accident board went to the Boeing plant at Wichita, Kansas where the type of failures I described to them were duplicated on an aircraft pulled directly from the assembly line. Aileron failure was duplicated by both mechanical and electrical means and the ailerons "locked" 100 percent of the time. The lock could not be broken by any action other than having someone disconnect the hydraulic line at the power control unit located in the wing.

I went through the torture of meeting with the family and friends of my former crew members and there probably will always be doubts in some minds as to whether or not I deserted my crew to save my own life. If that were the case I would have never flown again. I have great sorrow for the loss of my crew but that grief is not related to any self doubt as to my own actions during this tragedy.

There are those who may not be aware that the B-47, unlike most bomber aircraft, has a tandem seating arrangement. The pilot sits forward in front of the co-pilot. Both positions are equipped with individually operated ejection seats. Seat ejection can only be activated by the seat occupant. The navigator is seated in a downward ejection seat in the nose of the aircraft. That ejection seat is out of the view of the pilot. Since the pilot seat is in front of the co-pilot the actions of the co-pilot are also out of view. If an ejection or bailout order is given the pilot has no control over the ejection actions of the other two crew members.

One Boeing representative told me during the investigation that my testimony had provided information that could account for five other B-47 accidents where the cause was unknown or never satisfactorily explained and there were no survivors to verify any of the data obtained during the accident investigations. Perhaps I can gain some solace in that I was able to describe the events that occurred and thus contributed to a solution that may have saved others.

The accident was determined to be due to mechanical failure that made control of the aircraft impossible. As a result of my testimony and the follow-up investigation by the Accident Investigating Board, all B-47's in the fleet were provided with corrective measures that eliminated any possibility of a recurrence of an accident of this type.

The accident investigation board could only list a most probable cause for failure of my crew members to exit the aircraft. "G" forces or the Force of Gravity exerted on the individuals in the aircraft were estimated to be between 3 and 4 "G's." This force was sufficient to completely incapacitate the aisle passenger and possibly be the reason the ejection seats were never activated.

After the accident investigation was completed I once again flew the B-47 with a new crew. When the B-47's were replaced by the B-52, my B-47 crew remained with me as we made the transition to the new aircraft.

Richard Martin

Max Workman

Donald Petty

PART IV AFTER LIBERATION 263

Accident Investigation Team Members
Canada - December, 1956

My survival gear - Recovered in 1972
Discovered by Herb Shaefer, a Canadian hunter

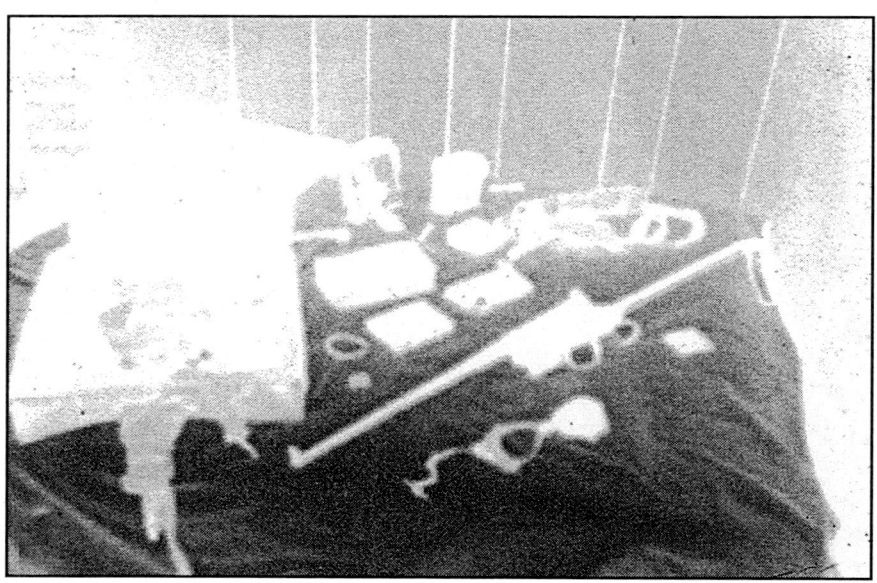

Military Synopsis

I accrued 3000 hours in the B-52 flying as an aircraft commander and as an instructor pilot. I was the Vice Wing Commander of the B-52 Wing at Plattsburg Air Force Base in New York when I volunteered for a combat assignment to South East Asia in 1970. I was scheduled to be the Wing Commander of the 553rd Reconnaissance Wing at Korat, Thailand. This unit was equipped with a special sensor-surveillance capability and was flying reconnaissance sorties in EC 121R aircraft (the old prop driven, Lockheed "Super Constellations").

I requested an early date to start flight training so that I might leave as soon as possible as my intention was to replace the present Vice Wing Commander and to be in place and combat qualified when I replaced the Wing Commander. Everything went as planned. I checked out early in the "Super Constellation" and replaced the Vice Commander a full two months before he was due to be replaced and I settled in as the new Vice Wing Commander.

The day finally arrived when I was to replace the Wing Commander. I had already flown about 25 combat sorties and felt confident that I was fully prepared to assume the duties and responsibilities of the Wing Commander. There was a formal "change of command" ceremony - complete with a parade and an aircraft "Flyover."

As fortune would have it, about 10 days after the big change of command ceremony, my "Wing" was downgraded to a "Group" and I was a "Wing Commander ' without a "Wing." Such are the fortunes of "War and Peace."

The last four years of active duty in the military; I was assigned duty as a Base Commander. I was first assigned as the Base Commander at Bien Hoa Air Base in Vietnam after the 553rd Reconnaissance Wing assignment in Thailand. Upon return to stateside duty I assumed Base Commander duty at Carswell AFB, Texas. My last duty assignment was as the Base Commander at Barksdale AFB, Louisiana.

My career in the Army Air Corps and the Air Force was to continue for a total of 32 years, 10 months and 22 days. I volunteered for and flew combat missions during both the Korean and Vietnam conflicts, accruing 116 additional combat missions to add to the 4 missions flown during World War II. Combat hours totaled 561.

My war time assignment in Europe was for a period of 22 months The war time assignment to Korea was for a 12 month period. and the one to Vietnam was also for 12 months. I served my military time without ever having the benefit of an overseas assignment during peacetime.

Slane's B-52 Crew Members, 1958.
L-R: Slane - Aircraft Commander, Edgerton - Co-pilot,
Royer - Radar Navigator, Harris - Navigator,
Barnes - Electronic Warfare Officer, Silva - Gunner

The Later Years

In late 1972, while I was still on active duty, my wife, Lee, received a telephone call from a man in Canada. He was trying to locate, "Major Slane." I was the Base Commander at Barksdale AFB at the time of the call. The Canadian, from Thunder Bay, Canada, had been on a hunting trip north of Thunder Bay and had discovered the campsite where I left my survival equipment after being rescued by helicopter on December 1st, 1956. I was a Major at the time of the B-47 accident and was flying a B-47 jet bomber from Barksdale.

Upon making the find, this man, Herb Schaefer, had discovered that I was the pilot and survivor of the accident and by going through old newspaper files he had the complete story of the crash and my survival of a tragedy that had occurred sixteen years earlier.

It was purely by chance that, after an absence of almost nine years, I was assigned back to Barksdale AFB, Louisiana. I was at my office on the base when his call was transferred to me. Mr. Schaefer said that he had found the .22 Hornet rifle "leaning against a tree." He also had sections of the parachute and had discovered parts of the life raft. He was very excited and amazed that he had actually found me.

Retirement brings changes in life style and perspective. One benefit is that there is now time to try and accomplish some of the activities that have been on the back burner for many years. This is also a period in our lives when we can look back and then go forward with our dreams - at least those dreams that are not restricted by health problems or restrained by lack of adequate monetary support.

In 1986, 14 years after receiving the phone call from Herb Schaefer, Lee and I made a trip that included a visit to the Schaefer family in Thunder Bay, Ontario, Canada. The Canadian government had permitted Herb to retain the .22 Hornet rifle. He gave me a piece of my parachute. It is particularly significant that every year since that visit I have received a phone call from Herb Schaefer on the 30th of November.

It was also in 1986 that I received a forwarded letter from Louis Brown, who had been my B-17 ball turret gunner during the war. He had mailed his letter to an address in Arkansas where I owned a lake house. This was my first contact since 1945 with any of the enlisted members of my World War II, B-17 crew. Through Lou Brown, I was able to also establish contact with Victor Kuhlman, the radio operator and Sherman Sly, the engineer and top turret gunner. Louis Brown and Sherman Sly had, over the years, maintained a close relationship with each other and had attended reunions of former prisoners from Stalag-17B. Inspired by the renewed connection with my former crew members, Lee and I attended our first "Second Schweinfurt Memorial" Association reunion in Las Vegas, Nevada. At this reunion we met Louis and his wife Claire. It had been 41 years since my last meeting with Louis in La Havre, France.

It was through my meeting other members of the 2nd Schweinfurt Memorial Association that I established contact with a German who was corresponding with some of the members of this Association. Volker Wilkins, a native of Munich, has provided help to many former airmen seeking to solve some of the mysteries that linger after loss of an aircraft and fellow airmen in hostile territory. Volker, as a teenager, helped man the flak batteries that surrounded Schweinfurt during the war years. He provided me with a map of the general area between the cities of Metz and Nancy in eastern France. Volker also put me in contact with a young Frenchman named M. Coquillat Guy. In my correspondence with Guy, he indicated that he had an interest in helping me locate the area where I had crash-landed the B-17 on October 14th, 1943. We agreed to meet when Lee and I make our planned trip to England and France.

In the latter part of May 1991, we were finally able to make the trip of our dreams. The purpose of the trip was threefold.

First on the agenda was to visit with the Harveys, the owners of the land in East Anglia, England, where I crash-landed the B-17, "Sir Baboon McGoon," on October 10th, 1943. The Harveys' were now operating a "Bed and Breakfast" in a beautiful old home, called Tannington Hall, which is located on the same property where five of my crew members and I spent the night after surviving the crash-landing. The night of the crash-landing, we were quartered in Braisworth Hall, another beautiful home that is now occupied by one of the Harvey sons.

The second goal on this trip was to locate the site where I made the crash landing in France on the return flight from the mission to Schweinfurt, Germany on October 14th, 1943. Our third mission was to locate and visit the grave site at St. Avold, France where my brave tail gunner, Claud J. Smith was buried. Although we had limited time, we were able to accomplish all three goals.

When my wife and I arrived at the Harvey home, we were pleasantly surprised by a visit from Tom Perkins. At the time of the crash-landing in 1943, Tom was a fifteen-year-old youngster who had been riding his bicycle on a pathway adjacent to the beet field where I crash-landed the B-17. He and a companion heard the roar of the aircraft engines followed by the sounds of the crash-landing. The fog was so dense that they didn't see the aircraft, but they were close enough that they feared for their own lives. These two young men were among the first of the locals to arrive at the aircraft and they had a short visit with some of the crew before the "Home Guard" arrived to secure the aircraft.

During this visit, Tom presented me with a beautiful "booklet" that contains the story of the recovery of the B-17, "Sir Baboon McGoon," from the beet field. That story, complete with color photographs, was reproduced from the June 1944 issue of Popular Science. The article is devoted to the various stages of work performed by the mobile repair unit and it provides the names of people involved in the recovery effort. The two young Harvey sons had been excited witnesses to this entire operation, which included viewing the aircraft as it was flown off their land to a distant recovery depot. The flight was made on December 5th, 1943 – less than two months after my gear-up landing on that foggy day in October.

We greatly enjoyed our visit with the Harvey family and we spent considerable time discussing events of the past. One son was a collector of beautiful, antique carriages. He also hosted a meeting at a local Pub and we arrived at the Pub in a horse drawn carriage. The pub where we had refreshments was "The Kings Head," one of the oldest in England.

With Tom as our escort, we were taken to the 390th Bomb Group Memorial Museum, where Tom is an active member in the restoration and preservation of the tower museum. It so happens that on that same day, Mr. Arthur Tye was visiting the museum. I was re-introduced to the man who was the first person to arrive at the crash-landing site. After 47 years, I was able to discuss events that we all remembered with remarkable clarity. Mr. Tye had been assigned to guard the aircraft that night and had remained on guard duty until a recovery unit arrived to relieve him the next morning – October 11th, 1943.

Our next adventure took us to the "White Cliffs of Dover" where it was unbelievably cold. We spent the night in Dover and crossed the channel to Calais, France by hovercraft the following morning. Traveling by hovercraft was also a new and exciting experience. From Calais we went by train to Paris where we spent two nights in a quaint little hotel not too far from the railroad station. While in Paris, I contacted Coquillat Guy and arranged for him to meet us in Metz. Our hotel in Metz was the Hotel La Globe, nothing fancy, but clean and the management was friendly. It was just across the street from the historic Metz railroad station, "The La-Gare."

Coquillat Guy had offered his services as an interpreter and guide. He was in the French military and had evidentially gained access to a report that had extracts of information provided by my navigator, Lt. Glenn Foster, during his interrogation after leaving Switzerland and after reporting back to Allied control.

Guy was also very interested in the mapping of locations where aircraft parts might be recovered from crash sites.

After arriving at the hotel, I requested the lady at the registration desk to place a call to Guy's residence and provide his wife with our location. Guy was living some distance away near the city of Dijon, but would be at work at his military installation. We arranged to meet with Guy the next morning at 9AM to begin our search of the countryside.

Guy arrived on schedule the next day - May 30th, 1991. We were immediately impressed with this bright and very personable young man. He spoke excellent English and had made some initial contacts with various people in the villages to the east of Metz. He said he would be available to assist us all day and evening. Guy had also obtained the correct burial number for the location of Claud Smith's grave in the Lorraine American Cemetery at St. Avold, France.

Since much of Alsace-Lorraine had been German territory prior to World War I, the Germans had returned during World War II to regain their claimed territory. Many of the residents were displaced by the German occupation force and taken to Germany to serve as laborers in German factories. Most of the present occupants of the villages were not in those villages during World War II, which added to the difficulty in obtaining reliable information.

Guy was particularly interested in a location near the railroad city of Delm, but I ruled out that location as I still had a clear vision of the terrain where I made the crash-landing and knew that I had not crash-landed near a railroad. I was taken to two locations where locals had indicated the aircraft had crash-landed. Neither of these locations met my criteria for the landing site. There were no villages within view at these two locations.

Finally, late in the afternoon, I reviewed the map and indicated to Guy where I thought the landing site should be located. We headed for a village called Viviers. As we crossed a shallow valley, I had Guy stop the car. I got out of the vehicle and looked in all four directions. There was a village in a raised area to my left and a slight rise in the ground to my right and about half a mile away in that same direction was a hilly forested area. Ahead of me some distance away was a ditch or canal. I told Guy "this is the place!"

We continued into the town of Viviers and found a man who indicated he had heard that during the war a bomber had crashed near the village, but he was not a resident at the time. During this discussion, a Mr. Schulte, a German resident of the nearby town of Oran who had volunteered to help find the aircraft location, told me that there was a man who wanted to see me. This man claimed that he was present and had witnessed the entire event both before and after the crash-landing.

Although he was bed-ridden and suffering from cancer, this man was insistent that I talk to him. The man was Jacques Heller. Using Guy as an interpreter, Mr. Heller accurately described my tight circling flight from altitude, emphasizing that the flight path was a spiral. He told of events that only an eyewitness could know. He discussed the shattered side window and windshield on the co-pilot's side of the aircraft. He stated that fuel was pouring from the right wing root and that the right outside engine had a propeller that was positioned different than the others. (Our number 4 engine was feathered.) He informed us that the open bomb doors had gouged deep ruts in the ground and these ruts had remained for years. (Our bomb-bay doors were open during the crash-landing. They had been opened with the emergency release handle to permit bailout from that location. Once the doors were released by emergency means, they must be reengaged manually before they can be closed.)

Finally, Mr. Heller pointed to me and said in French, "you took out a fence!" When Guy interpreted Mr. Heller's remark about the fence, I could feel chills running down my back. I am the only person who knew about the fence; I had never mentioned the fence to anyone. The fence had been overlooked in any of my reports because it had no particular significance to me - until now! There will never be any doubt in my mind that Mr. Heller was a witness to the crash landing.

Mr. Heller indicated that he saw me captured and taken away by the local "Gendarmes" and that he had been present when

Sgt. Smith was removed from the aircraft later that evening. When questioned about Sgt. Claud Smith and where he was buried after I was captured, he informed me that he was initially buried in a cemetery in Delm, a larger city located about 6 miles southwest of Viviers.

When asked about the disposition of the aircraft, Mr. Heller said that the Germans dismantled the aircraft, piece by piece, and loaded the parts on vehicles for transport to another city. He continued with information that the aircraft was reassembled and for many years remained on display in the town of Chateau-Salins which is located south-east of Viviers. Mr. Heller went on to say that many of the local area residents had taken photographs of this aircraft and that I could probably obtain a photo from someone in that city (Chateau-Salins).

Note of Special interest:
Just this year - 2003, I received an e-mail from Glenn Foster's grandson, Drew Van Duren. In the message to me, Drew stated that, while performing a web search, he found the aircraft that my crew was flying on October 14th, 1943. (The one that I crash-landed in France.) It appears from the photograph and information contained in the German web site, http://www.beuteflugzeuge.de/B-17.htm that my crews' aircraft - # 42-5714 was in fact recovered and possibly restored to a flyable condition by German technicians.

The interview with Mr. Heller provided me with even more information than I expected to uncover. What wasn't clearly explained was how he could have had so much knowledge of these events. He told us that he was a shepherd and was out in the fields the day I crash landed. I had seen no cattle or sheep in the area either from the air or after being on the ground, but Mr. Heller's portrayal of events was as clear and concise as my own. I had an indefinable feeling that Mr. Heller was more than just a 'Shepard.'

Although very ill, there was something about his appearance

and demeanor that reminded me of one of the men who drove out to the crash-landing site and captured me in the vicinity of the aircraft. Mr. Heller was a tall man and his features were similar to those of the man who had the Slavic prisoner in the back seat of his Ford when I was captured. I will let this subject remain a mystery, as I am just grateful to Mr. Jacques Heller and to Coquillat Guy for the information provided me during this very busy day.

The day following the visit to Viviers, Lee and I rode a bus from Metz to St. Avold, the location of the Lorraine American Cemetery and Memorial. We were delayed as we had trouble getting a taxi from St. Avold to the cemetery and arrived so late in the afternoon we feared that the gates to the cemetery would be closed. The gates were closed, but with the help of our cab driver we were able to flag down a French worker and ask if we could gain entrance. After a few minutes, a golf-style vehicle arrived driven by a retired American Army Major, John Ferguson. Major Ferguson, the assistant caretaker for the cemetery, quickly put us at ease, saying that the cemetery was never closed "to any visiting American" and that we could spend as much time as we needed at the gravesite.

Major Ferguson put us aboard his golf cart and drove directly to the burial location. Lee and I were left alone, in front of the cross marking Claud's grave. Standing there on sacred ground, looking at the marker with his name and surrounded by row after row of white crosses nestled in this amazingly beautiful cemetery, was an overwhelming, emotional experience. We just stood there for awhile holding hands, unable to stop the flow of tears.

It took some time to regain our composure. I took pictures of Claud's grave and the surrounding area. The serene, quiet beauty of the cemetery grounds is difficult to describe. We said our prayers, and kissed the stone that marked the grave site of a brave young American. When John Ferguson arrived to return us to the gate we were ready to leave. It was strange, but both of us left that cemetery knowing that this location was where Claud should be buried.

On the way back to the gate, John Ferguson told us that many people come to visit with the intention of returning their loved one back to the United States for re-burial. After visiting the burial location and viewing the surrounding area most families made the decision that this was the place where their loved one belonged.

Sgt. Claud J. Smith's grave site. Lorraine Cemetery, St. Avold, France

Beutetypen der Luftwaffe

Eine B-17F, Werksnummer: 425714, Kennung DR+PE, fotografiert im Mai 1944 bei Magdeburg, der Verbleib dieser Maschine ist unbekannt, wer weiß mehr dazu

The aircraft I crash landed near Viviers, France on 14 October, 1943. It appears from this copy of a photograph that the aircraft was recovered and restored by the German Luftwaffe.

PART IV AFTER LIBERATION   277

Epilogue

It was sometime after making contact with Louis Brown, Victor Kuhlman and Sherman Sly that I discovered that they, like the majority of prisoners of war in Germany, had not received any type of recognition for the missions flown prior to being shot down or for their heroic actions during the Schweinfurt mission on the day we were shot down. I could understand how this could happen as I was in the same situation. The only recognition that I had received for my military experiences in England and Germany during World War II was the "Defense Service" and Campaign medals, (The "been-there" ribbons.)

I certainly do not speak for all of the prisoners of war during World War II, but I am not aware of any special program designed to recognize those individuals who performed with valor and courage on the mission that was to be their last or those who attempted escape or who actually escaped while in prisoner status and were recaptured.

I am also not aware of any special recognition provided for others who displayed unusual qualities of leadership while incarcerated. I am certain that there are some exceptions to my statement, particularly among deserving senior officers who held positions of leadership during their captivity.

My combat crew was typical of the many young Americans who were volunteers to fly and fight for the cause of freedom. My crew was also typical of the many crews lost to enemy action in hostile territory and captured before they had any opportunity to escape. No longer assigned to a military unit, their deeds and identity as individuals was of no concern to the enemy. Their former military unit had very little, if any, information regarding the activities of a crew that was shot down and thus unable to relate their experiences or receive verification regarding claims of enemy aircraft destroyed.

Like most returning ex-prisoners of war, the majority of my crew members were caught up in the hysteria of demobilization after the war and were separated from the military to begin new lives and new occupations. Some may have wondered at the lack of recognition for their heroism, but most ex-prisoners of war were just grateful for their lives and return to freedom. At that time little thought was given to medals or awards.

I learned from Glenn Foster, that among other awards he was presented a Purple Heart, Distinguished Flying Cross and the Air Medal for his three missions over Germany. He had escaped to Switzerland where he had had opportunity to provide the proper authorities with his story on a timely basis. After his release from Switzerland in late 1944 he was flown to England where he was debriefed and could present his story to Military Authority.

Since I was the commander of our combat crew, I decided it was my responsibility, even at this late date, to at least attempt to obtain the Air Medal for my remaining crew members. I began a research program. It took almost two years of waiting for various agencies to finally provide the information that I felt was needed to verify our eligibility for award of the Air Medal.

The first submission of material to support a request for award of an Air Medal for all of my former B-17 crew members, was made through the office of a local Congressman on January 14th, 1993. After a long wait, I received a response through the Congressman's office that the Air Force was "researching" my request and should have a decision within 60 days. The final response to my request arrived in June 1993 when I was notified that "Public Law 81-507 established May 2, 1951, was the deadline date to place recommendations based on World War II achievements." End of Action!!

This answer was aggravating. It had taken five months for the Air Force to "Research" my request when an answer could have been provided in one day. I was also concerned that my original letter request, with all of my attachments had not been returned. I had been aware of the particular public law quoted to me before I submitted the recommendations. It was my awareness of this law that had compelled me to send along as one of my attachments a letter I had received from a fellow prisoner who had just recently been able to get the pilot of his crew awarded the Silver Star. His request had been submitted through the office of Congressman Dornan, who had personally pushed for approval of the award. Prior to Congressman Dornan's intervention, the Air Force had denied my friends request, citing this same Public Law.

I resubmitted my request through the office of my local Congressman on July 3rd, 1993. My attachments were never returned and although every few months I received notice that the request was being considered, the request was never approved. I was forced to acknowledge that I knew of no avenue where I could receive help in obtaining awards for my crew members.

In the interim period a new medal was authorized for all former American Prisoners of War. I received this award, as did all four members of my crew with whom I was still able to contact. I note, however, that the order of precedence or priority for the POW Medal is twenty-four. This means that twenty-three other medal awards are considered to have higher priority or prestige. The AF Organizational Excellence Award, listed as No.23, is an award of greater significance than the POW Medal. The order of precedence for awards begins with the "Medal Of Honor." The Distinguished Flying Cross (DFC) is No. 8 and the Air Medal is No.14. Considering the priority given the POW Medal, it may be just another "been there" notice to others, but to the ex-prisoner of war, the medal, regardless of priority, is a symbol of an experience that will be remembered for a lifetime.

In 1997, I became aware of a new policy change with respect to award of the Air Medal. It had been established that any crew member who flew in air combat during World War II, regardeless of the number of missions, was eligible to receive the Air Medal; however, there remained the problem of obtaining a records search to insure that the individual was actually in combat and that the award had not previously been made. In accordance with the policy change, all requests for an award could only be made if the award recipient had given written permission for his or her records to be reviewed. If the recipient was deceased, only next of kin could grant this permission. I obtained the necessary record release forms, sent them out to my three ex-crew members, and then re-submitted the request for approval of the Air Medals.

A Second Schweinfurt Memorial Association reunion was held in October of 1997, which presented an excellent opportunity for my remaining surviving crew members and their wives to meet in a joyous reunion and relive some of our own personal history. Locating Joe Johnson, Charles Groth and Robert Soloman was unsuccessful then and it remains so today. They have not been located and their status is unknown.

Glenn Foster and his wife, Gloria, Vic Kuhlman and his wife, Janet, and Louis Brown and his wife, Claire, were present at the reunion. Of course, my wife, Lee, was also at my side. It was a memorable occasion for all of us. Sherman Sly intended to be at the reunion but he had the wrong date for the reunion and he arrived in Omaha the day after the reunion had ended.

On October 20th, 1998, I was advised by the Air Force Personnel center at Randolph AFB, Texas that a new law, enacted on February 10th, 1996, waived the timeline previously restricting acceptance of World War II award requests. With this knowledge, I typed up a narrative to accompany the citation that was to be used as justification for award of the Distinguished Flying Cross to Louis Brown who had shot down two ME109 German fighters during the Schweinfurt mission. In accordance with this new directive, as Louis Brown's aircraft commander, I was authorized to initiate the recommendation for award of the Distinguished Flying Cross (DFC), but the request was required to be submitted through a Congressional office.

Master Sergeant Alberto E. Salinas at the Air Force Personnel Center at Randolph AFB, Texas assisted in receiving approval of the Air Medal awards and on March 8th, 1999, I received a "courtesy" notice that the awards were to be made. Victor Kuhlman did not live long enough to personally receive the award he so richly deserved. He died on January 2nd, 1999. His wife, Janet, accepted his award on the 9th of March, 1999. The award arrived three months too late.

After a wait of 55 years, Sherman Sly received his Air Medal. It was presented to him by his proud Pastor who wanted his entire church congregation to be witness to a true hero.

I had submitted the renewed request for award of the Distinguished Flying Cross for Louis Brown through the office of a Congressman on December 4th, 1998. The original request was submitted in 1993 through that same office. I didn't receive a response to this latest award request until August 17th, 1999, some seven months after submission of the request to the office of my local Congressman. The report read as follows:

"The Secretary of the Air Force Personnel Council (SAFPC) advised that the recommendation, though commendable, did not meet the requirements for the DFC." "This action does not preclude a request for reconsideration if Colonel Slane can provide significant additional justification, such as verification that the navigator, MR. Glen Foster, received the DFC for this mission and a sworn affidavit from Mr. Foster on behalf of Mr. Brown. A request for reconsideration must be submitted within one year from the date of disapproval, July 23rd, 1999."

When I received this correspondence, I immediately contacted Glenn Foster to verify his receipt of the DFC. Contrary to what I said in the recommendation, Glenn informed me that he had *not* received the DFC for his exploits during the Schweinfurt mission. This was a shock to me as I was certain that he had told me, after I returned home from Germany, that he had received the award. In any event, I had unknowingly included an erroneous statement in my recommendation and I acknowledged that fact. It was and still is my opinion, however, that whether Glenn Foster received the DFC or did not receive the DFC should be immaterial to the determination of the merits of awarding the DFC to Louis Brown.

Glenn did provide the sworn affidavit, but also added his version of a citation and added additional comments with respect to each crew member. He sent all of this information directly to the Office of the Secretary of the Air Force. The material was returned to him, stating that he must go back through Congressional channels, thus resulting in additional delay. Upon receipt of this information Glenn then sent the packet of information to me. I, in turn, channeled the new packet including all of Glenn's data on to the local Congressional office that had handled my previous requests. That resubmission was on February 29th, 2000.

I heard nothing more on the status of the DFC award recommendation until April 25th, 2001 and again on July 3rd, 2001 when I received word that the National Personnel Records Center, once again, needed Mrs. Claire Brown's signature on the release form so that Louis Brown's records could be released. Claire had signed the first release as "Mrs. Louis Brown" in April and that signature was rejected. Two months later the records center wanted her signature again. Claire signed the second release form as "Claire K. Brown" and the form was forwarded back to the National Personnel Records Center. All of these new requirements had been imposed simply because Louis Brown died during the sixteen-month period when the recommendation was still being "reviewed." This chapter was finally closed shortly after the second signature was obtained.

Louis Brown had lived just long enough to receive his Air Medal, but he died four months later on July 31st, 1999. The request for award of the DFC for Louis Brown had been resubmitted in December of 1998 and he had every reason to be hopeful that the award would be approved. The final 'disapproval' of his award of the DFC was received sixteen months later. I pray that his reward will be in Heaven.

Glenn Foster died on October 1st, 1999, following heart surgery.

Sherman Sly, a widower, lived in Fairland, Oklahoma. We "kept in touch." throughout the years after 1986. I received a report of his death from his son, Mark, on the 28th of November, 2003. The information is received as this book is in the process of being published. Sherman was my last direct contact with any of my World War II, B-17 crew members.

PART IV AFTER LIBERATION 283

Former B-17 Crew Members
L to R: Foster, Brown, Slane, Kuhlman. October 1997
Meeting together 54 years after their Schweinfurt mission.

The Author, Robert Slane